Communications
in Computer and Information Science 576

Commenced Publication in 2007
Founding and Former Series Editors:
Alfredo Cuzzocrea, Dominik Ślęzak, and Xiaokang Yang

More information about this series at http://www.springer.com/series/7899

Olivier Camp · Edgar Weippl
Christophe Bidan · Esma Aïmeur (Eds.)

Information Systems Security and Privacy

First International Conference, ICISSP 2015
Angers, France, February 9–11, 2015
Revised Selected Papers

 Springer

Editors
Olivier Camp
MODESTE/ESEO
Angers
France

Christophe Bidan
Supélec
Cesson
France

Edgar Weippl
SBA Research
Wien
Austria

Esma Aïmeur
Université de Montréal
Montreal, QC
Canada

ISSN 1865-0929   ISSN 1865-0937   (electronic)
Communications in Computer and Information Science
ISBN 978-3-319-27667-0   ISBN 978-3-319-27668-7   (eBook)
DOI 10.1007/978-3-319-27668-7

Library of Congress Control Number: 2015957037

Printed on acid-free paper

This Springer imprint is published by SpringerNature
The registered company is Springer International Publishing AG Switzerland

Preface

The present book includes extended and revised versions of a set of selected best papers from the First International Conference on Information Systems Security and Privacy (ICISSP), which was held in February 2015, in Angers, France. This conference reflects a continuing effort to increase the dissemination of recent research results among professionals who work in the areas of information systems security and privacy.

The program of this conference included several outstanding keynote lectures presented by internationally renowned distinguished researchers who are experts in the various ICISSP areas. Their keynote speeches contributed toward increasing the overall quality of the program and significance of the themes of the conference.

The conference topics define a broad spectrum in the key areas of information systems security and privacy. This wide-view reporting made ICISSP appealing to a global audience of engineers, scientists, business practitioners, ICT managers, and policy experts. The papers accepted and presented at the conference demonstrated a number of new and innovative solutions for information systems security and privacy, showing that the technical problems in these closely related fields are challenging and worth approaching from an interdisciplinary perspective such as that promoted by ICISSP.

ICISSP 2015 received 56 papers, with contributions from 23 different countries in all continents, which demonstrates its success and global dimension. To evaluate each submission, a double-blind paper evaluation method was used: Each paper was blindly reviewed by at least two experts from the international Program Committee. In fact, most papers had three reviews or more. The selection process followed strict criteria in all tracks. As a result only 10 papers were accepted and orally presented at ICISSP as full papers (18 % of submissions) and 19 as short papers (34 % of submissions). Additionally, 12 papers were accepted for poster presentation. The strict acceptance ratio shows the intention to preserve the high quality of this event, which we expect to improve even further in the years to come.

We hope that you will find this collection of the best ICISSP 2015 papers an excellent source of inspiration as well as a helpful reference for research in the aforementioned areas.

September 2015

Olivier Camp
Edgar Weippl
Christophe Bidan
Esma Aïmeur

Organization

Conference Chair

Olivier Camp   MODESTE/ESEO, France

Program Co-chairs

Edgar Weippl   SBA Research/TU Wien, Austria
Christophe Bidan   SUPELEC, France
Esma Aïmeur   University of Montreal, Canada

Program Committee

Carlisle Adams   University of Ottawa, Canada
Gordon Agnew   University of Waterloo, Canada
Anis Ben Aissa   Université Tunis el Manar École Nationale d'ingenieurs de
                                Tunis, Tunisia
Magnus Almgren   Chalmers University of Technology, Sweden
Mario Alvim   Federal University of Minas Gerais (UFMG), Brazil
Morteza Amini   Sharif University of Technology, Islamic Republic of Iran
Frederik Armknecht   Mannheim University, Germany
Elias Athanasopoulos   FORTH, Greece
Kensuke Baba   Kyushu University, Japan
Joonsang Baek   Khalifa University of Science, Technology and Research,
                                UAE
Alessandro Barenghi   Polytecnic University of Milan, Italy
Catalin V. Birjoveanu   Al.I. Cuza University of Iasi, Romania
Simon R. Blackburn   Royal Holloway University of London, UK
Douglas Blough   Georgia Institute of Technology, USA
Carlo Blundo   Università di Salerno, Italy
Alessio Botta   University of Naples Federico II, Italy
Hervé Chabanne   Morpho and Télécom ParisTech, France
Serge Chaumette   Université de Bordeaux, France
Feng Cheng   Hasso Plattner Institute at University of Potsdam, Germany
Hung-Yu Chien   National Chi Nan University, Taiwan, Taiwan
Stelvio Cimato   Università degli studi di Milano Crema, Italy
Bernard Colbert   Deakin University, Australia
Miguel Correia   Universidade do Porto, Faculdade de Engenharia, Portugal
Mathieu Cunche   INSA-Lyon/Inria, France
Mohammad Dastbaz   Leeds Beckett University, UK
Mingcong Deng   Tokyo University of Agriculture and Technology, Japan

Hung-Min Sun	National Tsing Hua University, Taiwan
Shamik Sural	IIT Kharagpur, India
Tsuyoshi Takagi	Kyushu University, Japan
Nadia Tawbi	Université Laval, Canada
Cihangir Tezcan	Middle East Technical University, Turkey
Raylin Tso	National Chengchi University, Taiwan
Yasuyuki Tsukada	Nippon Telegraph and Telephone Corporation, Japan
Udaya Tupakula	Macquarie University, Australia
Shambhu J. Upadhyaya	University at Buffalo, USA
Adriano Valenzano	Consiglio Nazionale delle Ricerche, Italy
Craig Valli	Edith Cowan University, Australia
Rakesh M. Verma	University of Houston, USA
Hongjun Wu	Nanyang Technological University, Singapore
Ching-Nung Yang	National Dong Hwa University, Taiwan
Neil Y. Yen	University of Aizu, Japan
Amr Youssef	Concordia University, Canada
Moti Yung	Google Inc. and Columbia University, USA
Jianhong Zhang	North China University of Technology, China
Jie Zhang	Nanyang Technological University, Singapore
Wenbing Zhao	Cleveland State University, USA
Huafei Zhu	Institute for Infocomm Research (I2R), A-Star, Singapore

Additional Reviewer

Franck Youssef	NEC Europe Ltd., Switzerland

Invited Speakers

Steven Furnell	Plymouth University, UK
Bryan Ford	Yale University, USA
Günther Pernul	University of Regensburg, Germany
Edgar Weippl	SBA Research/TU Wien, Austria
Philippe Desfray	SOFTEAM, France

Contents

Invited Papers

From Passwords to Biometrics: In Pursuit of a Panacea

S.M. Furnell[(⊠)]

Centre for Security, Communications and Network Research,
Plymouth University, Plymouth, UK
sfurnell@plymouth.ac.uk

Abstract. User authentication is a fundamental aspect of security, and a standard requirement on many of the devices and services that people use on a daily basis. However, while a variety of associated technologies exist, none has yet been found to offer the ideal solution for all contexts. This paper examines the authentication landscape, considering passwords and other popular secret knowledge approaches, as well as the alternatives that go beyond this in terms of tokens and biometrics. In all cases, there is a balance to be struck between the security provided and the usability (or tolerability) of the resulting approach, and the discussion also proceeds to examine how further research can support this via non-intrusive authentication solutions operating on both single systems and across multiple devices. While there remains no technique that will perfectly serve all contexts, there is now a richer and more varied choice from which to deliver practical solutions for the user.

Keywords: Authentication · Passwords · Tokens · Biometrics · Usability

1 Introduction

Achieving effective and acceptable means of user authentication has been a long recognised challenge of IT security. While passwords are still dominant, today's authentication systems are exhibiting a much greater diversity of techniques and technologies, particularly in relation to those used on mobile devices. We can now readily see examples of alternative forms of secret-based approach, as well as techniques that replace or supplement secrets with tokens and biometrics. However, the rationale in some cases is not specifically to make the security stronger, but rather to make it more accessible and easier to use, which in turn increases the chances of users having some protection rather than none at all.

For many years, the situation for most users has remained relatively unchanged, and while other forms of authentication (e.g. via tokens and biometrics) may have been in use, they were very much in the minority and tended to remain the preserve of larger organisations. The picture today is rather more diverse, with lay users now being far more likely to encounter departures from the traditional password and PIN methods. Key examples here have been the use of alternative techniques on websites and mobile devices, with the consequence that the use of one-time codes, and gesture-based secrets, biometrics, and multi-factor approaches are all far more likely to have been

© Springer International Publishing Switzerland 2015
O. Camp et al. (Eds.): ICISSP 2015, CCIS 576, pp. 3–15, 2015.
DOI: 10.1007/978-3-319-27668-7_1

amongst the things that users have directly experienced rather than just heard or read about. This movement has been driven and enabled by at least two key factors. The first is the increased security needs of certain types of online service, alongside the likely expectation from users that these will receive protection beyond the normal baseline. A good example here is Internet banking, in which authentication is now frequently achieved via the use of one-time codes generated by an additional hardware device (serving to prevent threats such as keylogging, and giving users an additional level of assurance that the service is safeguarded against impostor access). The second key driver is the new opportunities afforded by the devices themselves. A good example here is the leveraging of the touchscreens on smartphone and tablet devices to enable approaches such as Android's Pattern Unlock and Windows Picture Password (both of which are examined further as part of later discussion). In addition, the default inclusion of features such as cameras and microphones on virtually all access devices (from smartphones through to desktops) now enables the more routine use of techniques such as face and voice verification, which would previously have depended upon the addition of specialist hardware. Having said this, the present situation still reveals passwords to be the dominant mechanism, particularly when it comes to online services. Unfortunately, despite years of recognition as a source of problems (due to both technical limitations and weak user practices), the general usage of passwords is still far from ideal.

This paper examines the authentication landscape as currently faced by many users. It begins by considering the situation around traditional passwords, recognising that they remain both popular and problematic, and evidencing some of the possible reasons for this. The discussion then moves to consider other forms of secret-based approach, using the particular example of graphical methods that have become popular on mobile devices. Consideration is then given to the opportunities that exist when going beyond reliance upon secrets, and into the realms of token and biometric approaches (with examples relating to online banking and mobile device access). The final segment then considers routes for moving beyond each of these individual approaches, examining how they can be leveraged to deliver non-intrusive (and hence more usable) authentication solutions on single systems and across multiple devices.

2   The Challenge of Traditional Passwords

Passwords represent an aspect of security that all users are almost guaranteed to encounter. Traditional methods are often regarded as very usable, insofar as it is easy to understand the idea, users become familiar with them across different systems, there is a high degree of cross-device applicability, and they are perceived to be low cost (at least insofar as not requiring any investment in additional technology). However, the perceived ease of use can very often be linked to the fact that users have not been required to use them properly. Indeed, practically every aspect of good password practice (e.g. enforcing length and composition criteria, requiring them to be changed regularly, avoiding reuse, not writing them down, etc.) makes them more difficult to use. Moreover, the need to use passwords across multiple systems amplifies the challenge. While password management tools can overcome some of the constraints, they can often be perceived to be inconvenient in their own right, because they add a resulting overhead to the process of retrieving and using the passwords.

Part of the problem with current password usage can be directly linked to the lack of support and guidance provided to users when attempting to do so. This applies to usage in both personal and organisational contexts, and can be well illustrated in the former case by examining the approaches taken on popular websites. To this end, Table 1 presents a summary of key findings from a related study that examined the password practices of ten leading websites in order to determine both the extent of guidance that they presented to users, and the degree to which standard aspects of password good practice were actually enforced [1]. In most cases there is a clear indication of whether sites pass or fail in relation to each criterion, but there are also a few cases of partial compliance (denoted as ∼). It should be noted that the table specifically summarises the provisions made during initial sign-up (which are particularly important insofar as none of the sites enforced password expiration by default, and so the user's initial choice could persist for years). However, the study also looked at the password update and reset aspects of each site, and it should be noted that the provisions there are not necessarily the same (e.g. more than half of the sites were found to provide password selection/management guidance at the reset stage, as opposed to only two that did so at sign-up). The overall picture here is certainly not one of users being supported to make good password choices, and so it would be unsurprising to find weak passwords being chosen.

Table 1. Password guidance and enforcement provisions at sign-up on leading websites.

Site	Guidance to users		Restrictions enforced					
	Selection guidelines	Password meter	Enforces min length	Prevents Surname	Prevents User ID	Prevents 'password'	Enforces Composition	Prevents dictionary words
Amazon	✗	✗	6	✗	✗	✗	✗	✗
Facebook	✗	Ratings	6	✓	✗	✗	✗	✗
Google	✓	✓	8	✓	✓	✓	✗	✓
LinkedIn	✗	✗	6	✗	✗	✓	✗	∼
Microsoft Live	✗	✗	8	✓	✓	✓	✓	✗
Pinterest	✗	✗	6	✗	✓	✓	✗	✗
Twitter	✗	✓	6	✗	✓	✓	✗	∼
Wikipedia	✗	✗	✗	✗	✓	✗	✗	✗
WordPress	✓	✗	6	✗	✓	✓	∼	✓
Yahoo!	✗	✗	8	✓	✓	✓	✓	✓

Annual findings from SplashData reveal that predictable password choices remain popular [2], and while news of this nature is regularly reported quite widely, little appears to occur in terms of ensuring better attention towards awareness and enforcement of good practice. Instead, the conclusion that often appears to be drawn is that people and/or passwords are bad, and the technology has to be changed. Nonetheless, where guidance *is* provided, prior research has shown that it can make a tangible difference to users' password selection practices – helping to ensure that better choices are made, irrespective of whether selection rules are actually *enforced*. For example, users were found to be significantly more likely to choose passwords of at least 8 characters and to incorporate non-alphanumeric characters into their passwords if actually guided to do so (with 85 % choosing longer passwords and 62 % using other characters when a brief list of guidance was presented on the password selection page, versus only 50 % and 7 % doing so when left to the make selections without further information) [3].

Having said all this, even with effective guidance and support, there are still some contexts in which password usage runs into practical challenges. One such case is on mobile devices such as smartphones, where the small size of the virtual keyboard can make it more awkward from outset, and even more so if good practice has been followed by selecting a password that incorporate multiple character types. In this context, one ends up not only having to take care typing on the small keys, but also switch between different keyboard layouts in order to access the characters required. This is illustrated in Fig. 1, which shows the entry of the string Pa$$C0de (admittedly not a great choice, but it still serves to demonstrate the full range of upper and lower case alphabetic, numeric and punctuation symbols) on an iOS device. Even with a relatively short and straightforward password such as this, the user needs to switch between keyboards four times in order to get to the required characters. So, while such as password would likely be fine for many people to enter while sitting at a desktop or laptop and using a normal keyboard, it could easily become frustrating to enter on a mobile device that is frequently used for short bursts, and often on the move. The possible user responses in many cases may be to use something simpler, disable the passcode altogether, or set it so that it is not requested on such a frequent basis – none of which are desirable routes from the security perspective. As such, even if we could get passwords to be chosen effectively, they would certainly not represent a usable solution in all contexts, and so it is still clearly relevant to consider the merits of other alternatives.

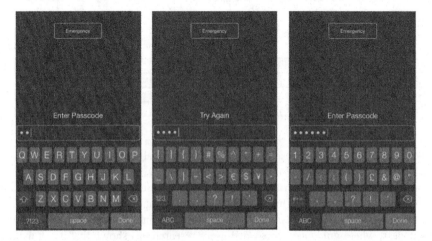

Fig. 1. Needing to switch across three virtual keyboard layouts to enter a password.

3 From Passwords to Other Secrets

Keeping the focus on the mobile device context, it provides some good examples of where the secret-knowledge approach to authentication has been applied with something other than passwords and PINs as the basis. Alternatives to these traditional approaches have been established for some time, with research having considered methods such as cognitive and associative challenges [4], as well as various forms of authentication based upon graphical or image-related secrets [5]. While approaches such as challenge questions can often be found in web-based services (particularly as the authentication fallback in a 'forgotten password' process), they would rarely find application as the frontline authentication approach. Graphical approaches, meanwhile, have made occasional appearances as a basis for website authentication, but have become particularly prominent in the context of protecting mobile devices such as smartphones and tablets. In this context, Windows Picture Password and Android Pattern Unlock are both examples of techniques that aim to take advantage of the devices they are running on in order to deliver authentication that is considered more usable – specifically by allowing the user to interact with a graphical approach using the touchscreen. As illustrated in Fig. 2a, the Android approach enables users to create a secret pattern using a series of nine on-screen dots. Meanwhile, the Windows approach (Fig. 2b) requires them to associate three gestures (which can be a mixture of drawing circles, straight lines, and taps) with particular parts of a chosen image.

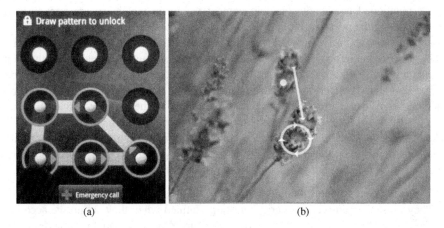

        (a)   (b)

Fig. 2. Secrets based upon graphical, touchscreen approaches, illustrated by (a) Android pattern unlock and (b) Windows picture password.

However, while both approaches are ostensibly user-friendly, and clearly suited to touchscreen devices, they do not come without potential downsides to consider. Firstly, both still run the risk of users selecting weak or obvious secrets (e.g. just drawing a simple line or a square as their unlock pattern, or tapping on three obvious 'hotspot' points in a picture password). Meanwhile, if they go for more complicated choices, they may find them harder to remember (perhaps particularly the case with the Windows Picture Password if a combination of circles, lines or taps has been used, and the device concerned is not used regularly enough for the sequence to become lodged in their memory). A further consideration is the discoverability of the patterns, as both are potentially more observable than passwords or PINs when they are being entered (this is particularly the case for the Android pattern if a relatively simple one has been used, and the user has left the device configured to show the pattern as it is entered). Moreover, the device screens themselves can leave clues, through residual smear marks from greasy fingers, meaning that a potential imposter picking up the device may actually be able to see the pattern that they need to trace. This can be overcome by choosing patterns that overlap or double-back on themselves (or indeed by cleaning the screen), but this then becomes something else that the user has to explicitly consider in their use of the techniques.

4 Going Beyond Secrets

Looking beyond the bounds of something the user knows, the other standard foundations of authentication are something that they have (e.g. tokens) and something that they are (i.e. biometric approaches). In contrast to the situation a decade ago (where biometrics were rarely encountered by average users and aside from payment cards even possession-based approaches were hardly commonplace), there are now readily identifiable examples of both in day-to-day life.

As mentioned above, the banking context is one in which we are already well versed in using the possession of physical identifier (the debit or credit card) as a means of authenticating ourselves (albeit typically in combination with a signature or a PIN, although someone in possession of a card alone could still use it to make unauthorised online purchases without requiring either of these aspects). As such, it is not surprising to find that banking websites have typically been at the forefront of going beyond standard secret-based approaches for granting access to their online services. As an example of this, Fig. 3 presents elements of the login process involved for HSBC's online banking service, for which account holders are provided with a small code-generating token that HSBC call the Secure Key. This introduces a multi-stage process for each login, the full details of which is as follows:

1. The user needs to enter their Banking ID.
2. They must then answer a security question, defined when they set up the account.
3. They then enter a 4-digit PIN code on the Secure Key device, and use the device to generate a 6-digit one-time code. Alternatively, the code may also be generated via a more recently introduced mobile app.

The 6-digit code is then entered into the web page in order to complete the information required to login.

Such a process is clearly more time-consuming and requires more cognitive effort than the potentially reflex action of typing a password. While many users will not object in a banking context (and indeed may get more confidence from seeing a more involved process to protect a site where their money is at stake), such an approach

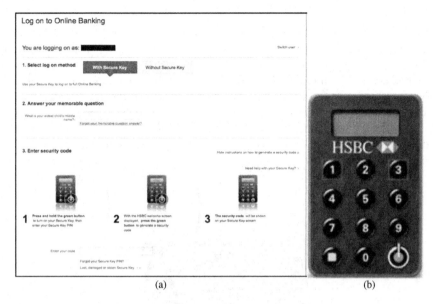

(a)   (b)

Fig. 3. Online banking login with HSBC, combining (a) website front-end and (b) Secure Key device.

would clearly not work for website authentication in general, particularly if the user ended up being provided with a variety of distinct tokens from the different providers.

As an aside, it is notable from Fig. 3a that there is also an option to log on without the Secure Key. This is achieved by answering an additional secret knowledge challenge (namely selected digits from a password), but doing so only grants access to a restricted set of online banking functionality (e.g. the user can view the account details but cannot perform financial transactions). As such, this is an example of differentiated access based upon the strength of user authentication that is considered to have been provided.

Moving to consider the final category of authentication, with approaches based upon biometrics, it is notable that mobile devices have again had a particularly prominent role in bringing these techniques into widespread use. Indeed, both of the leading smartphone platforms now offer biometric alternatives to traditional PINs or passwords, with Android having had Face Unlock since 2011 (as well as fingerprint and voice-based approaches on some devices), and iOS introducing the fingerprint-based Touch ID in 2013. While the underlying biometrics clearly predate the rise of smartphones, their popularity here goes back to the earlier observations around the difficulties of using traditional passwords, and the consequent need to find alternatives that users would consider tolerable to protect the increasingly sensitive content on their mobile devices. Indeed, the introduction of biometrics on both the Android and iOS platforms was marketed as an improvement in usability and convenience rather than claiming they provided stronger protection. Specifically, the promotional text for Apple's Touch ID said "You check your iPhone dozens and dozens of times a day, probably more. Entering a passcode each time just slows you down", while the advertising of Android Face Unlock claimed that it was "making each person's device even more personal" [6]. In fact, contrary to what one might have expected (given the many years of papers claiming that biometrics would improve upon the security of passwords), it is perhaps surprising to see that the biometric options are explicitly stated as being less secure than the PINs and passwords that they might replace, as indicated in Fig. 4. The reason for this is that the biometric implementations on the mobile devices are not necessarily as robust as the versions that may be found else where. For example, the early implementation of Face Unlock (introduced in Android Ice Cream Sandwich) could be easily fooled by showing it a static photo of the legitimate user, while the blinking-based liveness detection introduced in the next release (Android Jelly Bean) could be duped via an edited version of a photo, animated to show 'eyes open' and 'eyes shut' versions [7].

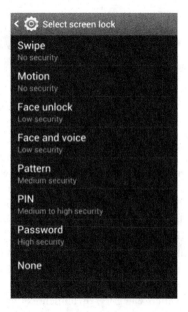

Fig. 4. Ranking the level of security provided by alternative Android lock mechanisms.

In addition to this, there are also scenarios in which some of the biometrics will not work. For example, Face Unlock will not work in low lighting or darkness, voice approaches may not work in noisy environments, and fingerprint approaches can fail in the event of moisture (e.g. sweaty hands or in the rain), dirty fingers, skin damage, or the user wearing gloves in cold weather! To account for such scenarios, it is notable that both the Android and iOS platforms revert to other authentication methods if the biometric authentication is unsuccessful (or indeed if the user chooses to bypass it). So, on iOS for example, the passcode (whether it be a simple 4-digit numeric code, or a more complex string) remains the ultimate fallback mechanism. As such, if the user has elected to use a 4-digit passcode and then made a weak choice such as 1234, an imposter can move directly to this by swiping past the Touch ID login and entering the PIN rather than worrying about fingerprint impersonation.

Having said all this, the inclusion of biometrics may still be regarded as a net gain for security if it encourages people to enable protection on their devices in the first place (i.e. weaker security that people will use is better than strong protection that they disable). In addition, whereas users with PINs or passwords might set them to activate after a grace period (e.g. 15 min of inactivity) before requesting them to be entered again, biometrics can be activated the moment device is put into standby without causing the user significant inconvenience to re-authenticate themselves (e.g. with iOS Touch ID, the authentication can occur entirely transparently when the user presses the home button to activate the device). In this way, biometrics can remove the window of exposure that might arguably exist with traditional methods.

5   Towards Seamless Authentication Solutions

The discussion to this point has essentially focused upon known and established technologies, and clearly all have their pros and cons in different contexts. Moving beyond this, it is relevant to consider how to bring authentication strength and convenience together in a more effective manner. Traditional authentication tends to deliver full access in one go, with secondary authentication sometimes required for specific applications or services. By contrast it is potentially desirable to differentiate the requirement based upon the nature of the device/system, data, or level of access concerned, but to manage it transparently wherever possible (i.e. such that the user is not made explicitly aware of the security unless it is necessary to do so). Such non-intrusive methods aim to maintain tolerability while offering opportunity to deliver authentication beyond Point of Entry, with the ability to obtain a continuous (or periodic) measure of the user's legitimacy. Moreover, this can be done by leveraging natural user interactions as a source for collecting authentication data. This is one of the principles underlying so-called Active Authentication approaches advocated by DARPA in order to overcome the weaknesses of traditional technologies. To quote from their call for research in early 2012: "The Active Authentication program seeks to address this problem by developing novel ways of validating the identity of the person at the console that focus on the unique aspects of the individual through the use of software based biometrics… This program focuses on the behavioral traits that can be observed through how we interact with the world" [8].

The generic framework for an associated transparent authentication approach is depicted in Fig. 5 [9]. It should be noted that in this case, the approach actually goes beyond simply the behavioural traits mentioned in the DARPA definition, and also incorporates physiological biometrics such as face and fingerprint recognition, recognising that it is also possible to use these in a non-intrusive manner if the associated samples can be captured as a natural consequence of other user activities (e.g. facial images acquired while the user is engaging in a video call, or as indicated above, fingerprints acquired during normal device activation). The framework incorporates five key elements:

- Capture of authentication samples, in order to acquire the candidate measures from the target device.

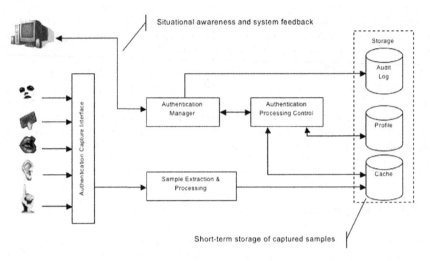

Fig. 5. A generic transparent authentication framework.

- Processing of authentication samples, in order to perform the necessary feature extraction for the captured biometrics.
- Short- and long-term data repositories, with the short-term representing recent samples that can contribute towards authentication decisions in the current session, and long-term being the reference profiles against which users are authenticated.
- Authentication Manager, which performs the comparison of samples against profiles in order to determine whether authentication is successful (i.e. a close enough match) and to what level of confidence.
- Response, in order to ensure that the system is able to respond according to the level of authentication achieved (which may include limiting the level of access granted, or making a request for further authentication in a more intrusive manner).

In normal operation the intention would be to enable ongoing transparent capture of authentication samples by the underlying system, minimising the requirement for explicit action or interruption of the legitimate user. The desirable outcomes in this context are therefore to reduce the authentication burden upon the user (which occurs by making the process more transparent to them), while at the same time improving the overall level of security being provided (which occurs as a result of enabling authentication to become a periodic, or even continuous process, rather than a one-off judgement at the start of the session). It is also possible to link the level of authentication required to the activity that the user is trying to perform (e.g. ensuring that multiple measures are used if the access request is related to an asset or activity that has been classed as sensitive, whereas lower-risk actions could be permitted with baseline authentication having been achieved). In this way it is possible to ensure that the approach is commensurate with the needs of the access request, and provide a more granular measure of identity confidence than a simple Boolean decision at point-of-entry.

The above approach can work within the context of a single device. However, it is also relevant to think beyond this and recognise the fact that many users today are operating across a multitude of devices, and often doing so concurrently (e.g. switching between smartphone and PC during the same activity). In this scenario, it is useful to consider how authentication performed on one device can be leveraged to also grant access to others. This has been investigated within the context of what we have termed the Authentication Aura; which can be imagined as a virtual authentication field surrounding the user, and allowing them seamless access to their different devices that are within close proximity. The strength of the Aura is affected by the success of prior authentication activities (whether they were performed explicitly or non-intrusively) and how recently they occurred. So, as a hypothetical example, if John is sitting down to use his PC, and has just authenticated himself using fingerprint recognition on his smartphone, then the PC (which normally requires a password) could allow access without requesting further authentication (on the basis that John is assumed to be present, having just proven himself to the phone, and has already verified himself using a technique that is considered strong enough to supersede the need for a password). If meanwhile a similar scenario were to occur but with John's smartphone authentication occurring via (say) pattern unlock, then the PC may still demand a password, as the contribution to the Authentication Aura arising from the pattern unlock alone might not be strong enough. However, having then authenticated explicitly on both the phone and PC within a short period of time via different methods, the Aura could now grant John transparent access to his tablet device. This approach has been evaluated in an experimental context, with 20 participants using devices for 14 days each. A resulting simulation, based upon 1.23 million collected samples, suggested that the use of the Aura would be able to deliver a 75 % reduction in the need for explicit authentication requests across different devices [10]. As such, this clearly has the potential to tangibly reduce the authentication burden compared to current practice.

6 Conclusions

Although the range of authentication opportunities has diversified, we are still some way from having a universally applicable and effective solution. This discussion has considered a variety of approaches, and none can be considered as the outright winners or losers. Even passwords, which are often dismissed altogether [10], can still provide suitable and effective protection for some contexts if used correctly. Meanwhile, none of the other approaches provide an ideal alternative either, as there are still drawbacks in terms of potential compromise and/or their applicability across the range of devices upon which authentication may need to be performed. While passwords and PINs are potentially lacking in terms of security, they can at least be used across almost all devices that the user is likely to encounter (i.e. all that they need is a keyboard of some form). Meanwhile, the more effective protection that some might argue can come from biometrics is only feasible if the device concerned has the necessary sensor(s) to capture them (and while these are certainly more commonplace, they are far from universal at this stage).

Where alternatives are now becoming more prominent, there is an interesting contrast to be drawn between whether their impact makes the resulting access more secure but less usable, or more usable but less secure. An example of the former is undoubtedly the case with some of the aforementioned online banking solutions. While the authentication process can frustrate a number of impostor and attack scenarios, it can also directly frustrate the legitimate user thanks to the complexity and overhead of the process compared to a normal login experience. By contrast, the current implementations of biometrics on mobile devices are explicitly not being presented as offering a stronger level of security than the methods that they can replace; they are instead offered as a means of enhancing the usability of the protection. However, given that this in turn can increase the likelihood that the safeguards are actually enabled (i.e. compared to users who would previously not have enabled a PIN or password), it can still mean devices are more protected than they otherwise might have been.

To conclude, it is possible to make some fairly confident statements about how things will be in the medium term future. Firstly, passwords are unlikely to disappear, and will certainly continue to be a key feature for several years to come. At the same time, the use of the alternative approaches (particularly biometrics) is certain to become more commonplace and experience a more accelerated uptake than we have previously seen to date. As such, the authentication landscape for the typical user will be far richer and varied than it has been in the past.

References

1. Furnell, S.: Password practices on leading websites – revisited, Computer Fraud & Security, pp. 5–11 December 2014
2. SplashData. 2015. "123456" Maintains the Top Spot on SplashData's Annual "Worst Passwords" List. SplashData press release, 20 January 2015. http://splashdata.com/press/worst-passwords-of-2014.htm
3. Furnell, S., Bär, N.: Essential lessons still not learned? examining the password practices of end-users and service providers. In: Proceedings of HCI International 2013, Las Vegas, Nevada, 21–26 July 2013
4. Haga, W.J., Zviran, M.: Question and answer passwords: an empirical evaluation. Information Systems **16**(3), 335–343 (1991)
5. Biddle, R., Chiasson, S., van Oorschot, P.: Graphical passwords: learning from the first twelve years. ACM Comput. Surv. **44**(4), 1–25 (2012)
6. Furnell, S., Clarke, N.: Biometrics: making the mainstream. Biometric Technol. Today **2014** (1), 5–9 (2014)
7. Racoma, J.A.: Android Jelly Bean Face Unlock 'liveness' check easily hacked with photo editing, Android Authority, 4 August 2012. http://www.androidauthority.com/android-jelly-bean-face-unlock-blink-hacking-105556/
8. DARPA: Broad Agency Announcement - Active Authentication DARPA-BAA-12-06. Defense Advanced Research Projects Agency, 12 January 2012
9. Clarke, N.L., Furnell, S.M.: Advanced User Authentication for Mobile Devices. Comput. Secur. **26**(2), 109–119 (2007)

10. Hocking, C., Furnell, S., Clarke, N., Reynolds, P.: Cooperative user identity very-fication using an Authentication Aura. Comput. Secur. **39**, 486–502 (2013). Part B
11. Fido Alliance: Lenovo, Nok Nok Labs, PayPal, and Validity Lead an Open Industry Alliance to Revolutionize Online Authentication, Press Release, 12 February 2013. https://fidoalliance.org/lenovo-nok-nok-labs-paypal-and-validity-lead-an-open-industry-alliance-to-revolutionize-online-authentication/

Privacy in Social Networks: Existing Challenges and Proposals for Solutions

Michael Netter, Günther Pernul[⊠], Christian Richthammer,
and Moritz Riesner

Department of Information Systems, University of Regensburg, Regensburg, Germany
{michael.netter,guenther.pernul,christian.richthammer,
moritz.riesner}@wiwi.uni-regensburg.de
http://www-ifs.uni-regensburg.de

Abstract. The significant change in our social lives and communication habits caused by the rise of Social Network Sites (SNSs) has not only brought along benefits but is also accompanied by privacy threats. In this paper we present our research efforts on SNS privacy and social identity management. First, we outline the results of an empirical study showing significant discrepancies between Facebook users' actual privacy settings and their perception as well as their preferences. Based on this evident need for improving privacy, we present a novel conceptualization of privacy that serves as the basis for tackling the challenges. Finally, the paper provides an overview of solutions we developed as part of our research efforts on privacy in SNSs.

Keywords: Social network sites · Privacy · Social identity management

1 Motivation

Since their emergence more than a decade ago, Social Network Sites (SNSs) are increasingly changing our social lives and communication habits. While social networks have always been an important part of human life, the advent of easy-to-use services and their ability to bridge boundaries – regarding both space and time – increasingly shifts social life to the online world. These networks enable communication with people from different social spheres (e.g. family, close friends, colleagues), ease interaction, and allow their users to stay in touch with existing contacts as well as to create new relationships.

However, the rise of SNSs also threatens the privacy of their users. On the one hand, people on SNSs inconsiderately share many personal items (e.g. status updates, location updates, photos) while they are not fully aware of their audience. There are numerous examples of SNS users posting inappropriate pictures and status updates and consequently offending people that have access to these items (such as one's boss or parents). On the other hand, few SNS providers exist that have collected a large amount of personal data in their databases raising surveillance and data protection concerns.

© Springer International Publishing Switzerland 2015
O. Camp et al. (Eds.): ICISSP 2015, CCIS 576, pp. 16–27, 2015.
DOI: 10.1007/978-3-319-27668-7_2

In [11], a differentiation is made between two types of privacy: protecting users from overly powerful SNS service providers and from other SNS users. Figure 1 clarifies the interdepencencies between SNS stakeholders and their implications on privacy. As can be seen, SNS service providers and SNS users are the two main stakeholders. From the provider perspective, the underlying business model is often based on selling services based on personal data of their users. Hence, the primary goal is to attract as many users as possible. At the same time, users have the contrary goal of preventing the disclosure of personal data to the SNS service provider. Yet simultaneously, SNS users depend on the functionality of the SNS platform to manage their social identities. In more detail, they are reliant on the provided functions to control the visibility of shared items in order to protect their privacy against other SNS users. In addition, users of SNSs need to cope with the properties of mediated communication such as persistence and searchability and take these into consideration [11].

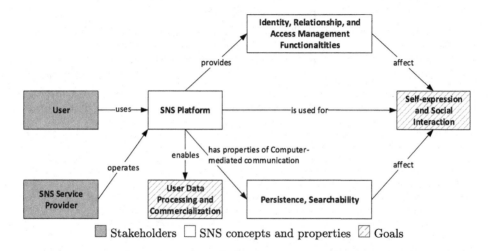

Fig. 1. Relation between SNS stakeholders, their goals, and core concepts [11]

While a variety of research focuses on protecting SNS users' privacy from overly powerful SNS service providers (e.g. [1–3,12]), this work concentrates on means to protect personal data from other SNS users. Its aim is to present existing challenges for SNS privacy and proposals for solutions by presenting our research efforts in this area. In the remainder, we conceptualize the problem of SNS privacy in Sect. 2. In Sect. 3, we further decompose it into sub-problems and present solutions to them. Finally, Sect. 4 concludes the paper.

2   Conceptualization of SNS Privacy

In this section, we conceptualize the notion of SNS privacy. First, we motivate the need for improving privacy by presenting the results of an empirical study. After that, we introduce three different perspectives to look at SNS privacy settings and decompose privacy into the two sub-problems of awareness and control.

2.1   The Need for Improving SNS Privacy

As already pointed out, SNSs require active participation and the disclosure of personal information. The more information the users share on the platform the more valuable the SNS becomes – both for the service provider who has more data for analyses at his disposal and for the users who can see more information about others. Since not every piece of personal information should be disclosed to all users of the platform (or to the entire Internet) but rather to one's personal contacts or a subset of them, SNS providers have introduced privacy settings that are similar to access control models known from identity and access management. Users can employ them to control who is able to see a shared item, which renders these settings the primary means to manage the information flow on SNSs. In general, these privacy settings enable the users to create multiple social roles for different audiences (such as family, friends, and professional life), to keep their roles separated and consistent, and thus to protect their privacy. However, in a study we were able to show that this idealized conception of managing information flows on SNSs is far from reality [14]. Access control models and privacy settings are difficult to understand and to use, especially for less technically-savvy users. As a consequence, the user's desired visibility of a particular item may differ from who can actually see the item.

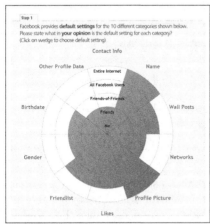

(a) Facebook's default settings

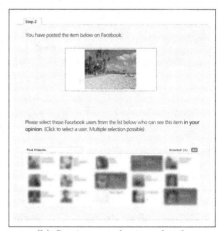

(b) Settings at the item level

Fig. 2. Conceptual designs of the questionnaires on visibility settings

In this study, we employed several questionnaires regarding privacy settings on Facebook. The first questionnaire targets Facebook's default visibility settings[1] (see Fig. 2(a)). The inner circles represent the different possible default settings on Facebook. The wedges of the circle represent the different categories of information on Facebook. First, the participants were asked to state how they believe the default settings to be for each information category by clicking in the respective area of the corresponding wedge. In a next step, they should state their preferred default settings for each category using the same interface. In our analysis we compared the perceived and actual visibility as well as preferred and actual visibility. The major findings are that users underestimated the scope of the default visibility settings and that they prefer more restrictive default visibility settings. The second questionnaire is concerned with the visibility settings of personal items (see Fig. 2(b)). At the top, the users are shown a personal item that they have disclosed on Facebook. At the bottom, they are shown a selection of contacts as well as randomly selected Facebook users. Similar to the first questionnaire, we gathered their perceived visibility by asking the participants to click on the contacts that in their opinion are able to see the item (perceived settings). Subsequently, the users should express their preferred visibility by clicking on the contacts to which they would actually like to show the item (preferred settings). Using real personal items instead of generic ones makes it easier for the participants to identify themselves with these tasks and thus constitutes an important difference to related studies. Our results show that for 17.9 % of the 8,505 binary visibility perceptions analyzed, there is a mismatch between the perceived and the actual settings. Moreover, 45 % of the 68 participants underestimate the visibility of at least one item. They also show that for 24.6 % of the 8,505 binary visibility perceptions analyzed, there is a mismatch between the preferred and the actual visibility settings. Moreover, 64 % of the 68 participants want more restrictive visibility settings for at least one item [14].

2.2 Decomposing Privacy into Awareness and Control

The results presented in [14] reveal two fundamental problems. First, users on Facebook underestimate the default visibility of items shared on the platform as well as the visibility of their own shared items. This shows that SNS users do not fully understand the privacy implications of the SNS access control models. The discrepancy between perceived and actual visibility can be interpreted as a lack of privacy awareness (see Fig. 3). Second, the demand for more restrictive privacy settings demonstrates that SNS users' preferred visibility settings differ from the actual ones. It shows that SNS users are not able to apply the preferred settings at all or at least with reasonable effort. This inability to align preferred and actual visibility can be seen as a lack of control. The interdependencies between perceived, preferred, and actual visibility are depicted in Fig. 3 and constitute one of the main contributions in [14]. In the following section, we show how to address the problems of awareness and control by developing new solutions for SNSs.

---

[1] The default settings used in the study were those of December 2011 and may have changed since then.

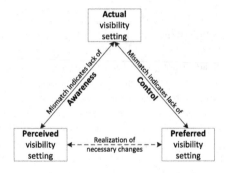

Fig. 3. Conceptualization of privacy as perceived, preferred and actual visibility [11]

3   Solutions to Address SNS Users' Lack of Awareness and Lack of Control

The previous sections demonstrate that the lack of awareness and the lack of control over who can see which personal items are one of the main threats to privacy on SNSs. We refer to these challenges of presenting different facets of the self to different contacts and keeping them consistent as *social identity management* [13]. Further decomposing these challenges shows that social identity management involves the management of one's different identities, one's relations to other users, and who has access to which identities [11].

In the following, we present solutions to address the problems of awareness and control and show how these improve identity, relationship, and access management in particular and social identity management in general.

3.1   Improving Awareness

Since users first need to know about SNS privacy risks and the effects of SNS privacy settings before making any adjustments, privacy awareness can be seen as a prerequisite for privacy control. In the following, we present approaches we developed to inform SNS users about SNS data types, assisting them with their privacy settings and educating them about privacy implications.

Understanding Social Network Data Types: A Taxonomy. Despite the large body of research regarding privacy issues in SNS, there are rather fundamental aspects that have received little attention and that should be addressed first such as the differentiation of social network data types. Since the lack of a generally accepted terminology may lead to confusion in related discussions, we fill this gap by proposing a comprehensive taxonomy in [18,19]. This is particularly important considering the fact that the popularity of SNSs has lead to an increased quantity and availability of sensitive data. The basis for our taxonomy is a thorough literature analysis clarifying discussions among researchers and

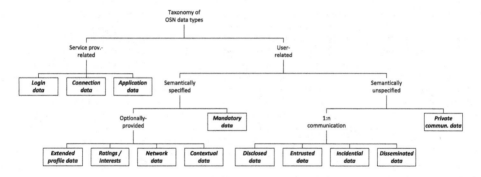

Fig. 4. Taxonomy of SNS data types

benefiting the comparisons of data types within and across platforms. However, we also include a conceptualization of common user activities on SNSs in the development process. We explicitly take the end users into consideration and aim at educating them about the characteristics and implications of different data types, thus raising their awareness regarding privacy in SNSs. Our proposed taxonomy is depicted in Fig. 4. We discover that privacy implications mainly depend on the interplay of a data element's content, the extent and the granularity of user control, and the concrete implementations of these factors on the respective platform. In the course of demonstrating the applicability of our taxonomy, we reveal the implementation-specific differences in privacy settings [18,19].

Raising Awareness Through Visualization: The Access Policy Grid.
One major issue in connection with SNS privacy settings is that translating them into human-understandable representations is not straightforward, especially considering the large number of items and contacts. Consequently, researchers (e.g. [9,17]) agree on the need for a holistic view on them. This is supposed to show the impact of users' privacy settings and to enable them to understand their social roles (i.e. their identity facets presented to different audiences) as well as to detect potential inconsistencies therein. In [15], we develop a novel matrix-based visualization approach called Access Policy Grid (APG) providing the users with a bird's-eye view on their privacy settings. This explicitly addresses the problem that users easily lose track of the visibility of items they have disclosed. The matrix-based visualization is appropriate for this purpose because it allows to examine the relations between a large number of objects without having to reduce the number of dimensions [5]. The concept of the APG along with the steps necessary to arrive at the final reordered matrix are illustrated in Fig. 5. In an initial step, the user's items as well as their visibility settings are retrieved from the SNS database. Then, the visibility settings are converted to a contact-permission matrix. The user's shared items $(i_1, \ldots, i_m)$ are represented as rows, while the user's contacts $(c_1, \ldots, c_n)$ are represented as columns. A cell c_{ij} is filled if item i_i is visible to contact c_j. Illustrating the visibility settings in a matrix already provides the user with a bird's-eye view on them. However, we

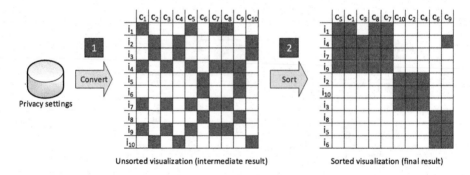

Fig. 5. Access Policy Grid generation process on a conceptual level [15]

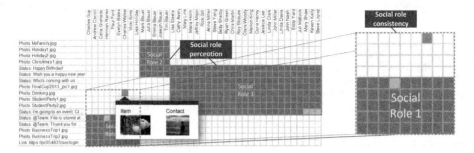

Fig. 6. Visualization of social roles and their consistency [15]

further sort the APG using a visual role mining algorithm presented in [6]. The algorithm arranges contacts with similar access rights next to each other. Thus, similar contacts are visualized in clusters and different social roles can easily be perceived by the user [15].

Figure 6 shows the implementation of the APG. In the given dataset, three social roles are easily conceivable. In addition, this visualization facilitates the discovery of possible errors such as missing privileges on the one hand and excessive privileges on the other hand. Figure 6 illustrates the discovery of such errors. As can be seen, item *Photo: Drinking.jpg* is visible to contact *Charles Walker* which makes *Social Role 1* inconsistent as this contact is the only contact of the role who can see the item [15].

Raising Awareness by Education: Friend Inspector. In order to playfully educate the users about SNS privacy settings, we introduce a serious game called "Friend Inspector" in [4]. The application relies on real Facebook data of the users, which makes it easier for them to identify themselves with the tasks that they are confronted with in the course of the application. Friend Inspector is developed for Facebook because it currently is the most popular SNS and offers very fine-grained privacy settings to its users. The reason for choosing the concept of a serious game is that we want to lay the focus on younger users (e.g.

teenagers, students) because they are the ones that are affected the most by threats like Internet mobbing, cyber stalking, and employers' online background research. Friend Inspector is based on the experiential gaming model introduced in [10], which combines experiential / inductive learning, flow theory, and game design [4].

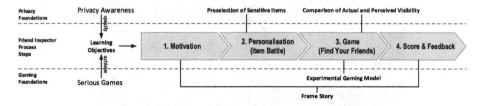

Fig. 7. Four-step process design of Friend Inspector [4]

The starting point of the experiential gaming model is the definition of the learning objectives. For Friend Inspector, the first of the two main goals is to enhance the users' privacy awareness. We want them to recognize the effects of their privacy settings, thereby decreasing the gap between perceived and actual visibility. The second goal is to educate the users about privacy settings. We want to empower them to improve their settings by providing them with personalized recommendations. With these learning objectives in mind, we design Friend Inspector as a four-step process. As can be seen in Fig. 7, the process integrates the concept of privacy awareness, which specifies the learning objectives, and the concept of serious games, which is used to achieve these objectives. Figure 8 shows the main game interface of Friend Inspector where users are asked to quickly choose the contacts that can see the item displayed [4].

3.2   Improving Control

Control over personal data in SNSs is enabled by offering SNS users' the functionality they need to manage their social identities in a privacy-preserving manner. This comprises the management of one's identities, one's relationships to other users, and the visibility of shared items. In the following, we outline our solutions for these three types of personal data control.

Managing Identities: Consistent Social Identities Across Multiple Platforms. On SNSs, the user is responsible to manage his various identities in a way that an appropriate facet is shown to a particular audience. However, we show in [20–22] that existing SNSs lack the required functionality to manage identities appropriately. This comprises the lack of means to create multiple representations of the self (i.e. multiple identity facets) and restrictions in shaping identities (e.g. providing only predefined SNS profile attributes). The problem increases when users aim to create consistent social identities across multiple

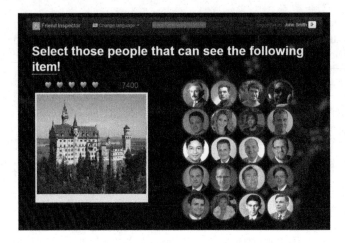

Fig. 8. Main game interface of Friend Inspector [4]

SNSs, such as Facebook, Twitter, and LinkedIn. In [23,24], we outline a single, global and provider-independent social identity model and show how to implement and decompose these identities on existing SNSs. Therein, decisions in the global model (e.g. sharing a particular item to a set of contacts) are translated to the local model of the SNS. In order to check if the changes have been implemented correctly, the provider-specific model is derived and compared to the global model. This results in a continuous cycle that applies changes from the global model to connected SNSs, evaluates the correct implementation, and updates the global model if necessary. We also show how the implementation of such a global model depends on the availability of suitable APIs on existing SNSs.

Managing Contacts: Assisted Audience Segregation. One of the major problems of existing SNSs is that all contacts (which are commonly referred to as friends) are treated equally and stored in one flat list [16]. Moreover, the default visibility of shared items is set to all contacts. This lack of differentiation between contacts from different social spheres (such as family, work, and close friends) hampers the targeted sharing of personal data. In [13], we propose to support users in pointing out segregated audiences among their SNS contacts. In more detail, a clustering algorithm is developed that discovers segregated audiences using the relationship between contacts as a criterion. The underlying assumption is that contacts that are mutual friends on the SNS are more likely to belong to the same social sphere (see Fig. 9). For instance, it is likely that classmates in my list of contacts have a mutual relationship, whereas it is more unlikely that one of my classmates is also friends with my parents who are also in my list of contacts. Once the algorithm has been executed, the clusters are presented to the user for refinement and approval [13].

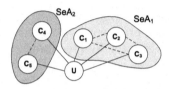

Fig. 9. Relationship between contacts [13]

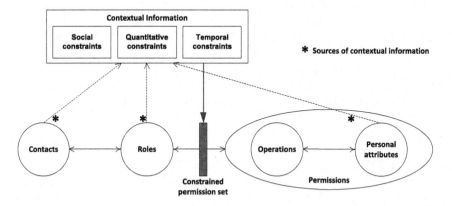

Fig. 10. Context-aware access control model [12], based on the Core RBAC model [7]

Managing Visibility: A Trust-Based Access Control Model. Besides managing contacts, one of the main drawbacks of existing SNSs is the underlying access control model which is used to define which contacts can see a particular item. Existing SNSs commonly use an access control model similar to the role-based access control (RBAC) [7] model. However, as stated by Grimmelmann "[people] think about privacy in terms of social rules and social roles, not in terms of access-control lists and file permissions" [8]. In order to incorporate the different levels of trust SNS users have in their contacts, in [12] we propose to extend the existing access control models by incorporating contextual information such as trust and time. Figure 10 depicts the extended access control model. For instance, the model allows to assign a trust value to each contact. Each time the SNS users share a new item, they define a minimum trust value required to see the item. Once a contact wants to access this item, the previously defined contextual constraint is evaluated. If the contact's trust value is higher than the trust value required to see the item, access is granted while otherwise access is denied [12].

4 Conclusions

The rise of SNSs and the accompanied change in our social lives and communication habits have not only brought along benefits but also worrying developments and considerable threats. Since then, privacy in SNSs has been an important topic both for academia and the general public. In this paper, we presented our research efforts concerning privacy in SNSs in general. First, we emphasized the need for improving SNS privacy by presenting the results of a user study we conducted. In this regard, we conceptualized privacy as awareness and control. Subsequently, we pointed out solutions to address these issues. Focusing on privacy awareness, we discussed the differences between SNS data types, introduced a novel matrix-based visualization to facilitate the users' understanding of their social roles, and presented a serious game to educate especially the younger users about the implications of their privacy settings. Regarding privacy control, we outlined a global and provider-independent social identity model to enable users to consistently manage their identities across multiple platforms, proposed a clustering algorithm discovering segregated audiences to assist the users in managing their contacts, and introduced a trust-based access control model to facilitate the management of the visibility of the users' items.

References

1. Beato, F., Kohlweiss, M., Wouters, K.: Scramble! your social network data. In: Fischer-Hübner, S., Hopper, N. (eds.) PETS 2011. LNCS, vol. 6794, pp. 211–225. Springer, Heidelberg (2011)
2. Bortoli, S., Palpanas, T., Bouquet, P.: Decentralised social network management. Int. J. Web Based Communities 7(3), 276–297 (2011)
3. Buchegger, S., Schiöberg, D., Vu, L.H., Datta, A.: PeerSoN: P2P social networking - early experiences and insights. In: Proceedings of the 2nd ACM Workshop on Social Network Systems (SocialNets), pp. 46–52 (2009)
4. Cetto, A., Netter, M., Pernul, G., Richthammer, C., Riesner, M., Roth, C., Sänger, J.: Friend inspector: a serious game to enhance privacy awareness in social networks. In: Proceedings of the 2nd International Workshop on Intelligent Games for Empowerment and Inclusion (IDGEI) (2014)
5. Chen, C.H., Härdle, W.K., Unwin, A.: Handbook of Data Visualization. Springer, Heidelberg (2008)
6. Colantonio, A., Di Pietro, R., Ocello, A., Verde, N.V.: Visual role mining: a picture is worth a thousand roles. IEEE Trans. Knowl. Data Eng. 24(6), 1120–1133 (2012)
7. Ferraiolo, D.F., Sandhu, R., Gavrila, S., Kuhn, D.R., Chandramouli, R.: Proposed NIST standard for role-based access control. ACM Trans. Inf. Syst. Secur. 4(3), 224–274 (2001)
8. Grimmelmann, J.: Saving Facebook. Iowa Law Rev. 94(8), 1137–1206 (2009)
9. Kelley, P.G., Brewer, R., Mayer, Y., Cranor, L.F., Sadeh, N.: An investigation into Facebook friend grouping. In: Campos, P., Graham, N., Jorge, J., Nunes, N., Palanque, P., Winckler, M. (eds.) INTERACT 2011, Part III. LNCS, vol. 6948, pp. 216–233. Springer, Heidelberg (2011)
10. Kiili, K.: Digital game-based learning: towards an experiential gaming model. Internet High. Educ. 8(1), 13–24 (2005)
11. Netter, M.: Privacy-preserving Infrastructure for Social Identity Management. Ph.D. thesis, University of Regensburg (2013)
12. Netter, M., Hassan, S., Pernul, G.: An autonomous social web privacy infrastructure with context-aware access control. In: Fischer-Hübner, S., Katsikas, S., Quirchmayr, G. (eds.) TrustBus 2012. LNCS, vol. 7449, pp. 65–78. Springer, Heidelberg (2012)

13. Netter, M., Riesner, M., Pernul, G.: Assisted social identity management - enhancing privacy in the social web. In: Proceedings of the 10th International Conference on Wirtschaftsinformatik (WI) (2011)
14. Netter, M., Riesner, M., Weber, M., Pernul, G.: Privacy settings in online social networks - preferences, perception, and reality. In: Proceedings of the 46th Hawaii International Conference on System Sciences (HICSS), pp. 3219–3228 (2013)
15. Netter, M., Weber, M., Diener, M., Pernul, G.: Visualizing social roles - design and evaluation of a bird's-eye view of social network privacy settings. In: Proceedings of the 22nd European Conference on Information Systems (ECIS), pp. 1–16 (2014)
16. Peterson, C.: Losing face: an environmental analysis of privacy on Facebook. SSRN eLibrary (2010)
17. Reeder, R.W., Bauer, L., Cranor, L.F., Reiter, M.K., Bacon, K., How, K., Strong, H.: Expandable grids for visualizing and authoring computer security policies. In: Proceedings of the 26th SIGCHI Conference on Human Factors in Computing Systems (CHI), pp. 1473–1482 (2008)
18. Richthammer, C., Netter, M., Riesner, M., Pernul, G.: Taxonomy for social network data types from the viewpoint of privacy and user control. In: Proceedings of the 8th International Conference on Availability, Reliability and Security (ARES 2013). IEEE (2013, accepted)
19. Richthammer, C., Netter, M., Riesner, M., Sänger, J., Pernul, G.: Taxonomy of social network data types. EURASIP J. Inf. Sec. **2014**(11), 1–17 (2014)
20. Riesner, M.: Provider-Independent Social Identity Management for Personal and Professional Applications. Ph.D. thesis, University of Regensburg (2013)
21. Riesner, M., Netter, M., Pernul, G.: An analysis of implemented and desirable settings for identity management on social networking sites. In: Proceedings of the 7th International Conference on Availability, Reliability and Security (ARES), pp. 103–112 (2012)
22. Riesner, M., Netter, M., Pernul, G.: Analyzing settings for social identity management on social networking sites: classification, current state, and proposed developments. Inf. Sec. Tech. Rep. **17**(4), 185–198 (2013)
23. Riesner, M., Pernul, G.: Maintaining a consistent representation of self across multiple social networking sites - a data-centric perspective. In: Proceedings of the Workshop on Security and Privacy in Social Networks (SPSN), pp. 860–867. IEEE (2012)
24. Riesner, M., Pernul, G.: Provider-independent online social identity management - enhancing privacy consistently across multiple social networking sites. In: Proceedings of the 45th Hawaii International Conference on System Sciences (HICSS), pp. 800–809 (2012)

Data and Software Security

MalCore: Toward a Practical Malware Identification System Enhanced with Manycore Technology

Taegyu Kim[1]([⊠]) and Ki Woong Park[2]

[1] School of Electrical and Computer Engineering, Purdue University,
West Lafayette, IN, USA
tgkim@purdue.edu
[2] Daejeon University, Daejeon, Republic of Korea
woongbak@dju.kr

Abstract. Many conventional control flow matching methods work well, but lead to obstructive latency for the operations as the number of malware variants has soared. Even though many researchers have proposed control flow matching methods, there is still a trade-off between accuracy and performance. To alleviate this trade-off, we present a system called MalCore, which is comprised of the following three novel mechanisms, each of which aims to provide a practical malware identification system: I-Filter for identical structured control flow string matching, table division to exclude unnecessary comparisons with some malware, and cognitive resource allocation for efficient parallelism. Our performance evaluation shows that the total performance improvement is 280.9 times. This work was undertaken on a real manycore computing platform called MN-MATE.

1 Introduction

Antivirus vendors have detected malware through signature-based detection. However, such malware detection has become ineffective as malware variant generation tools have been available [15]. Due to the availability of such tools, malware authors can easily create malware variants that are slight modifications of existing malware. Additionally, the number of new malware variants has increased at an exploding pace.

Malware classification and identification is therefore of immense importance to enable assessing damages after detection, and reinforcing disinfection mechanisms [14]. In addition, understudying groups and classes of malware would enable malware researchers to concentrate their efforts on specific sets of families to understand their intrinsic characteristics, and to develop better detection and mitigation tools for them.

As a remedy to this problem, Malwise [8] has proposed structured control flow string (SCFS) matching methods at a procedure level that classify malware variants by measuring similarities in existing malware samples. Their approaches are

O. Camp et al. (Eds.): ICISSP 2015, CCIS 576, pp. 31–48, 2015.
DOI: 10.1007/978-3-319-27668-7_3

effective in detecting malware variants because, unlike signatures, control flows of malware variants are much less changeable. Its authors have proposed two control flow matching methods. One of them is exact matching and the other one is approximate matching. However, there is a trade-off between the two methods. Exact matching is faster but less accurate than approximate matching because it is only necessary to check whether each control flow is identical. On the other hand, approximate matching is more accurate but has lower performance since this method compares all parts of each control flow in a fine-grained manner. In addition, both neither method considers parallelism even though many resources are available in recent high performance computers.

This study is an extension of our previous work [10,11], in which we focused on the conceptual design and implementation such as an acceleration of the approximate matching method and efficient parallelism. Our objective in this study however, is to achieve high accuracy and performance and apply parallelism, and integrate the overall components into MN-MATE platform, a novel resource management techniques for virtualization [16]. Consequently, MalCore acts as the key primitive for a practical malware identification system enhanced with manycore technology. As a result, we gained on average 280.9 times total performance improvements in our experiments.

The remainder of the paper is organized as follows: In Sect. 2, we review related works and analyze existing malware classification and identification systems. In Sect. 3, we present our motivation of this work. In Sect. 4, we illustrate the overall system design and components of the proposed system. In Sect. 5, we evaluate the performance of the proposed system. Finally, in Sect. 6, we present our conclusions.

2   Related Work

Malware identification through matching control flows has been proposed in order to solve the problem of not being able to detect malware variants. Of various analysis approaches, one of them is to match SCFSs of binaries [8]. The authors represented procedure-level control flows in a SCFS form and measure similarities to existing malware samples in databases. If the most similar malware is larger than the threshold value, the input binary is considered malicious. They suggested two matching methods: exact matching and approximate matching. However, exact matching has a lower accuracy, and approximate matching has a lower performance.

To increase the performance of string matching, bioinformatic researchers developed the fast string matching method to find identical strings to which proteins were converted. However, the conventional character-to-character (C2C) string matching is time-consuming due to large string sizes. In order to resolve this performance bottleneck, they proposed short filtering [13]. According to this algorithm, if a string shares a certain number of substrings, the pair is considered identical. Consequently, they could skip many character-to-character comparisons in the middle of matching processes. However, this approach is not applicable to matching malware programs because patterns of substrings in SCFSs depend on variable authors' coding styles.

From the view point of parallelism and resource management, there have been several approaches for large workload distributions in scientific calculation, such as matrix calculation [9]. It distributes workloads to multiple virtual machines (VM) which is useful to fully utilize computing resources. However, we distribute virtual CPUs (VCPU) instead of workloads. In an approach similar to our work, some researchers have proposed dynamic resource allocation [12]. These studies model workloads using resource usages, such as CPU usage, memory usage and so on. Our work utilizes an easier modeling variable, Q, which indicates how many workloads are distributed as well as CPU usage.

3   Motivation

In an attempt to achieve a practical malware identification system, we thoroughly analyze conventional operational routines for similarity measurement and identify three critical mismatches in the conventional routines. They are summarized as follows.

- **Inefficient SCFS Matching:** Before measuring set similarities, we need to measure string-to-string (S2S) similarities through C2C matching based on the edit distance algorithm [7]. However, this procedure is the main bottleneck of similarity measurements because C2C matching requires many computations. To resolve such a performance bottleneck, we found that there was a potential for improvement in matching identical SCFSs. The purpose of C2C matching is to find similar strings and measure how much similar two SCFSs are. When we determine whether SCFSs are identical, it is necessary to know whether they are identical to each other but unnecessary to measure how much similar they are because the similarity between matched identical SCFSs is 100 %. This approach can be frequently applied to C2C matching because malware variants in the same family share many identical SCFSs.

- **Brute-force Malware Comparison:** In the similarity measurement procedure, we need to match SCFSs of an input binary with all pre-analyzed malware samples in databases. However, the large number of malware samples causes the performance bottleneck. In order to reduce such comparison overhead, a rule to exclude malware samples that cannot be similar to an input binary before starting similarity measurements is necessary. Without such an exclusion rule, it is necessary to compare all malware samples in databases. This is because they are possibly similar.

- **Non-parallelized Malware Analysis:** According to the AV-TEST [1], malware authors created about 140 million new malware samples in 2014, and 88 % of them are malware variants [8], but it is hard to analyze all malware variants with the optimized methods because of the significant number of malware samples. However, we can utilize many resources in high performance computers to gain higher throughput. One way to use all resources for this purpose is parallelization of analysis which was not considered in the previous work [11]. Even though this is a valid approach to increasing total analysis throughput, this trial can waste resources without proper management. Therefore, we need find a way to efficiently use such resources for optimized parallelism.

4   Design of MalCore Identification System

The design of our system is motivated by three points as follows: inefficient SCFS matching, brute-force malware comparison and non-parallelized malware analysis. In this section, we describe the overview of our system and then how to solve these problems.

4.1   Overall System Design

We implemented the malware variant identification system on MN-MATE [16]. Our malware variant identification system consists of three parts: Convertor, Analyzer and Resource Manager. Both Convertor and Analyzer work on VMs but Resource Manager works on dom0, the privileged VM that can control hypervisor [17]. We describe our architecture in Fig. 1 and the flow chart in Fig. 2.

- **Convertor:** Convertor is responsible for converting input binaries into SCFSs. This conversion task is composed of unpacking, decompiling and structuring. Unpacking is for extracting hidden malicious codes, decompiling is to convert binary codes into high-level codes like C, and structuring is to represent branch instructions in decompiled codes into SCFSs. We describe the structuring rule in Fig. 3a and the example of SCFS conversion in Fig. 3b. After finishing the conversion process, converted SCFSs are sent to Analyzer.
- **Analyzer:** Analyzer plays a role in deciding whether input binaries are malicious through measuring set similarities with existing malware samples in databases. Analyzer uses SCFSs obtained from Convertor for similarity measurements. We designed Analyzer with three components: malware databases, I-Filter and C2C matcher. Malware databases consist of multiple tables, and we store pre-converted SCFSs and their metadata such as hash values in these tables. The role of I-Filter is to match identical SCFSs of an input binary with those in the databases. C2C matcher is responsible for measuring similarities of the remaining SCFSs that are not matched through I-Filter [11]. For malware databases, we use two types of databases: the global database and local database. We used the global database to match identical SCFSs through I-Filter. This database consists of several tables covering malware samples in certain ranges of the total number of SCFCs. Each table stores SCFSs and metadata of covered malware families, variant names, hash values and their total numbers of SCFCs of malware samples. The local database consists of multiple tables and stores the same data but only that of malware samples in one malware family. We store indexed hash values in both types of databases to use I-Filter more efficiently.

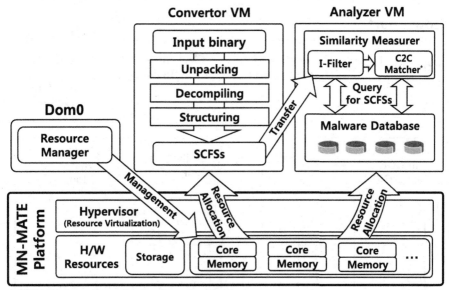

* C2C Matcher : Character-to-character Matcher

Fig. 1. Overview of our system on MN-MATE.

- **Resource Manager:** Each VM is responsible for conversion and analysis. However, their workloads vary according to the situation in which Analyzer does not work due to there being no SCFSs or Convertor generates so many SCFSs that Analyzer cannot process all of them. To prevent such a waste of resources, Resource Manager allocates a proper amount of resources to each VM. Therefore, we can conserve resources through manipulation of the processing speed of each VM through resource allocation. Also, we utilize VCPU pinning to dedicated nodes to enhance memory access performance through local memory access instead of remote memory access.

4.2 I-Filter

We pointed out that S2S matching for identical SCFSs is inefficient despite the high share ratio of identical SCFSs. In order to enhance the performance of S2S matching, we use I-Filter [11] to match identical SCFSs through hash value comparisons and then match only remaining SCFSs through edit distance algorithm. We use CRC-64 for generation of hash values.

Efficiency of I-Filter can be seen through comparisons between time complexities of both methods. In previous approach, all matching is done through edit distance algorithm. Its time complexity between two SCFSs is $O(mn)$. Both m and n are lengths of SCFSs, and their minimum value is 10 [7]. In order to accelerate matching for SCFSs, all SCFSs are stored in the BK-tree [6] indexed malware database in the previous work [8]. However, it is time-consuming to find

Flow Chart

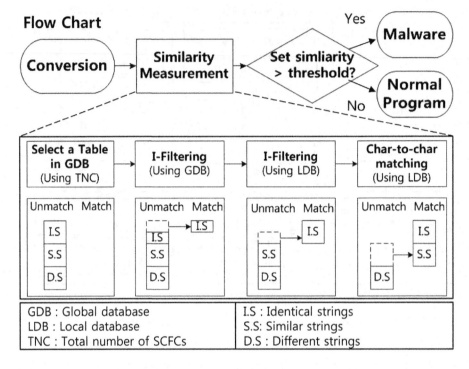

Fig. 2. Whole analysis flow chart.

Control flow	Result
Basic Block	B
Procedure Call	C
Break	K
Continue	T
Return	R
Goto	J
If	I
Else	E
Open Brace	{
Close Brace	}
Branch Condition: AND	A
Branch Condition: OR	O
Loop: Pre-tested	W
Loop: Post-tested	D
Loop: Infinite	F

(a) Grammar for structuring

Binary file

Decompiling

```
Procedure1              Procedure2
func1(){                func2(){
  Label1:                 if(a){
  if(a){                  }
    goto Label1;          else{
  }                         while(b){
  else{                       func1();
    func1();                }
  }                       }
  return;                 return;
}                       }
```

Structuring

Procedure1 : BI{BJB}E{BCB}BR
Procedure2 : BI{B}E{BW{BCB}B}BR

(b) Example of conversion

Fig. 3. Conversion rule and example [7].

valid SCFSs because each character of SCFSs should be checked. On the other hand, the searching time complexity of I-Filtering is $O(log\ s)$ where s is the number of SCFSs. For S2S matching for each SCFS, each matching is processed through hash value matching whose time complexity is $O(1)$ without character-to-character comparison. In addition, the number of comparisons is $O(log\ s)$ because we stored the hash values in B-tree. Therefore, we can induce the time complexity for finding one SCFS is $O(log\ s)$ from $O(1)O(log\ s) = O(log\ s)$. However, checks for identicalness are required to prevent hash collisions for all SCFSs whose hash values are identical. The time complexity for hash collision checking is $O(m)$ which is proportional to the lower length m in a string pair.

4.3   Table Division

When we match SCFSs in the global database, unnecessary comparisons with malware samples that cannot be similar cause redundant overhead costs. In order to reduce such costs, we make a rule for excluding malware samples that cannot be similar before starting similarity measurements. Because the set similarity, the final similarity result [7], is directly related to the total number of SCFCs, we can exclude such malware samples through dividing tables in the global database. Therefore, we can exclude many malware candidates through comparisons of the total number of SCFCs of an input binary. We describe such cases in Fig. 4. In the first case, malware x can be similar to malware y if all their SCFSs are matched. In the second case, malware x and y however are definitely dissimilar even if malware x and y consist of only identical SCFSs. Thus, malware x is eligible for comparison but malware y is ineligible according to the malware exclusion policy.

In order to apply the above policy, we divide the table of the global database into smaller tables according to the total number of SCFCs. Because our divided tables store only possibly similar malware samples, it is possible to compare a smaller number of entries. We describe the example of table division in Fig. 5. Before we analyze input SCFSs, we select one of tables in the global database based on the total number of SCFCs of each input binary. Although this selection may result in a small cost, we can gain greater performance benefits from it. Since each malware has on average 94 SCFSs in our malware samples, we can avoid comparisons of 94 SCFSs of the input binary with those of malware samples that cannot be similar in databases through one table selection. Through table division, we can reduce comparisons due to reduced depths of B-trees and I/O requests for loading unnecessary malware data from databases.

However, table division should guarantee that all possibly similar malware samples are in each divided table. This guarantee is based on the set similarity threshold value, 0.6 [7]. As described in Fig. 5, if the selected table covers malware D, E and F with the total number of SCFCs from 55 to 80, this table should have malware samples with the total number of SCFCs from 55 by 0.6 to 80 by 1.67. In such cases, we call the total number of SCFCs from 55 to 80 the cover range and from 33 to 55 and from 80 to 134 the guarantee range. Malware samples covered by guarantee range should be included in the divided

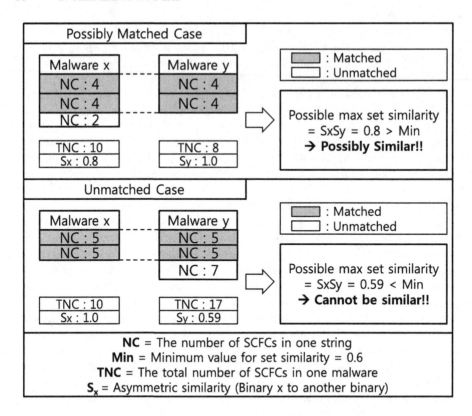

Fig. 4. Max similarity according to the total number of SCFCs.

tables. Otherwise, comparison only with a table cannot guarantee that all possibly similar malware samples are stored. From the perspective of performance, we need to divide a table into smaller tables because the number of hash entries can change according to sizes of cover ranges. However, excessive table division causes storage redundancy for guarantee ranges. Furthermore, they can be much larger than cover ranges if the cover ranges are too small. Therefore, we set the cover range from one of 3,000, 10,000 and 20,000 and dynamically divide tables to avoid excessive storage redundancy while maintaining a certain level of performance. If the difference in the number of hash entries is smaller than 110 % of the total number of hash entries with a larger cover range, we set the larger cover range since this 10 % difference does not cause meaningful performance degradation. After applying our table division policy, storage redundancy is not large compared to storage capacity of HDD. As a result of table division, depths are reduced from 50 % to 80 % and their average depth is 33 %.

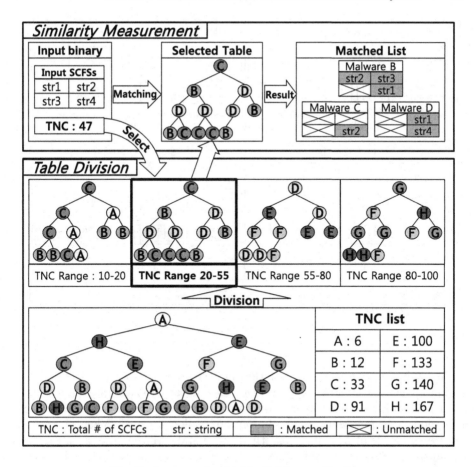

Fig. 5. An example of table division application.

4.4 Dynamic Resource Allocation

Our system consists of two main processing parts, Convertor and Analyzer. We describe this system in Fig. 6. There are two problems causing unbalanced core allocation. First one is processing speeds vary according to which binaries are analyzed, and the other one is that the required number of cores is not a natural number unlike the actual number of allocated cores. Therefore, naive static core allocation cause waste of CPU power. To prevent such a situation, we dynamically allocate cores according to the number of converted binaries. We define the value Q as the representation of the number of such binaries for dynamic core allocation modeling. To figure out whether core allocation is appropriate, we also define *Low* and *High* which are threshold values of Q which is periodically checked by Resource Manager. We categorize four states to determine whether we need core reallocation according to Q.

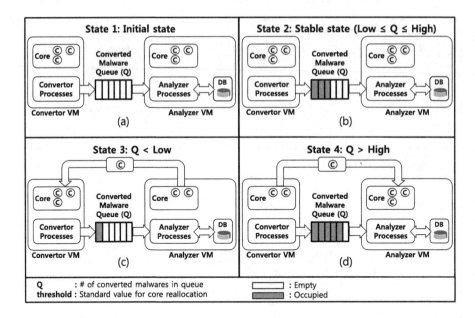

Fig. 6. Dynamic core allocation.

In detail, Fig. 6a refers to *State 1*, the initial core allocation state. In this state, we initially allocate cores using average core allocation of the previous result. If there is no such result, we can arbitrarily allocate cores. Even if it is wrong allocation, Resource Manger will appropriately allocate cores. When Q reaches the average value of *Low* and *High*, the current state will be *State 2*. In Fig. 6b, we illustrate *State 2*. In this case, we consider cores are properly allocated. Because the case where Q is higher than or equal to *Low* and lower than or equal to *High* indicates that jobs are appropriately assigned to Convertor and Analyzer. Consequently, Resource Manger does not reallocate cores. We describe *State 3* where Q is lower than *Low* in Fig. 6c. In this state, we reallocate cores to Convertor since Analyzer occupies too many cores compared to workloads. However, it is possible that frequent and unnecessary core reallocation can occur with this policy. To prevent such situation, Resource Manager temporarily store Q in *Low* when core reallocation occurs. In the next period, Resource Manger continuously control the number of cores with a new *Low* until the state is changed to *State 2*. On the other hand, *State 4* is the case where Q is lower than *Low* as described in Fig. 6d. In this situation, we reallocate cores since Convertor processed too many binaries. Similarly, Resource Manager temporarily store Q in *High*, when core reallocation occurs. Then, Resource Manger continuously maintains a new *High* until the state is changed to *State 2*.

4.5   Implementation

- **Convertor:** Convertor is responsible for unpacking, decompiling and structuring. For unpacking, we use the unpacking function of UPX [5] because malware authors widely use it to pack malware programs. After the unpacking process, we decompile unpacked binaries using REC decompiler [4]. Then, we convert decompiled binaries into SCFSs using the rule in Fig. 3a.
- **Analyzer:** This module measures similarities between input binaries and malware samples. The matching process starts with the global database. We first select a table in the global database based on the total number of input SCFCs. With the selected global database, we match only identical SCFSs through I-Filter. In this step, we process near unique strings first and then match duplicated SCFSs. Because such near unique strings are not normally shared, they are useful in determining a specific malware candidate. If the set similarity exceeds the set similarity threshold T, matching processes are performed on the local database whose tables cover respective malware families. If the highest set similarity is lower than min_t even after all SCFSs are processed, we consider this binary unmalicious. Otherwise, the top five candidate malware samples with similarities higher than the others are selected. With the local database, we apply I-Filter first because all SCFSs could not be matched through I-Filtering. Then, the similarity of the remaining SCFSs is measured through C2C matching. We consider the target binary is malicious if its similarity is larger than T.

  In the above procedure, we define several parameters. We choose min_t as 0.1 and determine the number of candidates as 5 based on our experiments. We use 0.9 for T and 0.6 for t as used in related work [7]. However, we can change these values according to additional experiments.
- **Resource Manager:** In Resource Manager, we use the Q variable to predict workloads between Convertor and Analyzer. For actual parameters, we currently define $High$ as 30 and Low as 10. With these values, there was no waste of resources, such as too many converted SCFSs or no SCFSs for similarity measurements, during our experiments. If we increase this value, the occurrence wasted resources will be reduced. In this case, even though more binaries will not be analyzed, its effect is negligible in the long run. However, we should consider that the most important factor for threshold values of Q is whether their values can guarantee avoidance of unbalanced resource distribution. We can change threshold values considering such conditions. Also, we define the period of checking Q as 0.3 seconds. Although it can be changed, we should choose checking period while considering core reallocation frequency. With a small value, it cause performance degradation because core reallocation flushes caches. With a large value, it cannot balance core distribution.

  When we reallocate cores, we reassign VCPUs to allocate cores to VMs. For efficient resource utilization, we assign memory on one node to each VM and set the VCPU affinity to the node in order to avoid remote memory access. Moreover, Resource Manager reallocates VCPUs to Analyzer and operates one more analyzer process according to CPU usage.

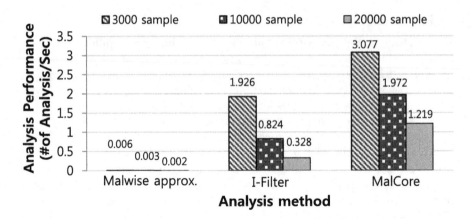

Fig. 7. Analyzer performance with a single core.

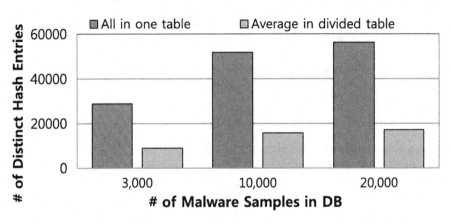

Fig. 8. The number of hash entries in each database.

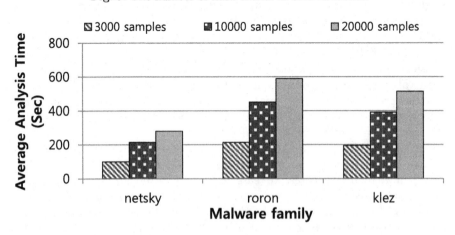

Fig. 9. Analyzer performance with approximate matching of Malwise.

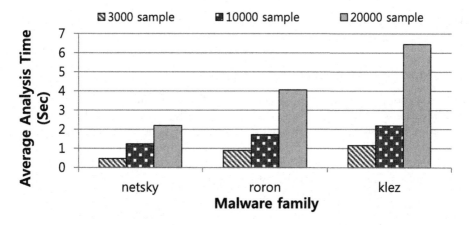

Fig. 10. Analyzer performance with approximate matching and I-Filter.

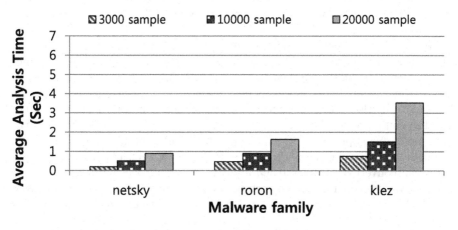

Fig. 11. Analyzer performance with MalCore.

5   Performance Evaluation

This section presents module performance improvements, total performance improvements, similarities between malware variants and validation of normal program threshold. The experimental environment consists of the AMD Opteron Processor 6282SE 64 core 2.6 Ghz, 128 GB RAM, SAS 10kbytes HDD, Cent OS 6.4 64 bit with Kernel 3.8.2 version, MN-MATE [16] and MySQL 14.14 for the database, but we utilized 16 cores and 16 GB RAM. We implemented our databases on MyISAM [2] which is a type of disk-based database. On the other hand, Malwise [8] consists of BK-tree [6] indexed memory databases. In all experiments, MalCore refers to application of I-Filter, Table division and Dynamic Resource Allocation. But Dynamic Resource Allocation is not applied to single process experiments. Also, MN-MATE means that we experimented on MN-MATE. Without MN-MATE, we experimented on Xen 4.2.1. Finally, we used

3,000 malware samples [3] and generated additional malware variants using the code mutation tool.

5.1 Module Performance Improvements

In this section, we evaluate the performance of each module in malware variant identification systems. This evaluation does not reflect the effect of dynamic core allocation because it focuses on each module with a single core, but, we consider the effect of VCPU pinning. First, we compare the performance of analyzer in Fig. 7. For the Analyzer performance, the performance improvements between approximate matching of Malwise [8] and application of all of our techniques on MN-MATE are from 512 to 657 times. For comparison between I-Filter application and MalCore, the performance improvements are from 60 % to 272 % and the improvement increases as the number of malware samples increases. These improvements are largely from table division because table division reduces on average 33 % numbers of table entries for identical SCFSs matching procedure as described in Fig. 8.

We describe the performance improvements in Figs. 9, 10 and 11. We can discern several performance trends in these figures. The trends of performance improvements are different from the malware families. This difference results mainly from the number of SCFCs in each malware and each string. For Malwise, the trend of performance difference between malware families results from the fact that computation time depends on string matching measurements. On the other hand, our approach relies on the number of hash entries in databases.

Finally, we describe the performance of Convertor. With a single core, Convertor can convert on average 0.365 input malware binaries per second. As the speed of Analyzer increases, the performance of Convertor creates a larger bottleneck. Moreover, its performance trend is different from Analyzer because it depends on how many instructions; not only branch instructions but also other types of instructions, variables and other factors are included. This different trend of processing speed causes unbalanced workload distributions even with perfect static core allocation. This is why core allocation, a part of dynamic resource allocation, is necessary.

5.2 Total Performance Improvements

In this section, we evaluate the total performance of the malware variant identification systems. We applied our Convertor to Malwise [8] because Malwise does not have dynamic resource allocation functions. We randomly choose malware samples for our experiments and show the performance evaluation in Figs. 12 and 13.

Performance improvements of MalCore with MN-MATE are on average 280.9 times compared to approximate matching proposed in Malwise and 71 % improvements compared to only I-Filter application. Although improvements are mostly from I-Filter for matching identical SCFSs and table division, the performance gain is limited by Convertor performance and a waste of resources

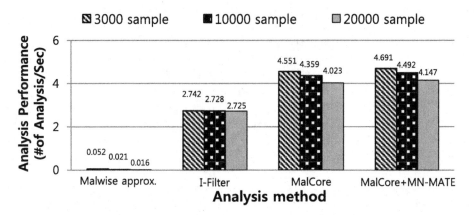

Fig. 12. Total performance (50 % of resource to Convertor and 50 % of resource to Analyzer).

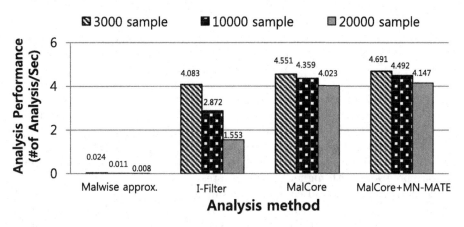

Fig. 13. Total performance (75 % of resource to Convertor and 25 % of resource to Analyzer).

due to unbalanced resource distribution. However, our system can balance the performance of each VM with our dynamic allocation.

5.3 Similarity of Malware Variants

In this experiment, we measure similarities using our approach. To determine whether input binaries were malicious, we used the same set similarity threshold value, 0.6, used in the related work [8]. Table 1 shows similarities between malware variants in *Klez*, *Roron* and *Netsky* malware families.

According to our experiments, *Klez*, *Roron* and *Netsky* had 43, 62, 66 percent matching rates. As the matching rates increase, new malware variants will more probably be classified. However, we still can classify malware variants with low

Table 1. Similarities between malware variants.

| | : Matched | | : Unmatched |

	12	25	35	37	ao	b39	b50
12		0.5	0.53	0.53	0.66	0.5	0.39
25	0.5		0.84	0.89	0.56	0.93	0.63
35	0.53	0.84		0.94	0.64	0.9	0.63
37	0.53	0.89	0.94		0.6	0.95	0.63
ao	0.66	0.56	0.64	0.6		0.57	0.43
b39	0.5	0.93	0.9	0.95	0.57		0.63
b50	0.39	0.63	0.63	0.63	0.43	0.63	

Roron

	a	b	c	d	e	g	h	i
a		0.73	0.91	0.65	0.5	0.49	0.5	0.45
b	0.73		0.8	0.87	0.54	0.53	0.54	0.52
c	0.91	0.8		0.7	0.5	0.49	0.5	0.45
d	0.65	0.87	0.7		0.52	0.5	0.52	0.51
e	0.5	0.54	0.5	0.52		0.94	0.91	0.91
g	0.49	0.54	0.49	0.5	0.94		0.93	0.92
h	0.5	0.54	0.5	0.52	0.91	0.93		0.99
i	0.45	0.52	0.45	0.51	0.91	0.92	0.99	

Klez

	ab	b	c	k	p	u	w	x
ab		0.74	0.84	0.91	0.64	0.75	0.7	0.6
b	0.74		0.76	0.72	0.54	0.58	0.55	0.53
c	0.84	0.76		0.86	0.6	0.67	0.63	0.59
k	0.91	0.72	0.86		0.61	0.7	0.66	0.58
p	0.64	0.54	0.6	0.61		0.68	0.6	0.88
u	0.75	0.58	0.67	0.7	0.68		0.85	0.64
w	0.7	0.55	0.63	0.66	0.6	0.85		0.57
x	0.6	0.53	0.59	0.58	0.88	0.64	0.57	

Netsky

matching rates. For instance, the matching rates of the *Klez* family were only 43 percent. However, let us suppose a, b, c and d *Klez* variants are group A and the other ones, e, g and i, *Klez* variants, are group B. In this case, one malware sample from group A and the other one from group B are enough to classify all *Klez* malware variants in Table 1. But, there is more chance to classify unseen malware programs with higher matching rates.

Furthermore, we should compare our similarity results since the purpose of our work is to accelerate Malwise. However, because we use REC decompiler which is different from Malwise [8], we measure similarities in both Malwise and our approach with REC decompiler. As a result, most similarities are identical, and they are lower than 0.01, even if the similarities are different. The reason for this small difference is that we match identical SCFSs first and then similar SCFSs but Malwise matches similar SCFSs.

5.4 Validity of Normal Program Threshold

As we mentioned in implementation of Analyzer, we use a normal program threshold, 0.1. If the set similarity is lower than 0.1, we consider the input as a normal program after matching identical SCFSs with the global database. To validate our parameter, we measure similarities of 3,256 normal programs from the Windows system folders with malware samples. The result of our experiments confirm that our threshold value is valid because set similarities of only 0.0012 % of normal programs exceeded 0.1 as shown in Fig. 14.

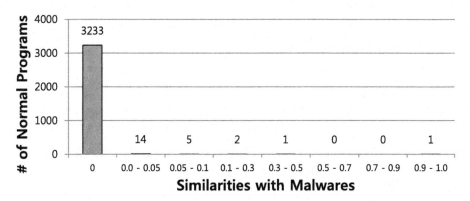

Fig. 14. Similarity between normal programs and malwares.

6 Conclusion

Many researchers have proposed many control flow matching methods. However, there is a trade-off between accuracy and performance. To solve such problems, we designed MalCore which is composed of I-Filter, table division and dynamic resource allocation and apply them incrementally on a real manycore computing platform called MN-MATE. As a result, we gained the total performance improvement of on average 280.9 times in our experiments; especially, the performance improvement of Analyzer is 593.2 times on average.

References

1. AV-TEST. http://www.av-test.org
2. MySQL reference. http://dev.mysql.com/doc/refman/5.7/en/index.html
3. Offensive computing. http://www.offensivecomputing.net
4. Reverse Engineering Compiler. http://www.backerstreet.com
5. Ultimate Packer for eXecutables. http://upx.sourceforge.net
6. Baeza-Yates, R., Navarro, G.: Fast approximate string matching in a dictionary. In: Proceedings of South America Symposium on String Processing and Information Retrieval, SPIRE 1998, pp. 14–22. IEEE (1998)
7. Cesare, S., Xiang, Y.: Classification of malware using structured control flow. In: Proceedings of Australasian Symposium on Parallel and Distributed Computing, AusPDC 2010, pp. 61–70. ACM (2010)
8. Cesare, S., Xiang, Y., Zhou, W.: Malwise–an effective and efficient classification system for packed and polymorphic malware. IEEE Trans. Comput. **62**(6), 1193–1206 (2013)
9. Gusev, M., Ristov, S.: Matrix multiplication performance analysis in virtualized shared memory multiprocessor. In: Proceedings of 35th International Convention, MIPRO 2012, pp. 251–256. IEEE (2012)
10. Kim, T., Hwang, W., Kim, C., Shin, D.J., Park, K.W. Park, K.H.: Malfinder: accelerated malware classification system through filtering on manycore system. In: Proceedings of 1st International Conference on Information Systems Security and Privacy, ICISSP 2015, pp. 1–10 (2010)

11. Kim, T., Hwang, W. Park, K.W., Park, K.H.: I-Filter: identical structured control flow string filter for accelerated malware variant classification. In: Proceedings of International Symposium on Biometrics and Security Technologies, ISBAST 2014. IEEE (2014)
12. Kundu, S., Rangaswami, R., Dutta, K., Zhao, M.: Application performance modeling in a virtualized environments. In: Proceedings of 16th International Symposium on High Performance Computer Architecture, HPCA 2010, pp. 1–10. IEEE (2010)
13. Li, W., Godzik, A.: Cd-hit: a fast program for clustering and comparing large sets of protein or nucleotide sequences. Bioinformatics **22**(13), 1658–1659 (2006)
14. Mohaisen, A., West, A.G., Mankin, A., Alrawi, O.: Chatter: Classifying malware families using system event ordering. In: Proceedings of 2nd Communications and Network Security, CNS 2014, pp. 283–291. IEEE (2014)
15. OKane, P., Sezer, S., McLaughlin, K.: Obfuscation: the hidden malware. IEEE Secur. Priv. **9**(5), 41–47 (2011)
16. Park, K.H., Hwang, W., Seok, H., Kim, C., Shin, D.J., Kim, D.J., Maeng, M.K., Kim, S.M.: MN-MATE: elastic resource management of manycores and a hybrid memory hierarchy for a cloud node. ACM J. Emerg. Technol. Comput. Syst. **12**(1), 5 (2015)
17. Paul, B., Boris, D., Keir, F., Steven, H., Tim, H., Alex, H., Rolf, N., Ian, P., Andrew, W.: Xen and the art of virtualization. In: Proceedings of the 19th ACM Symposium on Operating Systems Principles, SOSP 2003, pp. 164–177. ACM (2003)

How to Discover High-Quality Roles?
A Survey and Dependency Analysis of Quality Criteria in Role Mining

Michael Kunz[1]([⊠]), Ludwig Fuchs[2], Michael Netter[2], and Günther Pernul[1]

[1] Department of Information Systems, University of Regensburg,
Regensburg, Germany
{michael.kunz,guenther.pernul}@ur.de
http://www-ifs.uni-regensburg.de
[2] Nexis Gmbh, Regensburg, Germany
{ludwig.fuchs,michael.netter}@nexis-secure.de
http://www.nexis-secure.de

Abstract. Roles have evolved into the de facto standard for access control in Enterprise Identity Management. However, companies struggle to develop and maintain a role-based access control state. For the initial role deployment, role mining is widely used. Due to the high number and complexity of available role mining algorithms, companies fail to perceive which is selected best according to their needs. Furthermore, requirements on the composition of roles such as reduction of administration cost are to be taken into account in role development. In order to give them guidance, in this paper we aggregate existing role mining approaches and classify them. For consideration of individual prerequisites we extract quality criteria that should be met. Later on, we discuss interdependencies between the criteria to help role developers avoid unwanted side-effects and produce RBAC states that are tailored to their preferences.

Keywords: Role quality · Role mining · RBAC · Identity Management

1 Introduction

Regulating access to resources is an elementary function of every Identity Management System (IdMS). Not just as a result of governmental regulations or compliance requirements like the Sarbanes-Oxley Act [47], Basel III [2], or the EU General Data Protection Regulation in its revised form [13], especially medium- and large-sized companies are forced to control access to sensitive information. Over the past decades, Role-Based Access Control (RBAC [45]), has become the de facto standard for managing access to resources in IT systems. In RBAC, roles act as intermediary between users and permissions, essentially reducing access control complexity. Despite being widely used, RBAC struggles with the dynamic evolution of role models over time. Besides the daily user administration, the

© Springer International Publishing Switzerland 2015
O. Camp et al. (Eds.): ICISSP 2015, CCIS 576, pp. 49–67, 2015.
DOI: 10.1007/978-3-319-27668-7_4

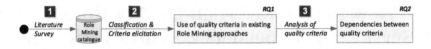

Fig. 1. Research methodology.

central challenge after setting up a role model is its strategic maintenance. Role system maintenance focuses on updating and cleansing role configurations, discarding unused, and defining new roles. Changing business processes, organizational structures, employee positions, or security policies and newly imposed regulations force the administrators to quickly react and adapt the access control structures in place. Commonly, this leads to an increasing number of roles, an overall reduction of the role model quality and the advent of security vulnerabilities due to erroneously assigned roles or outdated role definitions.

In order to mitigate the risk of increasing security vulnerabilities in RBAC, one cornerstone of ensuring a high role model quality is the periodic assessment of the role model components, such as the user-role assignments (UA), the role-permission assignments (RA), or role hierarchy structures. Role mining approaches that support organizations during their initial setup of an RBAC model have attracted the attention of researchers in the last decade. Over the last four years, for instance, a variety of research groups have published approaches to come up with an initial set of roles. However, despite the fact that reports like the Ponemon Cyber Crime Study 2013[1] emphasize the importance of implementing strategic policies and procedures for controlling access control structures, hardly any attention has been drawn to the challenge of maintaining an existing role model. Recently, the need for investigating and cleaning role model structures has been highlighted by [18]. However, the core challenge of measuring the current quality of a role model and select criteria for its optimization still remains unsolved. Due to the development of the area and its importance for access control it is likely that role mining approaches are re-applied by organizations periodically in order to ensure role model correctness. Our work builds on both, the in-depth investigation of the research area as well as our practical experience from several industry projects within medium- and large sized companies dealing with the setup and management of a role-based IdMS. Similar to the work presented in [18], we argue that the practical project requirements cannot be considered to a sufficient extent by the available role mining approaches. In particular, we address the following two research questions:

– *RQ1: Which quality criteria are employed in existing role mining approaches?*
– *RQ2: Which dependencies between those quality criteria do exist?*

Hence, the contribution of this work is threefold. In order to close the existing research gap, this paper firstly analyzes the development of role mining,

---

[1] http://www.hpenterprisesecurity.com/ponemon-2013-cost-of-cyber-crime-study-reports.

presenting a short survey of the field and underlining the rapid development in the area. In this respect, it builds on an existing survey of the area published in the year 2011. During execution, various role mining algorithms rely on some sort of quality criteria to different extents. As a result, this paper secondly analyzes and extracts potential criteria for rating the quality of role models included in current role mining approaches. It points out the differences among the various approaches and underlines the need for a structured quality rating process. Thirdly, this paper focuses on the mutual dependencies between the different quality criteria. With this contribution, we aim at stimulating the research community and engage them to enrich existing role mining approaches considering quality criteria in a structured manner.

The remainder of the paper is structured as follows: In Sect. 2 we present the RBAC concept and related work. Section 3 outlines the applied methodology before Sect. 4 shows the conducted survey and categorizes role mining approaches according to their underlying techniques. Subsequently, in Sect. 5 quality criteria are extracted from existing role detection mechanisms. We discuss their dependencies and show which criteria are mutually exclusive, which are complementary, and which have no effect on others. Finally, Sect. 6 concludes the paper and outlines future work.

2   Related Work

In todays medium and large-sized companies, RBAC has become the state-of-the-art standard for controlling user access to resources. As a result of the large amount of research output, several surveys of the general area of roles in IT security have been presented (e.g. [21,64]). Authors lately agreed upon the growing importance of role development in general and automated role mining in specific. Fuchs et al., for instance, provided an evaluation of role development approaches in [19,20]. Since their publications, the research output in the area has grown more than double, requiring a survey update in order to give an in-depth understanding of recent developments.

During the initial setup of a role model, role mining algorithms inherently rely on different quality criteria to various extents. Nevertheless, no structured analysis considering those criteria has been executed so far. It has rather been shown that popular role mining approaches like [23,43] or [48] do not offer the guidance required to judge the correctness of role definitions and role models [18]. In practice, however, it is very likely that companies re-apply role mining techniques in order to ensure role model correctness after having employed a role mining approach for the initial role setup. Yet, none of the related work in the field focuses on quality criteria applied during role system maintenance. In [42], the authors investigated the usage of selected metrics like the Weighted Structural Complexity (WSC) for analyzing role system states. [20] described mechanisms for periodically evaluating a role systems quality but do not consider the scalability of their approach in large real-world scenarios. [18] recently proposed the integration of a distinct quality rating and role classification phase in their

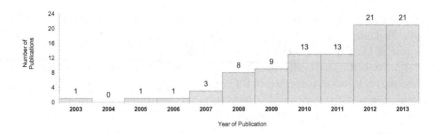

Fig. 2. Development of the research area.

role optimization process model. However, they do not present an overview of available quality criteria and their application. As a result, the core challenge of measuring the current quality of a role model still remains unsolved.

In the following this paper improves the state of the art by firstly presenting a survey of role mining approaches and their considered quality metrics. A consecutive analysis of the quality criteria and their combined applicability aims at stimulating future research to integrate them into role mining in a modular manner. Based on company-specific quality criteria this would allow organizations to select the best fitting role mining approach in the first place and re-use it during periodic role model reviews.

3   Methodology

Our methodology to answer the research questions presented in Sect. 1 is depicted in Fig. 1. At first, we survey the research area and create a catalog of role mining approaches that serves as the basis for further analyses (step 1). For this literature survey, we follow the methodology proposed by [32]. We carried out a bibliographic database search including the ACM Digital Library[2], DBLP[3], IEEE Digital Library[4], and Google Scholar[5] using the keyword "role mining". To arrive at a complete catalog of role mining approaches, author and reference search for each publication was applied to identify previously undiscovered research. Finally, papers that do not present role mining techniques were removed from the catalog (e.g. [42]). Consecutively, we classify recent role mining publications according to the scheme presented by [19]. Additional clusters were added for role mining approaches that used new techniques. Note, that approaches that rely on more than one role mining technique were clustered based on the predominant technique being used. At this stage we completed our first contribution by extending the existing survey and highlighting the rapid increase of research within the last three years as well as the further diversification of role mining techniques used.

---

[2] http://dl.acm.org/.
[3] http://www.dblp.org/search/index.php.
[4] http://www.computer.org/.
[5] http://scholar.google.com/.

During step 2 of our methodology we answer RQ1 by investigating the usage of quality criteria in role mining algorithms. Note that we do not consider quality criteria known from other fields such as quality management in general as our work aims at stimulating research regarding role system maintenance in specific. General quality management indicators or processes can be incorporated in future research but are not required to rate the initial situation regarding quality criteria used during role system maintenance in the role mining community. Finally, we conduct an in-depth analysis of the identified quality criteria and their dependencies (step 3). To answer RQ2, our results are presented as an impact matrix, showing positive, negative, or no mutual influence.

4   Development of Role Mining Research

This section extends a survey on role mining research conducted by [19]. Figure 2 underlines the importance of an updated interpretation of role detection approaches due to the increase in researchers' attention during the last three years. Between 2011 and 2013, 55 papers related to role mining have been published, representing an increase of 141 percent compared to the number of publications from 2003–2010 (39).

While role mining in general consists of a pre-processing phase, a role detection phase, and a post-processing phase [19], the remainder of this survey focuses on the role detection phase as the core element of every role mining algorithm. During this phase, suitable roles are created based on an existing set of user-permission assignments (UPA). The algorithms can be grouped according to the underlying technique (see Table 1). While the first six techniques have been previously introduced in [19], we identified three additional techniques (Visual Role Mining, Boolean Matrix Decomposition, and Attribute-based Role Mining) being applied to solve the role mining problem for the first time. Additionally to the 21 algorithms published in [19], 26 out of the 55 approaches from 2011 to 2013 have been categorized, while the rest is related to either pre- or post-processing phase. Subsequently, each technique and representative publications are presented:

Subset Enumeration aims to discover roles through creating all possible intersections of permission sets. Due to the exponential complexity of enumerating all possible subsets, algorithms such as [58] use heuristics for role candidate selection. Hence, role mining algorithms based on this technique strive to balance complexity and quality of results. With 13 available algorithms, this is the most frequently used technique in role mining.

Clustering is a role mining approach that is directly derived from data mining [17]. Using a UPA-matrix as input, this technique searches for clusters with similar permissions. However, clustering approaches struggle with limitations such as requiring users or permissions to be only part of one single cluster [17]. To solve these challenges, several clustering variants exist. Examples include iterative application of the technique or reduction of the input [28,34].

Graph Optimization uses bipartite graphs to represent the UPA [8]. As roles represent an intermediary between the two disjoint vertices of users and

Table 1. Overview of role mining techniques.

Technique	Description
Subset enumeration	Calculates all possible intersections of permissions in the initial UPA
Clustering	Creates clusters with similar permissions that indicate role candidates
Graph optimization	Convert an initial bipartite graph into a tripartite graph whereby middle vertices indicate role candidates
Frequent permission set mining	Discovers permissions that frequently occur together in access control data
Formal concept analysis	Discovery of a hierarchical structure for representing the UPA-matrix through mathematical concepts
Heuristic matrix selection	Iteration through the rows of a UPA-matrix and selecting rows as roles based on heuristics
Visual role detection	Sorting and visualizing the UPA-matrix for detecting roles visually
Boolean matrix decomposition	Decomposition of the UPA-matrix into two consistent sub-matrices
Attribute-based role mining	Leveraging attributes to construct roles

permissions, those approaches aim at converting the bipartite into a tripartite graph or a representation with sub-graphs. Roles are then represented by the middle vertex [8] or each necessary sub-graph [40].

Frequent Permission Set Mining has its roots in marketing analysis and algorithms of generic frequent set mining [1]. Initially used for the study of consumers' purchase behavior, it is applied by role mining algorithms in order to discover permissions that frequently occur together. The presumption is that permission sets that appear together can be interpresed as role candidates.

Formal Concept Analysis is a data mining technique similar to clustering, overcoming the limitation of only assigning entities to one group [42]. Related algorithms build a concept lattice from the UPA-matrix and reduce duplicate information. A concept lattice is a construct similar to a graph and represents roles and their connection in a partially ordered collection of clusters which again consist of permissions and users.

Heuristic Matrix Selection is similar to Subset Enumeration without the initial role set being based on intersections of permissions. Instead, it iterates through rows (or columns) and picks role candidates successively according to the highest number of given assignments (e.g. permissions assigned to a user). Initially, each row/column is treated as a role. Subsequently, a cross-check for duplicate roles is conducted [3].

Visual Role Mining is a fairly new technique initially proposed in [10]. It reorders rows and columns of the input UPA-matrix in order to create clusters of adjoined permissions. Displayed to an administrator, the underlying assumption is that humans' cognitive capabilities and context knowledge are better suited to discover proper roles compared to purely algorithm-based approaches.

Boolean Matrix Decomposition is an approach that directly addresses the Role Mining Problem (RMP) introduced by [51]. This formal definition of role mining and targets at decomposing the boolean UPA-matrix into two separate matrices, a UA-matrix and a PA-matrix. By dividing the initial UPA-matrix into two consistent sub-matrices, the columns of the UA-matrix and the rows of the PA-matrix build up the set of roles.

Attribute-based Role Mining such as [16] are trying to incorporate business information through attributes into role mining. They rely on the assumption that additional semantic data is available and can be taken into account. Attribute-based approaches combine other techniques and enrich them with attribute-based mechanisms to arrive at an improved role set.

5   Quality-Related Criteria

5.1   Criteria

After their classification we examined role mining algorithms regarding their decision making processes of including certain role candidates in their final output. We argue that this central decision making provides well-suited indicators for quality management in RBAC. This assumption is based on the claims of several publications (e.g. [56,63]) of outperforming competitive approaches in terms of the quality of generated roles.

A total of 23 different quality criteria can be identified. They either focus on the quality of the overall RBAC state, the quality of single roles, or both. At first we focus on RBAC state quality criteria. Secondly, we examine criteria that deal with the quality of an individual role (cf. Table 2). Note that for some criteria (e.g. *Exclude Unused Permissions*) additional input information is required. In the following, we present a detailed interpretation of the quality criteria and group them according to their focus.

Achieve Completeness. Completeness refers to the exact representation of the original access control state, i.e. the goal is to cover the initial UPA-matrix with the resulting set of roles. In contrast to most approaches (e.g. [3,53,60]), some techniques allow to deviate to a certain extent from the initial UPA-matrix based on a given threshold (the so called $\delta - RMP$ [51]) [5,35]. Completeness therefore measures the quality of a RBAC state by measuring the degree to which a resulting role set represents the initial access control situation.

Reduce Number of Roles. Initially formulated in the RMP, the goal of having as few roles as possible is based on the assumption that complexity of RBAC is directly connected to the number of roles maintained. Thus, the number of roles in a given RBAC state is a quality criteria usable to rate the estimated administrative efforts to manage the role model. Depending on the size of a company in terms of its employees, user accounts, permissions and UPA, this measure can be normalized in order to allow for a comparison of role models in different organizations.

Decrease Role Set Similarity. Quality criteria related to Role Set Similarity measure the distance between two given sets of roles. They are mainly used for the measurement of the dissimilarity of RBAC states (e.g. in [62]) or the difference between a current RBAC state and a targeted state. In [29], for instance, the permission similarity is measured using the Euclidean Distance. Furthermore, the Jaccard Similarity is a popular metric used in a variety of approaches [5,40,57].

Minimize Users/Permissions per Role & Minimize/Maximize Roles per User/Permission. Quality criteria assigned to this category target at two main objectives. First, the definition of an upper bound per role limiting the amount of users assigned to one role. Second, the objective of finding as few as possible permissions that are placed in a role. This can, for instance, be applied in case an organization aims at defining a larger number of small roles for employees that exactly fit their specialist tasks. On the contrary, maximizing the number of users or permissions per role can be beneficial other scenarios, e.g. when organizations aim at defining a small set of large roles. Moreover, Minimizing/Maximizing the roles per element (user or permission) is applied in seven existing role mining approaches (e.g. see [34,39]). This can be useful in case the overall role model complexity in terms of relationships among the role model elements should be minimized.

Fullfill Role Constraints. Role Constraints impose restrictions on the definition of roles. For instance, [38] consider Segregation of Duty (SOD) policies that entail mutually exclusive permissions in the RBAC state. Other policies, such as the four-eye-principle, that affect the user assignments of a role are also conceivable.

Reduce WSC. In contrast to most other quality criteria the so called Weighted Structural Complexity (WSC) is a widely-used heuristic to rate the complexity of a RBAC model. Originally introduced by [42], it applies weights to different optimization objectives. It can be seen as one of the most advanced measures that solely relies on the components of an RBAC state. It is usable for both, individual roles and role sets, and thus allows for a good comparability of RBAC states. As a result of its popularity, several existing role mining approaches are able to consider the WSC.

Optimize Matrix Sorting. Matrix sorting aims at covering an initial access control state by sorting the input UPA-matrix based on user accounts with similar permissions and permissions that are assigned a similar set of user accounts. [10] introduced the ADVISER and EXTRACT algorithms that generate a matrix representation of the initial UPA-matrix that clusters permissions and user accounts together. As a result, large areas covering initial UPA can be visually detected by a human role engineer.

Similarities & Redundancy. Well-known similarity metrics can be applied to the various elements of a RBAC state in order to measure its quality. [48] gives an overview of possible applications of the Jaccard Similarity in the context of role management. He discusses three similarity metrics that can be applied on the assignment types of a role (user, permission and role hierarchy). They can further be used to compute the similarity of two role sets (cf. Decrease Role Set Similarity). Besides examining the similarity of assignment types of a role, similarity metrics are applied to attributes of role components. They can, for instance, be used to create a role set based on the location attribute of all user accounts. Distance measures are applied to identify redundant roles [5].

Increase Role Coverage. The Role Coverage is formally defined in [61] as the fraction of role-covered UPA by the initial UPA. Companies aim at achieving a high role coverage in order to foster the benefits of RBAC compared to other access control models. The implication of reducing administrative costs through RBAC is represented through this criterion.

Attribute-related Criteria. Attribute-related criteria evaluate the quality of a role based on its attributes or attributes of its components. Permission usage derived from access logs, for example, can be used to display the actual usage of privileges by employees. It offer insights into unused PA that can potentially be removed during the next refinement of a role [44]. Furthermore, restrictions on the composition of a role, e.g. by allowing only certain attributes of users in a role are possible [56].

5.2   Discussion

This work is motivated by the gap between the recent uprising of role mining and the practical need for periodic quality assessment of the resulting role models. The presented survey underlined the significant growth (141 %) of published papers in the recent past. We have shown that every role mining approach relies on one or more quality criteria, mostly implicitly without providing a structured integration of quality management. In the following we present a short discussion of our quality-related findings from Fig. 2.

Firstly, it can be seen that the main quality criterion in role mining is to arrive at an exact representation of existing access control states. This criterion is – to a varying extent – considered by all available approaches, except for [29] which derive the roles solely from access history logs. Secondly, Fig. 2 shows that a large number of approaches focus on generating as few roles as possible (**Reduce Number of Roles**). Interestingly, as the WSC is a potential criterion which is able to represent this and other measures (by modifying its weight factors), recent approaches try to use this metric as a heuristic for producing high quality

Table 2. Quality Criteria (QC) in existing approaches.

Technique / Focus	Paper	QC — State: Achieve Completeness	Reduce Number of Roles	Decrease Role Set Similarity	Individual Role: Minimize Users per Role	Maximize Users per Role	Minimize Roles per User	Minimize Roles per Permission	Minimize Permissions per Role	Maximize Permissions per Role	Fulfill Role Constraints	Reduce WSC	State + Individual Role: Optimize Matrix Sorting	Decrease Permission Similarity	Reduce Role Redundancy	Increase User Similarity	Decrease Permission Attribute Similarity	Increase Role Coverage	Exclude Unused Permissions	Consider Timestamp	Consider Role Attributes	Consider User Attributes	Group by Attributes
Subset Enumeration	[5]		■			■							■										
	[6]		■						■			■											
	[28]		■						■									■					
	[34]		■				■																
	[41]		■																■				
	[44]	■																■					
	[53]		■				■																
	[51]		■																				
	[50]		■																				
	[52]		■																				
	[56]								■						■								■
	[58]		■																				
	[62]			■														■					
Clustering	[14]					■										■							
	[17]		■																				
	[15]		■															■			■		
	[31]								■														
	[46]		■																				
Graph Optimization	[8]		■																				
	[9]		■																				
	[11]					■			■														
	[22]		■												■			■					
	[26]		■															■					
	[40]			■														■					
	[60]											■											
Frequent Permission Set Mining	[7]		■												■								
	[29]			■										■									
	[37]				■			■				■											
	[38]				■			■															
	[39]						■											■					
	[61]											■											
Formal Concept Analysis	[42]		■																				
	[54]		■																				
	[55]		■															■					
Heuristic Matrix Selection	[3]		■																				
	[4]					■			■		■												
	[27]						■			■													
Visual Role Mining	[10]														■			■					
	[12]						■																
Boolean Matrix Decomposition	[30]						■																
	[36]	■																					
	[35]	■																					
	[49]	■																					
	[59]											■											
Attribute-based Approaches	[16]	■																					■
	[25]	■																					■
	[33]					■																	

Uses criteria: ■ Yes ☐ No

roles [12,58,59]. This can be interpreted as an indicator that research is already trying to integrate sophisticated measures – such as the WSC – into role mining.

Other interesting results are, that criteria with practical relevance up to now are only considered by few existing approaches (see Fig. 2). Timestamps as an attribute of permissions are, for instance, only considered by one approach [41]. However, their integration into role mining seems promising as they heavily can influence role design. Sets of permissions activated together within a certain period of time can e.g. represent good candidate permissions for a role. We argue that the low availability of timestamp information might be the main reason for its low acceptance in the community.

We furthermore noted that several quality criteria well-known in practice have not yet been included in any role mining approach at all. This includes criteria like the

- Maximum allowed number of roles in a role model
- Role usage
- Hierarchy restrictions

It seems straightforward to integrate a maximum threshold of roles to be found through automatic role discovery in order to ensure the maintainability of the whole role set. Intuitively, result sets can always be limited by just taking the desired number of roles after sorting them according to a predefined criterion. However, we argue that a dedicated parametrization of a role mining approach needs to be possible so that it considers this upper bound during the process of role generation. Furthermore, the usage of UA over a certain period of time (i.e. the activation of roles) can hint at outdated role definitions. Several approaches are able to take existing roles into consideration (e.g. [42]) but do not integrate usage data. Moreover, restrictions on the hierarchy of a RBAC state can represent one way to reduce complexity and increase the quality of either a single role or the whole RBAC state. In practice, deployed RBAC states feature unlimited depth, sometimes even resulting in hierarchy loops. Limiting the maximum allowed number of parent or child roles of a role or the maximal hierarchy depth can ease administrative staff's understanding of the overall role model. Note that [15] already considers RBAC hierarchies. However, they only introduce an overall hierarchy depth of two and indicate the possibility to extend their probabilistic approach with more layers. Several post-processing approaches already outline the need for an inspection of the role hierarchy (e.g. [24,48]). However, they only focus on removing duplicate hierarchy depiction and finding the minimal set of hierarchical assignments, not on cardinality restrictions.

5.3   Relationships Between Quality Criteria

After having presented the set of quality criteria currently used in role mining, in this section we analyze the relationships between different quality criteria in order to answer RQ2. By showing how the various quality categories affect each other (see Fig. 3), we point at potential combinations that can be applied during strategic role model maintenance. Knowledge about quality criteria and their mutual influence can support companies during the selection of the best fitting approach in a given scenario. It is of major importance to consider strategic role maintenance efforts before designing the initial role model. A company might select a certain role mining approach (that even may require a higher initial role definition effort) as its future maintenance is expected to be significantly lower in the long run. Up to now, such a qualified role mining selection is not possible.

Figure 3 illustrates mutual dependencies between quality criteria. A positive influence implies that fulfilling one criteria impacts another criteria in a way that it can be easier or more efficiently achieved (and vice versa). Negative influence means that focusing on one criteria impairs the fulfillment of the other criteria. A white background is used, if no definite statement can be made. For our analysis, we focus on direct implications between two criteria and evaluate those effects if possible. While we are aware of potential differences in the impact intensity, the goal of our research is not to examine the degree of influences. It rather is to provide a first overview of dependencies and stimulate further research in the area. We argue that without the knowledge of the currently applied quality criteria, a structured integration – above all considering criteria combinations – into role mining approaches is hardly possible.

The matrix presented in Fig. 3 reveals that in order to **Achieve Completeness**, negative impacts on all other except attribute-based criteria are the consequence. Intuitively, an algorithm that aims at covering the input UPA matrix with roles leaves few possibilities to optimize other criteria such as maximizing the number of users per role. A complete coverage of an input UPA state leads to an increased role count and a decreased number of users per role.

Similarly, **Reduce the Number of Roles** negatively impacts an optimization towards most other quality criteria. Exceptions are the maximization of users and permissions per role as reducing the number of roles inherently entails an increase of users and permissions per role. Likewise, a small number of roles has a positive influence (e.g. on the WSC) since the number of roles is given less weight.

Given the goal to **Decrease Role Set Similarity** has several side-effects on the fulfillment of other criteria. As users and permissions two role sets have in common are used to measure similarity, minimizing the number of roles per user leads to more distinct roles. In general, a decreasing Role Set Similarity positively impacts the decrease of other similarity-related criteria as its calculation is commonly based on the similarity of role components. Among negative impacts is its influence on the reduction of the total role number and the completeness to be achieved. Both originate from the fact that regulations on the similarity of roles lead to an increased need of new role definitions for representing the access control.

Techniques that **Minimize Users per Role** positively impact the overall WSC. A decrease of UA, e.g., leads to a lower general WSC. On the contrary, negative dependencies exist between minimizing the number of users per role and minimizing the number of roles per user. Intuitively, fewer users per role

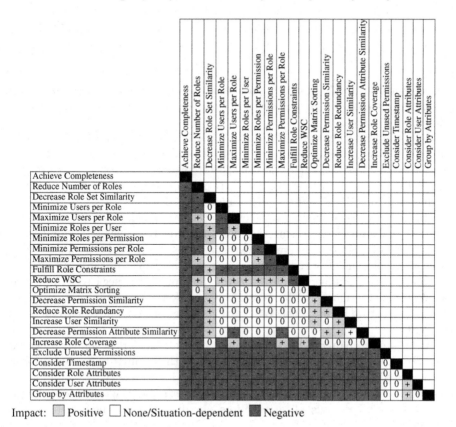

Impact: ☐ Positive ☐ None/Situation-dependent ■ Negative

Fig. 3. Dependencies between quality criteria.

require the assignment of more roles to a single user in order to arrive at the same number of privileges.

The goal of maximizing the number of users per role (**Maximize Users per Role**) impairs fulfilling other criteria also related to role configuration and role size. A positive impact on finding a minimum role set and role coverage can be inferred as maximizing the number of users per role leads to fewer and larger roles that cover a significant portion of the UPA-matrix.

Techniques that **Minimize Roles per User** positively influence the overall WSC in case URA are considered in the WSC calculation. Likewise, minimizing the number of roles requires more users to be assigned to a role. Yet, considering this criterion leads to negative effects on role coverage and role constraints. Fewer roles promote the use of direct UPA and lead to a lower role coverage. Role constraints are negatively impacted as role design becomes more difficult if only a few roles per user are allowed.

The goal of minimizing the number of roles per permission (**Minimize Roles per Permission**) affects other criteria in the same way. It leads to a reduced number of role-permission assignments which has a positive impact on the overall WSC. Negative impacts can be expected for role constraints due to increased role definition complexity and for role coverage due to a larger number of direct UPA.

Dependencies for **Minimize Permissions per Role** and **Maximize Permissions per Role** are similar to the respective minimization and maximization criteria for users per role.

Role mining techniques that aim to **Fulfill Role Constraints** in general struggle with optimizing most other criteria except for a decreased Role Set Similarity. The positive impact in this case stems from the fact that role definition constraints are often referring to SoD policies which in return are likely to produce a disjunctive – and thus dissimilar – set of roles.

Trying to **Reduce WSC** positively affects several other criteria, in particular those that aim at decreasing the number of role component assignments. A negative impact can be observed when using this criterion in combination with either the achievement of completeness or role constraints. Regarding completeness an increased number of roles to cover the input UPA negatively influences the WSC. Furthermore, as the percentage of UPA covered by roles has a significant impact on lowering the WSC, using role constraints in general increases the WSC.

As **Optimize Matrix Sorting** aims at creating clusters of similar users and roles, it is likely to have a positive impact on other similarity-related criteria. When sorted next to each other in a visualized UPA-matrix, a human role engineer is supported during tasks like merging or separating roles according to their similarity. Using visualization filters can allow the role engineer to display information according to similarity (e.g. similar job positions of employees) and model roles accordingly.

Decrease Role Permission Similarity-related techniques that focus on creating roles with distinct permissions inherently have a positive impact on reducing role redundancy as they decrease the number of overlapping roles. Similarly, they positively impact attribute similarity as they generate attribute-based roles. Commonly different attribute values (e.g. location or function of employees) lead to roles that are likely to bundle distinct sets of permissions.

As mentioned before, the goal to **Decrease Role Redundancy** positively affects all similarity-related criteria. Intuitively, minimizing redundancy has a negative impact on criteria such as completeness and finding the minimal number of roles. Completeness typically generates a large number of roles with redundant permissions in order to cover an initial UPA-matrix to a certain extent. Likewise, trying to reduce the overall number of roles inherently leads to larger roles with overlapping permissions.

Increase Role Coverage negatively affects the accomplishment of most other quality criteria. Exceptions include the maximization of users and permissions per role which are direct consequences of trying to maximize role coverage. Additionally, the fact that all UPA are covered by roles positively impacts the WSC as the usage of direct UPA increasing complexity is minimized.

Techniques aiming at the **Decrease of Permission Attribute Similarity** argue that permissions with similar attributes may be redundant and thus should not be included into one role. This implies a positive impact on Role Permission Similarity as roles are more likely to have distinct permissions. Consequently, the positive impact on Role Set Similarity stems from the fact that Role Set Similarity is often measured on the basis of the similarity of the permissions of a specific role [29, 63].

The remaining **Attribute-related Criteria**, namely **Exclude Unused Permissions, Consider Timestamp, Consider Role Attributes, Consider User Attributes**, and **Group by Attributes** share that they impose restrictions on the definition of the role catalog and thus have a negative impact on the fulfillment of most other criteria. For example, practical projects with partners show that over a certain period of time not activated permissions by the users of a role should not be included. However, the affected UPA still exist and therefore will be taken into account by role mining. An a priori cleansing of the input data through a structured role optimization process [18] can aid in avoiding such problems, but has not directly been placed into role detection mechanisms.

6 Conclusions and Future Work

Role-based Access Control as the de facto standard for managing access privileges in organizations struggles with the dynamic evolution of role models over time. As a result the quality of RBAC states initially modeled using role mining techniques decreases over time. In order to address this challenge, role mining mechanisms applied during role system maintenance need to be extended in order to integrate a dedicated quality management stage for rating and improving a role system state on the basis of company-specific quality criteria. In this paper we presented three contributions in that respect. We firstly provided a survey giving an overview of current role mining approaches. The significant increase of research activity and the growing number of applied techniques for generating roles during the last three years underlines the relevance and diversification of the area. By extracting criteria that are dedicated to improving role quality from currently available role mining approaches we were able to answer RQ1 in Sect. 4. In Sect. 5.3 we then analyzed the identified quality criteria and their mutual dependencies in order to answer RQ2. We have shown on which quality criteria current role mining approaches rely and revealed a number of practically relevant but yet untreated criteria in research. The results highlight the need for a structured integration of quality mechanisms into role mining in order to allow for an improved selection of role mining approaches in a given scenario based on company-specific quality criteria. Up to now, our findings are restricted to the field of role mining exclusively. Expanding the scope towards areas like Quality Management or Data Mining in general could yield additional criteria. In future work we are thus going to investigate the promising concept of integrating Quality Management Frameworks such as the EFQM Excellence Model[6].

Acknowledgements. The research leading to these results was supported by the "Bavarian State Ministry of Education, Science and the Arts" as part of the FORSEC research association. This work would not have been possible without our student Christian Wawarta.

References

1. Agrawal, R., Imieliński, T., Swami, A.: Mining association rules between sets of items in large databases. In: SIGMOD Record. vol. 22, pp. 207–216. ACM (1993)
2. Basel Comittee on Banking Supervisions: Basel III: Int. framework for liquidity risk measurement, standards and monitoring (2010)
3. Blundo, C., Cimato, S.: A simple role mining algorithm. In: Proceedings of the 2010 Symposium on Applied Computing (SAC). ACM (2010)
4. Blundo, C., Cimato, S.: Constrained role mining. In: Jøsang, A., Samarati, P., Petrocchi, M. (eds.) STM 2012. LNCS, vol. 7783, pp. 289–304. Springer, Heidelberg (2013)
5. Chu, V.W., Wong, R.K., Chi, C.H.: Over-fitting and error detection for online role mining. Int. J. Web Serv. Res. **9**(4), 1–23 (2012)
6. Colantonio, A., Di Pietro, R., Ocello, A.: A cost-driven approach to role engineering. In: Proceedings of the 2008 Symposium on Applied Computing (SAC). ACM (2008)
7. Colantonio, A., Di Pietro, R., Ocello, A.: Leveraging lattices to improve role mining. In: Jajodia, S., Samarati, P., Cimato, S. (eds.) Proceedings of The Ifip Tc 11 23rd International Information Security Conference, vol. 278, pp. 333–347. Springer, Heidelberg (2008)
8. Colantonio, A., Di Pietro, R., Ocello, A., Verde, N.V.: A probabilistic bound on the basic role mining problem and its applications. In: Gritzalis, D., Lopez, J. (eds.) SEC 2009. IFIP AICT, vol. 297, pp. 376–386. Springer, Heidelberg (2009)
9. Colantonio, A., Di Pietro, R., Ocello, A., Verde, N.V.: Taming role mining complexity in rbac. Comput. Secur. **29**(5), 548–564 (2010)
10. Colantonio, A., Di Pietro, R., Ocello, A., Verde, N.V.: Visual role mining: a picture is worth a thousand roles. IEEE Trans. Knowl. Data Eng. **24**(6), 1120–1133 (2012)
11. Ene, A., Horne, W., Milosavljevic, N., Rao, P., Schreiber, R., Tarjan, R.E.: Fast exact and heuristic methods for role minimization problems. In: Proceedings of the 13th Symposium on Access Control Models and Technologies (SACMAT). ACM (2008)
12. Eucharista, A., Haribaskar, K.: Visual elicitation of roles: using a hybrid approach. Orient. J. Comput. Sci. Technol. **6**(1), 103–110 (2013)
13. European Union: General data protection regulation (2012)
14. Frank, M., Basin, D., Buhmann, J.M.: A class of probabilistic models for role engineering. In: Proceedings of the 15th ACM Conference on Computer and Communications Security (CCS). ACM (2008)
15. Frank, M., Buhman, J.M., Basin, D.: Role mining with probabilistic models. ACM Trans. Inf. Syst. Secur. (TISSEC) **15**(4), 15:1–15:28 (2013)

---

[6] http://www.efqm.org/.

16. Frank, M., Streich, A.P., Basin, D., Buhmann, J.M.: A probabilistic approach to hybrid role mining. In: Proceedings of the 16th ACM Conference on Computer and Communications Security (CCS), pp. 101–111. ACM (2009)
17. Frank, M., Streich, A.P., Basin, D., Buhmann, J.M.: Multi-assignment clustering for boolean data. J. Mach. Learn. Res. **13**(1), 459–489 (2012)
18. Fuchs, L., Kunz, M., Pernul, G.: Role model optimization for secure role-based identity management. In: Proceedings of the 22nd European Conference on Information Systems (ECIS) (2014)
19. Fuchs, L., Meier, S.: The role mining process model - underlining the need for a comprehensive research perspective. In: Proceedings of the 6th International Conference on Availability, Reliability and Security (ARES). IEEE (2011)
20. Fuchs, L., Müller, C.: Automating periodic role-checks: a tool-based approach. In: Business Services: Konzepte, Technologien, Anwendungen: 9. Int. Tagung Wirtschaftsinformatik (WI), vol. 246. OCG, Wien (2009)
21. Fuchs, L., Pernul, G., Sandhu, R.: Roles in information security-a survey and classification of the research area. Comput. Secur. **30**(8), 748–769 (2011)
22. Gal-Oz, N., Gonen, Y., Yahalom, R., Gudes, E., Rozenberg, B., Shmueli, E.: Mining roles from web application usage patterns. In: Furnell, S., Lambrinoudakis, C., Pernul, G. (eds.) TrustBus 2011. LNCS, vol. 6863, pp. 125–137. Springer, Heidelberg (2011)
23. Giblin, C., Graf, M., Karjoth, G., Wespi, A., Molloy, I., Lobo, J., Calo, S.B.: Towards an integrated approach to role engineering. In: SafeConfig, pp. 63–70. ACM (2010)
24. Guo, Q., Vaidya, J., Atluri, V.: The role hierarchy mining problem: discovery of optimal role hierarchies. In: Proceedings of the 24th Computer Security Applications Conference (ACSAC). IEEE (2008)
25. Han, D.J., Zhuo, H.K., Xia, L.T., Li, L.: Permission and role automatic assigning of user in role-based access control. J. Central South Univ. **19**, 1049–1056 (2012)
26. Hingankar, M., Sural, S.: Towards role mining with restricted user-role assignment. In: 2nd International Conference on Wireless Communication, Vehicular Technology, Information Theory and Aerospace Electronic Systems Technology (Wireless VITAE) (2011)
27. Huang, C., Sun, J.I., Wang, X.Y., Si, Y.J.: Minimal role mining method for web service composition. J. Zhejiang Univ. SCIENCE C **11**(5), 328–339 (2010)
28. Huang, H., Shang, F., Zhang, J.: Approximation algorithms for minimizing the number of roles and administrative assignments in rbac. In: Proceedings of the 36th Annual Computer Software and Applications Conference Workshops (COMPSAC). IEEE (2012)
29. Jafari, M., Chinaei, A., Barker, K., Fathian, M.: Role mining in access history logs. J. Inf. Assur. Secur. **38** (2009)
30. John, J.C., Sural, S., Atluri, V., Vaidya, J.S.: Role mining under role-usage cardinality constraint. In: Gritzalis, D., Furnell, S., Theoharidou, M. (eds.) SEC 2012. IFIP AICT, vol. 376, pp. 150–161. Springer, Heidelberg (2012)
31. Kumar, R., Sural, S., Gupta, A.: Mining RBAC roles under cardinality constraint. In: Jha, S., Mathuria, A. (eds.) ICISS 2010. LNCS, vol. 6503, pp. 171–185. Springer, Heidelberg (2010)
32. Levy, Y., Ellis, T.J.: A systems approach to conduct an effective literature review in support of information systems research. Informing Sci. J. **9**, 181–212 (2006)
33. Li, R., Wang, W., Ma, X., Gu, X., Wen, K.: Mining roles using attributes of permissions. Int. J. Innovative Comput. Inf. Control **8**(11), 7909–7924 (2012)

34. Lu, H., Hong, Y., Yang, Y., Duan, L., Badar, N.: Towards user-oriented RBAC model. In: Wang, L., Shafiq, B. (eds.) DBSec 2013. LNCS, vol. 7964, pp. 81–96. Springer, Heidelberg (2013)

35. Lu, H., Vaidya, J., Atluri, V.: Optimal boolean matrix decomposition: application to role engineering. In: Proceedings of the 24th IEEE International Conference on Data Engineering (ICDE). IEEE (2008)

36. Lu, H., Vaidya, J., Atluri, V., Hong, Y.: Constraint-aware role mining via extended boolean matrix decomposition. IEEE Trans. Dependable Secure Comput. (TDSC) **9**(5), 655–669 (2012)

37. Ma, X., Li, R., Lu, Z.: Role mining based on weights. In: Proceedings of the 15th Symposium on Access Control Models and Technologies (SACMAT). ACM (2010)

38. Ma, X., Li, R., Lu, Z., Wang, W.: Mining constraints in role-based access control. Math. Comput. Model. **55**(1), 87–96 (2012)

39. Ma, X., Tian, Y., Zhao, L., Li, R.: Mining role based on ranks. Int. J. Res. Surv. ICIC Express Lett. Part B Appl. **4**(2), 319–326 (2013)

40. Mandala, S., Vukovic, M., Laredo, J., Ruan, Y., Hernandez, M.: Hybrid role mining for security service solution. In: Proceedings of the 9th International Conference on Services Computing (SCC). IEEE (2012)

41. Mitra, B., Sural, S., Atluri, V., Vaidya, J.: Toward mining of temporal roles. In: Wang, L., Shafiq, B. (eds.) DBSec 2013. LNCS, vol. 7964, pp. 65–80. Springer, Heidelberg (2013)

42. Molloy, I., Chen, H., Li, T., Wang, Q., Li, N., Bertino, E., Calo, S., Lobo, J.: Mining roles with semantic meanings. In: Proceedings of the 13th Symposium on Access Control Models and Technologies (SACMAT). ACM (2008)

43. Molloy, I., Chen, H., Li, T., Wang, Q., Li, N., Bertino, E., Calo, S., Lobo, J.: Mining roles with multiple objectives. In: ACM Transactions on Information and System Security (TISSEC). ACM (2010)

44. Molloy, I., Park, Y., Chari, S.: Generative models for access control policies: applications to role mining over logs with attribution. In: Proceedings of the 17th Symposium on Access Control Models and Technologies (SACMAT). ACM (2012)

45. Sandhu, R.S., Coyne, E.J., Feinstein, H.L., Youman, C.E.: Role-based access control models. Computer **29**(2), 38–47 (1996)

46. Schlegelmilch, J., Steffens, U.: Role mining with orca. In: Proceedings of the 10th Symposium on Access Control Models and Technologies (SACMAT). ACM (2005)

47. SOX: Sarbanes-oxley act of 2002, pp. 107–204, 116 stat 745 (July 2002)

48. Takabi, H., Joshi, J.B.: Stateminer: An efficient similarity-based approach for optimal mining of role hierarchy. In: Proceedings of the 15th Symposium on Access Control Models and Technologies (SACMAT). ACM (2010)

49. Uzun, E., Atluri, V., Lu, H., Vaidya, J.: An optimization model for the extended role mining problem. In: Li, Y. (ed.) DBSec. LNCS, vol. 6818, pp. 76–89. Springer, Heidelberg (2011)

50. Vaidya, J., Atluri, V., Warner, J., Guo, Q.: Role engineering via prioritized subset enumeration. IEEE Trans. Dependable Secure Comput. **7**(3), 300–314 (2010)

51. Vaidya, J., Atluri, V., Guo, Q.: The role mining problem: finding a minimal descriptive set of roles. In: Proceedings of the 12th Symposium on Access Control models and Technologies (SACMAT). ACM (2007)

52. Vaidya, J., Atluri, V., Guo, Q.: The role mining problem: a formal perspective. ACM Trans. Inf. Syst. Secur. (TISSEC) **13**(3), 27 (2010)

53. Vaidya, J., Atluri, V., Warner, J.: Roleminer: mining roles using subset enumeration. In: Proceedings of the 13th ACM Conference on Computer and Communications Security (CCS). ACM (2006)
54. Wang, J., Zeng, C., He, C., Hong, L., Zhou, L., Wong, R.K., Tian, J.: Context-aware role mining for mobile service recommendation. In: Proceedings of the 27th Annual Symposium on Applied Computing (SAC). ACM (2012)
55. Wong, R.K., Chu, V.W., Hao, T., Wang, J.: Context-aware service recommendation for moving connected devices. In: Proceedings of the International Conference on Connected Vehicles and Expo (ICCVE) (2012)
56. Xu, Z., Stoller, S.D.: Algorithms for mining meaningful roles. In: Proceedings of the 17th Symposium on Access Control Models and Technologies (SACMAT). ACM (2012)
57. Xu, Z., Stoller, S.D.: Mining attribute-based access control policies from rbac policies. In: Proceedings of the 10th International Conference and Expo on Emerging Technologies for a Smarter World (CEWIT). IEEE (2013)
58. Xu, Z., Stoller, S.D.: Mining parameterized role-based policies. In: Proceedings of the 3d ACM Conference on Data and Application Security and Privacy (CODASPY). ACM (2013)
59. Ye, W., Li, R., Li, H.: Role mining using boolean matrix decomposition with hierarchy. In: Proceedings of 12th IEEE International Conference on Trust, Security and Privacy in Computing and Communications (TrustCom). IEEE (2013)
60. Zhang, D., Ramamohanarao, K., Ebringer, T.: Role engineering using graph optimisation. In: Proceedings of the 12th Symposium on Access Control Models and Technologies (SACMAT). ACM (2007)
61. Zhang, D., Ramamohanarao, K., Ebringer, T., Yann, T.: Permission set mining: Discovering practical and useful roles. In: Proceedings of the 24th Annual Computer Security Applications Conference (ACSAC). IEEE (2008)
62. Zhang, W., Chen, Y., Gunter, C., Liebovitz, D., Malin, B.: Evolving role definitions through permission invocation patterns. In: Proceedings of the 18th Symposium on Access Control Models and Technologies (SACMAT). ACM (2013)
63. Zhang, X., Han, W., Fang, Z., Yin, Y., Mustafa, H.: Role mining algorithm evaluation and improvement in large volume android applications. In: Proceedings of the 1st International Workshop on Security in Embedded Systems and Smartphones (SESP). ACM (2013)
64. Zhu, H., Zhou, M.: Roles in information systems: a survey. IEEE Trans. Syst. Man Cybern. (SMC) **38**(3), 377–396 (2008)

An Evasion Resilient Approach to the Detection of Malicious PDF Files

Davide Maiorca[✉], Davide Ariu, Igino Corona, and Giorgio Giacinto

University of Cagliari, Piazza d'Armi, 09123 Cagliari, Italy
{davide.maiorca,davide.ariu,igino.corona,giacinto}@diee.unica.it

Abstract. Malicious PDF files still constitute a serious threat to the systems security. New reader vulnerabilities have been discovered, and research has shown that current state of the art approaches can be easily bypassed by exploiting weaknesses caused by erroneous parsing or incomplete information extraction. In this work, we present a novel machine learning system to the detection of malicious PDF files. We have developed a static approach that leverages on information extracted by both the structure and the content of PDF files, which allows to improve the system robustness against evasion attacks. Experimental results show that our system is able to outperform all publicly available state of the art tools. We also report a significant improvement of the performances at detecting reverse mimicry attacks, which are able to completely evade systems that only extract information from the PDF file structure. Finally, we claim that, to avoid targeted attacks, a more careful design of machine learning based detectors is needed.

Keywords: PDF · Evasion · Malware · Javascript · Machine learning

1 Introduction

Malicious PDF files still constitute a major threat to computer systems, as new attacks against their readers have recently been released. The integration of the PDF file format with third-party technologies (e.g., Javascript or Flash) is often exploited to execute them. Despite the efforts of software vendors such as Adobe, PDF readers are vulnerable to zero-day attacks, as the creation of ad-hoc patches is often a complex task. Antivirus products also exhibit problems at providing protection against novel or even known attacks, due to the various code obfuscation techniques employed by most of the attacks [1].

Javascript is often adopted by attackers to exploit PDF vulnerabilities, by resorting to popular techniques such as Return Oriented Programming and Heap Spraying [2,3]. Some vulnerabilities also employed different attack vectors, such as ActionScript. For example, CVE 2010-3654 exploits a vulnerability in Adobe Flash Player by means of a "Just in Time Spraying" approach [4]. Some attacks also use advanced encryption methods for hiding malicious code or malicious embedded files [5].

© Springer International Publishing Switzerland 2015
O. Camp et al. (Eds.): ICISSP 2015, CCIS 576, pp. 68–85, 2015.
DOI: 10.1007/978-3-319-27668-7_5

Most of commercial anti-malware tools resort to signature-based approaches that are based on heuristics or string matching. However, they are often not able of detecting novel attacks, as they are inherently weak against polymorphism [6]. For this reason, recent research works analyzed malicious PDF files from two different perspectives: first, they examined malicious Javascript code within PDF files, through both static and dynamic (behavioral) analysis [7–9]. Then, they focused on the external structure of the PDF files to detect malicious ones regardless of the exploit they carried [10–12]. The latter approach is considered to be more effective than the former, as it allows to detect a wider variety of attacks, including non-Javascript ones.

However, further research proved that such strategy is extremely vulnerable against targeted attacks [13,14]. Its vulnerabilities are related to two aspects: (a) *File parsing*, as the logical connection among objects is often ignored and embedded contents are overlooked; (b) *Weak information*, i.e., data that can be easily crafted by an attacker. For this reason, new efforts have been made to provide a better detection of malicious Javascript code [15,16] and to harden security through the adoption of *sandboxes* [17].

In this work, we present a novel machine learning-based system to the detection of malicious PDF files that extracts information both from the *structure* and the *content* of the PDF file. Information on the file *structure* is obtained by examining: (a) basic file structure properties and (b) objects structural properties, in terms of *keywords*. *Content-based* information is obtained from: (a) malformed objects, streams and codes, (b) known vulnerabilities in Javascript code and (c) embedded contents such as other PDF files. We leverage on two well-known tools for PDF analysis, namely, PeePDF[1] and Origami[2], to provide a reliable information extraction process and to avoid parsing-related vulnerabilities.

With this approach, it is possible to accurately detect PDF malware deployed in the wild (including non-Javascript attacks), with very low false positives. At the same time, we report a significant improvement on detecting targeted attacks in comparison to the other state of the art approaches. We also show that a careful choice of the learning algorithm is crucial to ensure a correct detection of evasion attacks. We therefore encourage further research on this aspect, as we believe it can provide remarkable improvements to the security of machine learning systems. This work is an extension of a previously presented paper presented by us [18]. In this version, we provide a detailed analysis of the evasion attacks that might be perpetrated against a malicious PDF file detector, as well as a deeper insight into the solutions we have adopted to detect them.

Contributions. We summarize the contributions provided by this work in four points:

---

[1] http://eternal-todo.com/tools/peepdf-pdf-analysis-tool.
[2] http://esec-lab.sogeti.com/pages/origami.

- We develop a novel, machine learning based system to the detection of malicious PDF files that extracts information from the *structure* and the *content* of a PDF file;
- We experimentally evaluate the performances of our system on a dataset containing various PDF-related vulnerabilities. We compare our results to the ones obtained using publicly available tools;
- We evaluate the robustness of our system against evasion attacks that are able to completely bypass most of the released PDF files detectors;
- We discuss the limits of our system and the importance that the *learning algorithm* has to ensure a good robustness. In relation to that, we provide research guidelines for future work.

Structure. This work is divided into six Sections beyond this one. Section 2 provides the basics to understand the structure of the PDF files. Section 3 presents related works on malicious PDF detection. Section 4 describes our general methodology to the detection of malicious PDFs, and our strategies to tackle evasion attacks. Section 5 provides the experimental results. Section 6 discusses the limits of our approach and provides guidelines for future research work. Section 7 provides the conclusions of our work.

2 PDF File Format

A PDF file is a hierarchy of objects logically connected to each other. Its structure is composed by four parts [19]:

- **header:** a line that gives information on the PDF version used by the file.
- **body:** the main portion of the file, which contains all the PDF objects.
- **cross-reference table:** it indicates the position of every *indirect* object in memory.
- **trailer:** it gives relevant information about the *root object* and number of revisions made to the document. The root object is the first, in the logical hierarchy, to be parsed by the reader. New revisions (also called *versions*) are created every time the user causes changes to the PDF file. This leads to the generation of a new trailer and an updated cross-reference table, which will be appended at the end of the file.

The objects contained in the body can be of two types. *Indirect* ones are typically introduced by the expression `ObjectNumber 0 obj` and can be referenced. *Direct* objects, on the contrary, cannot be referenced and are typically less complex than the former ones. Most of indirect objects are *dictionaries* that contain a sequence of coupled *keywords* (also called *name objects*), which are introduced by a /. Keywords provide a description of the data inside the object itself or in one of its references (e.g., in case of an attack, the keyword `/Javascript` can be related to the presence of malicious code). An object might also include a *stream*, which usually contains compressed *data* that will be parsed by the reader and visualized by the user (e.g., in case of an attack, a malicious code can be compressed into a stream that will be deployed along with the object containing the keyword /Javascript). For more information on the PDF structure, please check the PDF Reference [19].

3 Related Work

First approaches to malicious PDF detection resorted to static analysis on the raw (byte-level) document, by employing *n-gram* analysis [20, 21] and *decision trees* [22]. However, these approaches were not focused on detecting PDF files, as they were developed to detect as many malware as possible, such as DOC and EXE based ones. Moreover, they are vulnerable to modern obfuscation techniques, such as AES encryption [5], and they can be also evaded by polymorphic malware that employ techniques like Return Oriented Programming, Heap Spraying or JIT Spraying [2–4].

Being Javascript the most popular attack vector contained in PDF files, subsequent works focused on its analysis. Many solutions have been proposed in the context of web security. For instance, Jsand [7], Cujo [23], Zozzle [24], Prophiler [25] are popular tools for the static and dynamic analysis of Javascript code. These tools are often adopted to detect threats embedded in different document formats.

Wepawet[3], a popular framework for the analysis of web-based threats, relies on JSand to analyze Javascript code within PDF files. Jsand [7] adopts HtmlUnit[4], a Java-based browser simulator, and Mozilla's Rhino[5] to extract dynamic behavioral features from the execution of Javascript code. The system is trained on samples containing benign code and resorts to *anomaly detection* to detect malicious files, by leveraging on the strong differences between legitimate and dangerous ones.

A similar approach is adopted by MalOffice [26]. Mal Office uses pdftk[6] to extract Javascript code, and CWSandbox [27] to analyze the code behavior: Classification is carried out by a set of rules (CWSandbox has also been used to classify general malware behavior [28]). MDScan [9] follows a different approach as malicious behavior is detected through Nemu, a tool able to intercept memory-injected shellcode. A different approach, with some similarities to the previous ones, has been developed in ShellOS [29].

Dynamic detection by executing Javascript code in a virtual environment is often time consuming and computationally expensive, and it is vulnerable to evasion when an attacker is able to exploit code parsing differences between the attacked system and the original reader [9]. To reduce computational costs, PJScan [8] proposed a fully static lexical analysis of Javascript code by training a statistical classifier on malicious files.

---

[3] http://wepawet.iseclab.org/index.php.
[4] http://htmlunit.sourceforge.net.
[5] http://www.mozilla.org/rhino.
[6] http://www.pdflabs.com/tools/pdftk-the-pdf-toolkit.

In 2012 and 2013, malicious PDF detectors that extract information on the *structure* of the PDF file, without analyzing Javascript code, have been developed. We usually refer to them as *structural systems* [10–12]. PDFRate[7] is the most popular, *publicly available* approach. It is based on 202 features extracted from both document metadata and structure and it resorts to random forests to perform classification. Such approach allows to detect even non-Javascript vulnerabilities such as Actionscript based ones. Moreover, it provided significantly higher performances when compared to previous approaches. However, recent works [13,14] showed that such systems are easily attackable by exploiting, for example, parsing vulnerabilities.

As structural systems might be unreliable under targeted attacks, research focused on improving malicious Javascript code detection. New approaches resorted to discriminant API analysis [15], code instrumentation [16] and *sandboxing* [17]. Recently, a complete state of the art survey of malicious PDF files detectors has been proposed [30].

4   Proposed Detection Approach

As stated in Sect. 3, the vast majority of recent works on malicious PDF detection focused on the analysis of either the Javascript code (*content-based systems*) or the PDF file structure (*structural systems*). Such information is usually processed by a *machine learning* system, i.e., it is converted into a *vector* of numbers (*features*) and sent to a mathematical function (*classifier* or *learner*), whose parameters have been tuned through a process called *training*. Such training is performed by using samples whose classes (benign or malicious) were already known.

However, systems developed until now suffer from several weaknesses, which can be summed up in three categories:

- **Design Weaknesses:** some systems might be designed to only detect a specific type of attack (e.g., Javascript-based ones). However, such choice might make the system easy to evade when, for example, ActionScript is used [10].
- **Parsing Weaknesses:** some systems resort to what we define as *naive parsing*, i.e., analyzing the whole file content without considering its *logical* structure. This might lead to examining, for example, objects that will never be parsed by the reader. This might expose such systems to *evasion attacks*, as it is very easy to introduce changes that will deceive the systems without having any impact on the reader. Moreover, ignoring the logical structure also leads to overlooking *embedded* content, such as other PDF files [11,13].
- **Features Weaknesses:** some features might be easily crafted by an attacker. For example, a system might rely on the number of lowercase or uppercase letters of the file. Modifying such elements is a straight-forward task and might simplify the system evasion.

---

[7] http://pdfrate.com/.

To overcome these weaknesses, we propose a new machine learning-based approach that extracts information from the *structure* and the *content* of a PDF file. This method is purely *static* and, as the file is not executed by a PDF rendering engine.

Figure 1 shows the high-level architecture of our system. To extract information, we created a *parser* that adopts `PeePDF` and `Origami`. These tools perform an in-depth analysis of PDF files to detect known exploits, suspicious objects, or potentially malicious functions (for example, see vulnerability `CVE-2008-2992`). Moreover, they will extract and parse, as a separate sample, any *embedded* PDF file. When combined, these tools provide a reliable parsing process in comparison to other ones, such as `PdfID`, which naively analyzes PDF files ignoring their logical properties, thus allowing attackers to easily manipulate them [13].

Each PDF file will be represented by a vector composed by: **(a)** 8 features that describe the *general structure* of the file in terms of number of objects, streams, etc.; **(b)** A *variable* number of features (usually not more than 120, depending on the training data) related to the *structure of the PDF objects*. Such features are represented by the occurrence of the most *frequent keywords* in the training dataset; **(c)** 7 features related to the *content* of the PDF objects. In particular, the PDF objects are parsed to detect *known vulnerabilities, malformed objects*, etc.

The remaining of this Section is organized as follows. Section 4.1 provides a detailed description of all the features that we extract to discriminate between benign and malicious PDF files. Section 4.2 describes and motivates the chosen classification algorithm. Section 4.3 describes the evasion problem and the strategies that have been adopted to counteract it.

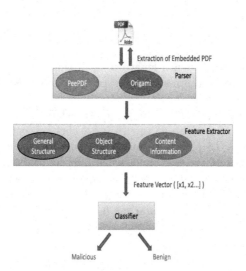

Fig. 1. High-level architecture of our system.

4.1   Features

General Structure. We extract 8 features that contain information about: **(i)** The *size* of the file; **(ii)** The number of *versions* of the file; **(iii)** The number of *indirect objects*; **(iv)** The number of *streams*; **(v)** The number of *compressed objects*; **(vi)** The number of *object streams*[8]; **(vii)** The number of *X-ref streams*[9]; **(viii)** The number of *objects containing* Javascript.

Whereas these features may not be discriminant when singularly used, they provide a good overview of the whole PDF structure when used together. For instance, malicious PDFs (and their number of objects/streams) are often smaller, in terms of size, than legitimate ones. This is reasonable, as malicious PDFs do not usually contain text. The smaller is the file size, the smaller is the time needed to infect new victims. The number of *versions* is usually higher than 1 in benign files, as a new version is typically generated when a user directly modifies or extends a PDF file. Malicious files usually exhibit a higher number of Javascript objects compared to benign files. This is because many exploits are executed by *combining* multiple Javascript pieces of code in order to generate the complete attack code. Finally, *object and X-ref streams* are usually employed to hide malicious objects inside the file, and *compressed objects* can include embedded contents, such as scripting code or other EXE/PDF files.

Object Structure. We extract the *occurrence* of the most *characteristic* keywords defined in the PDF language. *Characteristic* keywords are the ones that appeared in our training dataset D with a frequency that is higher of a threshold t. Other works, such as [12], obtained a similar threshold by arbitrarily choosing a reasonable value for it. We obtain t in a more systematic way, so that it is better related to the data in D. In order to do so, we:

1. Split D into D_m and D_l. D_m only contains *malicious* files and D_l only *legitimate files*. Obviously, $D = D_m \cup D_l$;
2. For each dataset, and for each keyword k_n of the PDF language, we define: $f_n = F(k_n)$, where f_n represents *the number of samples* of each dataset in which k_n appears at least once;
3. For each dataset, we extract the frequency threshold value t by resorting to a *k-means clustering* algorithm [31] with $k = 2$ clusters, computed through an euclidean distance. To precisely determine the sizes of the two clusters, the algorithm has been tested five times with different starting points[10]. In this way, basing on their f_n value, we split keywords into two groups. Thus, for each dataset, we extract the set of keywords K defined as: $K = \{(k_n)|f_n > t\}$. Therefore, for D_m we will obtain a set K_m and for D_l a set K_l;
4. Finally, we get the final set of characteristic keywords K_t by: $K_t = K_m \cup K_l$.

---

[8] Streams containing other objects.

[9] A new typology of cross-reference table introduced by recent PDF specification.

[10] The seed value has been set to the default value indicated here: http://weka.sourceforge.net/doc.dev/weka/clusterers/SimpleKMeans.html.

The number of keywords in K_t depends on the training data and on the clustering result. The reason why we considered characteristic keywords occurrences is that their presence is often related to specific actions performed by the file. For example, */Font* is a characteristic keyword in benign files. This is because it represents the presence of a specific font in the file. If this keyword occurs a lot inside one sample, it means that the PDF renderer displays different fonts, which is an expected behavior in legitimate samples. Selecting the most characteristic keywords also helps to ignore the ones that do not respect the PDF language standard. Including the occurrence of non-characteristic or extraneous keywords in the feature set might make the system vulnerable to evasion attacks, as an attacker could easily manipulate the PDF features without altering the file rendering process.

Content-Based Properties. We verify if a PDF file is accepted or rejected by either `PeePDF` or `Origami`. There are two features associated to this information, one for `PeePDF` and one for `Origami` and they are extracted by means of a *non-forced scan*[11]. Such scan evaluates the overall *integrity* of the file. For example, if the PDF file exhibits a bad or malformed header, it will be immediately rejected by the two tools. In more complex cases, rejecting a file usually means that it contains suspicious elements such as the execution of code, malformed or incorrect x-ref tables, corrupted headers, etc. However, such elements might as well be present in legitimate samples. Therefore, `PeePDF` and `Origami` cannot be used alone as malicious PDF files detectors, as they would report a lot of *false positives*.

There are also 5 features that provide information about *malformed* **(a)** objects (e.g., when scripting codes are directly put in a PDF dictionary), **(b)** streams, **(c)** actions (using keywords that do not belong to the PDF language), **(d)** code (e.g., using functions that are employed in vulnerabilities) and **(e)** compression filters (e.g., when compression is not correctly performed). This is done as malicious PDF files often contain objects with some of the aforementioned malformations, as the reader would parse them without raising any warnings about them.

4.2 Classification

We resort to a *supervised* learning approach, i.e., both benign and malicious samples are used for training, and we adopted decision trees classifiers [32]. Decision trees are capable of natively handling different types of features features, and they have successfully been used in previous works related to Malicious PDF files [10,11,15].

As classifier, we choose the *Adaptive Boosting* (`AdaBoost`) algorithm, which linearly combines a set of *weak* learners, each of them with a specific weight, to produce a more accurate classifier [33]. A *weak learner* is a low-complexity classification algorithm that is usually better than random guessing. The weights

---

[11] A scan that is stopped if it finds anomalies in the files. This definition is valid for `PeePDF`; in `Origami`, such scan is defined as *standard mode*.

of each weak learner are dependent on the ones of the training instances with which each learner is trained. Example of weak learners are decision stumps (i.e., decision trees with only one leaf) or simple decision trees (J48). Choosing an ensemble of trees usually guarantees more robustness against *evasion attacks* compared to a single tree, as an attacker should know which features are most discriminant for *each* tree of the ensemble to perform an optimal attack.

4.3   Evasion Detection

Introduction on Mimicry. Differently from current state of the art approaches, the features of our system, as well as its parsing mechanism, have been designed to consider the possibilities of *deliberate* attacks against structural systems. Typically, an attacker crafts a malicious file (for instance, by adding objects that will never be parsed by the reader) so that the feature values extracted by the analysis system are closer to the ones of a file that is treated as benign by the system itself. This approach is called *mimicry*.

As already observed by Biggio et al. [34], the effectiveness of the attack depends on the amount of *knowledge* possessed by the attacker. We usually distinguish between *perfect* and *imperfect* knowledge. In case of *perfect knowledge*, the attacker should be aware of the *features and the classification algorithm* employed by the system that is attacked. He should also be knowledgeable about how the features are computed. In case of *imperfect knowledge*, the attacker has incomplete information about the system features and classification algorithm. This attack is performed by means of algorithm such as *gradient descent* [34], but some simplified versions have been in other works, for example to test PDFRate [11].

Mimicry is an attack that is performed on the *feature* level. This means that first the attacker has to determine which features to modify and how many changes should be made on them. Then, he should *rebuild* the sample from the feature values he has determined. Finally, he has to ensure that the targeted system exactly extracts, from the rebuilt sample, the feature values he has obtained in the first step. Rebuilding the sample from specific feature values might be a very difficult task as some changes, although valid on the feature level, might *break* the functionalities of the file itself. For instance, keeping certain keywords is critical to assure the correct functionality of the file, and they cannot be removed. A possible solution to this problem has been proposed by Snrdic et al. [14], by limiting the changes to only *adding* features on a certain area of the file. Although effective, the authors also state that this changes might easily be detected.

Reverse Mimicry. To address the problems introduced by employing *mimicry*, an attacker can perform a variant of this attack called *reverse mimicry*, i.e., crafting a *benign* sample by injecting malicious contents in a way that its features receive as few changes as possible. To achieve this, the malicious content is injected so that the structure of the file (from which structural systems extract the file features) is only slightly changed. This has been shown to be

Fig. 2. A simplified example of the mimicry and reverse mimicry attacks. On the left (mimicry) it can be seen that the features of a malicious sample are changed to go into the benign region. On the right (reverse mimicry) a benign sample is injected with malicious content with few structural changes, so that the sample could keep staying in the benign region.

extremely effective against structural systems [13]. To better explain the differences between *mimicry* and *reverse mimicry*, Fig. 2 shows a graphical, simplified representation in a 2-D feature space of the two attacks.

Our previous work described three variants of reverse mimicry [13]: **(a)** *Java script (JS) Injection* (injecting a Javascript object that exploits a vulnerability), **(b)** *EXE Embedding* (injecting an executable that is automatically executed at runtime) and **(c)** *PDF Embedding* (injecting a malicious PDF file that is opened after the main file).

Detecting Reverse Mimicry. To tackle reverse mimicry attacks, we resort to different strategies. To counteract *PDF Embedding* we look for objects that, in their dictionary, contain the keyword /EmbeddedFiles. If such object is found, the relative object stream is decompressed, saved as a separate PDF and then analyzed. If this file is found to be malicious, then the original starting file will be considered malicious as well. To detect the other two attacks, it is important to correctly tune the *learning algorithm parameters* that we chose to train our system. In particular, we show that the robustness of the learning algorithm is strongly dependent on two aspects:

– The *weight threshold* (W) parameter of the AdaBoost algorithm (expressed, in our case, as a *percentage*) [33]. Thanks to this value, it is possible to select the samples that will be used, for each iteration of the AdaBoost algorithm, to tune the weights of the weak classifiers. In particular, for each iteration, the samples are chosen as follows:

1. We order the training set samples by their *normalized* weights (the lowest weight first). Samples that have been incorrectly classified at the previous iteration get higher weights. The normalized weights sum S_w is set to zero.
2. Starting from the first sample, we compute $S_w = S_w + w_s$, where w_s is the normalized weight of the sample. If $S_w < W$, then the sample will be employed for the training[12]. Otherwise, the algorithm stops.

---

[12] If W is in its percentage form, it must be divided by 100 first.

Fig. 3. A simplified example of the optimization effects on the decision function (original on the left, optimized on the right). In blue we represent a benign sample for which the classifier had to adapt its shape in order to correctly classify it (Color figure online).

The usage of a reduced weight threshold means that the weak classifiers will not be trained on samples that have been misclassified during previous iterations. This avoids that the global decision function changes its shape trying to correctly classify a particularly hard sample. This might also lead to more false positives.
– The *training data quality*. The *reverse mimicry* attacks directly address the *shape* of the classifier decision function [13], which depends on the weights of each weak classifier. Some functions might be particularly vulnerable after being trained, i.e., might have a combination of weights that could be particularly sensitive to *reverse mimicry* attacks. An empirical way to fix this problem is tuning the function weights by using *resampling*, i.e., generating *artificial training data* from the samples set obtained, given a specific weight threshold W. However, tuning the weights of an already robust function might create a *vulnerable* shape. Therefore, this empirical correction should only be used *after* having checked the weights of the function and *after* having verified its vulnerability. We call this correction *function optimization*.

Figure 3 shows a simplified example of possible performance optimizations effects. From this Figure we can observe that, when performances are optimized, the shape of the decision function will not try to adapt to the blue benign training sample. This results in a simplified decision function shape. As a further consequence, the blue sample will be misclassified. However, benign samples (in green) are now much closer to the boundary, and this will make a *reverse mimicry* attack applied on these samples most likely fail, as even with slight changes they would end up in the malicious region.

5   Experimental Evaluation

We start this Section by discussing the dataset adopted in our experiments, as well as the training and test methodology for evaluating performances. Then, we describe *two* experiments. In the first one, we compared the general performances of our approach, in terms of detection rate and false positives, to the ones of the other state of the art tools. In particular, we focused on PJScan, Wepawet, and PDFRate, as they can be considered the most important and *publicly available* research tools for detecting malicious PDF files. The second experiment tested our system against the *reverse mimicry attacks* that have been described in Sect. 4.3, and compared its results to the ones provided by the tools described in the previous experiment. We do so by producing a high number of *real, working* attack samples.

Dataset. We executed our experiments using real and up-to-date samples of both benign and malicious PDFs in-the-wild. Overall, we collected 11,138 unique malicious samples from `Contagio`[13], a well-known repository that provides information about latest PDF attacks and vulnerabilities. Moreover, we *randomly* collected 9,890 benign PDF samples, by resorting to the public `Yahoo search engine API` (http://search.yahoo.com). We kept a balance between malicious and benign files to ensure a good supervised training.

For the second experiment, we created 500 attack samples variants for each of the three attacks described in Sect. 4.3: *Javascript Injection, EXE Embedding* and *PDF Embedding*. Hence, we generated a total of 1500 real attack samples.

Training and Test Methodology. For the *first experiment*, to carefully evaluate the performances of our system, we randomly split our data into two different datasets:

- A training set composed by 11,944 files, split into 5,993 malicious and 5,951 benign files. This set was used to train the classifier.
- A test set composed of 9,084 files, split into 5,145 malicious and 3,939 benign files. This set was used to evaluate the the classifier performances.

This process was repeated *three* times: we computed the mean and the standard deviation of the True Positives (TP) and False Positives (FP) over these three replicas. As a unique measure of the classification quality, we also employed the so-called *Matthews Correlation Coefficient* (MCC) [35], defined as:

$$MCC = \frac{TP \cdot TN - FP \cdot FN}{\sqrt{(TP + FP)(TP + FN)(TN + FP)(TN + FN)}}$$

where TN and FN refer to the number of true and false negatives, respectively.

In our experiments, we trained an `AdaBoost` [33] ensemble of J48 trees, whose parameters were optimized with a 10-fold cross validation. We selected this classifier as it showed the best accuracy compared to single classifiers (we also experimented with random forest and SVM) or other ensemble techniques on our dataset.

For the *second experiment*, we employed the *same* training sets of the first experiment to train the system but, as a test set, the 1500 attack samples described before have been adopted.

5.1 Experiment 1: General Performances

In this experiment we compared the performances of our system to three public research tools for the detection of malicious PDFs: `Wepawet`, `PJScan` and `PDFRate`

---

[13] http://contagiodump.blogspot.it.

Table 1. Experimental comparison between our approach and other academic tools.

System	TP(%)	FP(%)	MCC
Our System	**99.805** (±.089)	**.068** (±.054)	**.997**
PDFRate	99.380 (±.085)	.071 (±.056)	.992
Wepawet	88.921 (±.331)	.032 (±.012)	.881
PJScan	80.165 (±1.979)	.013 (±.012)	.798

(see Sect. 3). As PJScan employs a *One Class SVM*, we did not use any benign files to train the system. PJScan was trained with the same malicious samples used for our system. PDFRate was trained with a balanced dataset of 5000 benign and 5000 malicious samples, the latter collected from Contagio. We point out that there are three different instances of PDFRate: Each of them employs the same classifier, but is trained with different data. To provide a fair comparison with our system, we considered only the one trained on the Contagio dataset, as Contagio is the same source from which we collected our malware samples. We also observe that the training size of Wepawet is unfortunately unknown[14]. Even though a perfect comparison would require the same exact training set for all the systems, we believe that, in this situation, our a set up was a very good compromise with which we could provide useful information about their performances.

In Table 1 we show the results of the comparison between our system and the other tools. For each system, we show the average percentage of true positives (TP), false positives (FP), the related standard deviation within parentheses, and the MCC coefficient computed on mean values for TP and FP. We point out that Wepawet was not able to analyze all the samples. In particular, it examined 5,091 malicious files and 3,883 benign files. We believe there were some parsing problems that affected the system, as it did not fully implement all the Adobe specifications and only simulated the execution of embedded Javascript code and executables. We also observe that PJScan considered as *benign* all the samples for which it could not find evidence of *Javascript* code usable for the analysis.

From this Table, it is evident that our system completely outperformed Wepawet and PJScan. PJScan showed the smallest false positive rate, but exhibited a much lower detection rate compared to the other systems. Wepawet performed slightly better than our solution in terms of FP rate, but it provided a lower TP detection rate. We also observe than our system performed better than PDFRate. In fact, results are superior both in terms of TP and FP rate, with a higher MCC coefficient. We point out that our approach was better to PDFRate while adopting a significantly lower number of features. In fact, PDFRate resorts to 202 features to perform its analysis [11], whereas our system has never gone beyond 135 (considering the variable number of object-related features).

---

[14] Being Wepawet and PDFRate online services, we could not train such systems with our own samples.

5.2   Experiment 2: Evasion Attacks

In this experiment we produced, for each attack described in Sect. 4.3, 500 attack variants for a total of 1500 samples, as the number of samples created in our previous work was not enough for deeply assessing their efficiency against the various systems [13]. The vulnerabilities exploited in these attacks are similar to the ones presented in our previous work, with some differences[15].

Table 2 shows the performances, in terms of *true positives* (TP), of the systems tested during the previous experiment (trained with the same data and with the same *splits* as before). It can be observed that `Wepawet` exhibited excellent performances on *EXE Embedding* and *JS Injection*. That was expected because *reverse mimicry* addresses *static structural systems*. However, `Wepawet` was not able to scan *PDF Embedding* attacks due to parsing problems. As we pointed out in the previous experiment, we believe that `Wepawet` did not fully implement the Adobe PDF specifications, and was therefore not able of analyzing some elements of the file. `PJScan` also exhibited several parsing problems in this experiment and was not able of analyzing *any* of the samples we provided. This is because `PJScan` could not analyze embedded files, i.e., PDFs or other files such as executables, and only focused on *Javascript* analysis (which also failed, in this case). Finally, `PDFRate` poorly performed, thus confirming the results of our previous work [13].

With respect to our system, we notice that it was able to detect all *PDF Embedding* attacks, thanks to its advanced parsing mechanism. As shown in Table 2, using the default weight threshold, namely, $W = 100$ (the one adopted in Experiment 1) with no function optimization, we obtained performances that were already better than `PDFRate`, yet not fully satisfactory. With $W = 1$ and an optimized decision function, performances were almost two times better, completely outperforming all the other static approaches. Using $W = 1$ on the test data of Experiment 1, we also noticed that false positives increased up to 0.2 %. This was predictable, as explained before, as a simplified decision function shape might lead to more mistakes in the detection of benign files. It is a small trade off we had to pay for a higher robustness. The standard deviation values deserve a deeper discussion in the next section.

Table 2. Comparison, in terms of true positives (TP), between our approach and research tools with respect to *evasion* attacks (%).

System	PDF E.	EXE E.	JS INJ.
Our System (W = 1, Optimized)	**100** ($\pm$0)	**62.4** ($\pm$12.6)	**69.1** ($\pm$16.9)
Our System (W = 100)	**100** ($\pm$0)	**32.26** ($\pm$9.18)	**37.9** ($\pm$10.65)
PDFRate	0.8	0.6	5.2
Wepawet	0	99.6	100
PJScan	0	0	0

---

[15] For *EXE Embedding* we exploited the `CVE-2010-1240` vulnerability and for *PDF Embedding* and *Javascript Injection* we exploited the `CVE-2009-0927`.

6   Discussion

Results attained in the second experiment showed that the features we had chosen allowed for a significantly higher robustness when compared to the state of the art. However, the high standard deviation attained in Experiment 2 also showed some limits in our approach: In this work we mainly focused on defining improving robustness by defining a more powerful set of features, but we did not *design* a *robust* decision function so that its shape would guarantee more robustness against targeted attacks. Therefore, the performances optimizations we have introduced in the previous section are only *empirical*, i.e., they are strongly dependent on the training data that are used. As future work, it would be interesting to design of a more robust *decision function* that, regardless of the quality of the training data, was able to reliably detect targeted attacks. This aspect has been often overlooked, especially in computer security applications and has been pointed out, for example, by Biggio et al. [34,36,37]. It would be also interesting to analyze the effects of *poisoning attacks* on the classifier detection, as our approach only focused on *test-time* evasion attacks [38,39]. Moreover, recent works have shown that clustering algorithms can also be vulnerable against evasion and poisoning attacks [40,41]. Since our method resorts on a clustering phase, possible future works might also address its resilience against such attacks.

7   Conclusions

Malicious PDF files have become a well-known threat in the past years. PDF documents still constitute a very effective attack vector for cyber-criminals, being their readers often vulnerable to zero-day attacks. Despite all the detection approaches that have been developed during the years, research has shown how it is possible to craft PDF samples so that it is easy for an attacker to evade even the most sophisticated detection system. In this work, we presented a new approach that leveraged on both structural and content-based information to provide a very accurate detection of PDF malware. Our approach has been designed to cope with evasion attacks, thus significantly improving the detection of reverse mimicry attacks. Finally, our work pointed out the need of secure learning techniques for malware detection, as vulnerabilities of machine learning systems seriously affect their performances at detecting targeted attacks.

Acknowledgement. This work is supported by the Regional Administration of Sardinia, Italy, within the project "Advanced and secure sharing of multimedia data over social networks in the future Internet" (CUP F71J11000690002). Davide Maiorca gratefully acknowledges Sardinia Regional Government for the financial support of his PhD scholarship (P.O.R. Sardegna F.S.E. Operational Programme of the Autonomous Region of Sardinia, European Social Fund 2007–2013 - Axis IV Human Resources, Objective 1.3, Line of Activity 1.3.1.).

References

1. Symantec: Internet Security Threat Reports. 2013 Trends. Symantec (2014)
2. Buchanan, E., Roemer, R., Sevage, S., Shacham, H.: Return-oriented programming: exploitation without code injection. In: Black Hat 2008 (2008)
3. Ratanaworabhan, P., Livshits, B., Zorn, B.: Nozzle: a defense against heap-spraying code injection attacks. In: Proceedings of the 18th Conference on USENIX Security Symposium (2009)
4. Bania, P.: Jit spraying and mitigations. CoRR abs/1009.1038 (2010)
5. Adobe: Adobe Supplement to ISO 32000. Adobe (2008)
6. Esparza, J.M.: Obfuscation and (non-)detection of malicious pdf files. In: S21Sec e-crime (2011)
7. Cova, M., Kruegel, C., Vigna, G.: Detection and analysis of drive-by-download attacks and malicious javascript code. In: Proceedings of the 19th International Conference on World Wide Web (2010)
8. Laskov, P., Šrndić, N.: Static detection of malicious javascript-bearing pdf documents. In: Proceedings of the 27th Annual Computer Security Applications Conference (2011)
9. Tzermias, Z., Sykiotakis, G., Polychronakis, M., Markatos, E.P.: Combining static and dynamic analysis for the detection of malicious documents. In: Proceedings of the 4th European Workshop on System Security (2011)
10. Maiorca, D., Giacinto, G., Corona, I.: A pattern recognition system for malicious pdf files detection. In: Proceedings of the 8th International Conference on Machine Learning and Data Mining in Pattern Recognition (2012)
11. Smutz, C., Stavrou, A.: Malicious pdf detection using metadata and structural features. In: Proceedings of the 28th Annual Computer Security Applications Conference (2012)
12. Šrndić, N., Laskov, P.: Detection of malicious pdf files based on hierarchical document structure. In: Proceedings of the 20th Annual Network and Distributed System Security Symposium (2013)
13. Maiorca, D., Corona, I., Giacinto, G.: Looking at the bag is not enough to find the bomb: an evasion of structural methods for malicious pdf files detection. In: Proceedings of the 8th ACM SIGSAC Symposium on Information, Computer and Communications Security (2013)
14. Šrndic, N., Laskov, P.: Practical evasion of a learning-based classifier: a case study. In: Proceedings of the 2014 IEEE Symposium on Security and Privacy, SP 2014, pp. 197–211. IEEE Computer Society, Washington, D.C. (2014)
15. Corona, I., Maiorca, D., Ariu, D., Giacinto, G.: LuxOr: detection of malicious pdf-embedded javascript code through discriminant analysis of API references. In: Proceedings of the 7th ACM Workshop on Artificial Intelligence and Security (AiSEC). Scottdale, Arizona, USA (2014)
16. Liu, D., Wang, H., Stavrou, A.: Detecting malicious javascript in pdf through document instrumentation. In: Proceedings of the 44th Annual International Conference on Dependable Systems and Networks (2014)
17. Maass, M., Scherlis, W.L., Aldrich, J.: In-nimbo sandboxing. In: Proceedings of the 2014 Symposium and Bootcamp on the Science of Security, HotSoS 2014. ACM, New York, pp. 1:1–1:12 (2014)
18. Maiorca, D., Ariu, D., Corona, I., Giacinto, G.: A structural and content-based approach for a precise and robust detection of malicious pdf files. In: Proceedings of the 1st International Conference on Information Systems Security and Privacy (ICISSP 2015), pp. 27–36. INSTICC (2015)

19. Adobe: PDF Reference. Adobe Portable Document Format Version 1.7. Adobe (2006)
20. Li, W.J., Stolfo, S., Stavrou, A., Androulaki, E., Keromytis, A.D.: A study of malcode-bearing documents. In: Proceedings of the 4th International Conference on Detection of Intrusions and Malware, and Vulnerability Assessment (2007)
21. Shafiq, M.Z., Khayam, S.A., Farooq, M.: Embedded malware detection using markov n-grams. In: Proceedings of the 5th International Conference on Detection of Intrusions and Malware, and Vulnerability Assessment (2008)
22. Tabish, S.M., Shafiq, M.Z., Farooq, M.: Malware detection using statistical analysis of byte-level file content. In: Proceedings of the ACM SIGKDD Workshop on CyberSecurity and Intelligence Informatics (2009)
23. Rieck, K., Krueger, T., Dewald, A.: Cujo: efficient detection and prevention of drive-by-download attacks. In: Proceedings of the 26th Annual Computer Security Applications Conference (2010)
24. Curtsinger, C., Livshits, B., Zorn, B., Seifert, C.: Zozzle: fast and precise in-browser javascript malware detection. In: Proceedings of the 20th USENIX Conference on Security (2011)
25. Canali, D., Cova, M., Vigna, G., Kruegel, C.: Prophiler: a fast filter for the large-scale detection of malicious web pages. In: Proceedings of the 20th International Conference on World Wide Web (2011)
26. Engleberth, M., Willems, C., Holz, T.: Detecting malicious documents with combined static and dynamic analysis. In: Virus Bulletin (2009)
27. Willems, C., Holz, T., Freiling, F.: Toward automated dynamic malware analysis using cwsandbox. IEEE Secur. Priv. **5**, 32–39 (2007)
28. Rieck, K., Holz, T., Willems, C., Düssel, P., Laskov, P.: Learning and classification of malware behavior. In: Proceedings of the 5th International Conference on Detection of Intrusions and Malware, and Vulnerability Assessment (2008)
29. Snow, K.Z., Krishnan, S., Monrose, F., Provos, N.: Shellos: enabling fast detection and forensic analysis of code injection attacks. In: Proceedings of the 20th USENIX Conference on Security (2011)
30. Nissim, N., Cohen, A., Glezer, C., Elovici, Y.: Detection of malicious PDF files and directions for enhancements: a state-of-the art survey. Comput. Secur. **48**, 246–266 (2015)
31. MacQueen, J.B.: Some methods for classification and analysis of multivariate observations. In: Cam, L.M.L., Neyman, J., (eds.) Proceedings of the Fifth Berkeley Symposium on Mathematical Statistics and Probability, vol. 1, pp. 281–297. University of California Press (1967)
32. Quinlan, J.R.: Learning decision tree classifiers. ACM Comput. Surv. **28**, 71–72 (1996)
33. Freund, Y., Schapire, R.E.: A decision-theoretic generalization of on-line learning and an application to boosting. J. Comput. Syst. Sci. **55**(1), 119–139 (1997). doi:10.1006/jcss.1997.1504
34. Biggio, B., Corona, I., Maiorca, D., Nelson, B., Šrndić, N., Laskov, P., Giacinto, G., Roli, F.: Evasion attacks against machine learning at test time. In: Blockeel, H., Kersting, K., Nijssen, S., Železný, F. (eds.) ECML PKDD 2013, Part III. LNCS, vol. 8190, pp. 387–402. Springer, Heidelberg (2013)
35. Baldi, P., Brunak, S., Chauvin, Y., Andersen, C.A.F., Nielsen, H.: Assessing the accuracy of prediction algorithms for classification: an overview. Bioinformatics **16**, 412–424 (2000)
36. Biggio, B., Fumera, G., Roli, F.: Security evaluation of pattern classifiers under attack. IEEE Trans. Knowl. Data Eng. **26**, 984–996 (2014)

37. Biggio, B., Corona, I., Nelson, B., Rubinstein, B., Maiorca, D., Fumera, G., Giacinto, G., Roli, F.: Security evaluation of support vector machines in adversarial environments. In: Ma, Y., Guo, G. (eds.) Support Vector Machines Applications, pp. 105–153. Springer, Heidelberg (2014)
38. Biggio, B., Nelson, B., Laskov, P.: Poisoning attacks against support vector machines. In: Langford, J., Pineau, J. (eds.) 29th International Conference on Machine Learning (ICML). Omnipress (2012)
39. Biggio, B., Fumera, G., Roli, F.: Multiple classifier systems for robust classifier design in adversarial environments. Int. J. Mach. Learn. Cybernet. 1, 27–41 (2010)
40. Biggio, B., Rieck, K., Ariu, D., Wressnegger, C., Corona, I., Giacinto, G., Roli, F.: Poisoning behavioral malware clustering. In: Proceedings of 2014 Workshop on Artificial Intelligent and Security Workshop, AISec 2014. ACM, New York, pp. 27–36 (2014)
41. Biggio, B., Pillai, I., Bulò, S.R., Ariu, D., Pelillo, M., Roli, F.: Is data clustering in adversarial settings secure? In: Proceedings of the 2013 ACM Workshop on Artificial Intelligence and Security, AISec 2013, ACM, New York, pp. 87–98 (2013)

Privacy and Confidentiality

Privacy Assessment of Data Flow Graphs for an Advanced Recommender System in the Smart Grid

Fabian Knirsch[1,2]([✉]), Dominik Engel[1], Cristian Neureiter[1],
Marc Frincu[3], and Viktor Prasanna[3]

[1] Josef Ressel Center for User-Centric Smart Grid Privacy, Security and Control,
Salzburg University of Applied Sciences, Urstein Sued 1, 5412 Puch/Salzburg, Austria
{fabian.knirsch,dominik.engel,christian.neureiter}@en-trust.at
[2] Department of Computer Sciences, Salzburg University,
Jakob-Haringerstr. 2, Salzburg, Austria
[3] Ming-Hsieh Department of Electrical Engineering,
University of Southern California, Los Angeles, USA
{frincu,prasanna}@usc.edu

Abstract. The smart grid paves the way to a number of novel applications that benefit a variety of stakeholders including network operators, utilities and customers as well as third party developers such as electric vehicle manufacturers. In order to roll out an integrated and connected grid that combines energy and information flows and that fosters bidirectional communications, data and information needs to be exchanged and aggregated. However, collecting, transmitting and combining information from different sources has some severe privacy impacts on customers. Furthermore, customer acceptance and participation is the key to many smart grid applications such as demand response. In this paper we present (i) an approach for the model-based assessment of privacy in the smart grid that draws on a formal use case description (data flow graphs) and allows to asses the privacy impact of such use cases at early design time; and (ii) based on that assessment we introduce a recommender system for smart grid applications that allows users and vendors to make informed decisions on the deployment, use and active participation in smart grid use cases with respect to their individual privacy.

1 Introduction

In a smart grid a number of stakeholders (actors) have to cooperate effectively. Interoperability has to be assured on many layers, ranging from high level business cases to low level network communication. Data and information is sent from one actor to another in order to ensure effective communication. Furthermore, the exchange of vast amounts of data is crucial for many smart grid applications, such as demand response (DR) or electric vehicle charging [1,2]. However, this data is also related to individuals and privacy issues are an upcoming concern [3,4]. Especially the combination of data, e.g., meter values and preferences for

© Springer International Publishing Switzerland 2015
O. Camp et al. (Eds.): ICISSP 2015, CCIS 576, pp. 89–106, 2015.
DOI: 10.1007/978-3-319-27668-7_6

DR can exploit serious privacy threats such as the prediction of personal habits. In system engineering, privacy is a cross-cutting concern that has to be taken into account throughout the entire development life-cycle, which is also referred to as *privacy by design* [1].

Model-driven privacy assessment is especially useful when applied in software engineering. In [5], the author thoroughly investigates the phases in software engineering and the expected costs for error correction and change requests. Costs double with every phase and once an application or a service is delivered, the additional adding of crosscutting concerns such as privacy is tied to enormous costs. As a result, design time privacy assessment is preferred in early phases of the software engineering process. Therefore, a framework is needed to (i) model the system, including high-level use cases and concrete components and communication flows; and (ii) to assess the system's privacy impact using expert knowledge from the domain. Related work in the domain of automated assessments in the smart grid mainly focuses on security aspects and is not primarily concerned with privacy and the modeling in adherence to reference architectures.

In this paper we address these issues and present an approach for the model-driven assessment of privacy for smart grid applications. The framework proposed in this paper is designed to assist system engineers to evaluate use cases in the smart grid in an early design phase. For evaluation only meta-information is used and no concrete data is needed. We use Data Flow Graphs (DFG) to formally define use cases according to a standardized smart grid reference architecture. The assessment is based on an ontology driven approach taking into account expert knowledge from various domains, including customer views on privacy as well as system engineering concerns. The output is a set of threats and a quantitative analysis of risks, i.e., a number indicating the strength of that threat. To evaluate the system we draw on insights from the University of Southern California microgrid. The primary contributions of this paper are (i) the use of DFGs to model use cases in the smart grid; (ii) the usage of DFGs for a quantitative privacy assessment; and (iii) the use of an ontology driven approach to capture domain knowledge.

The remainder of this paper is structured as follows: In Sect. 2 related work in the area of smart grid reference architectures, privacy evaluation and automated assessment tools is presented. In Sect. 3 the architecture of the proposed framework and its components are described. This includes the concept of DFGs for modeling use cases in the smart grid, the principal design of the ontology and the mapping of data flow graphs to the ontology, the methodology for defining threat patterns and finally, how these patterns are matched to use cases. The framework is evaluated with a set of representative use cases in Sect. 4. Section 5 shows a practical application for the proposed framework as a recommender system for the potential privacy impact when using applications and services in the smart grid. Section 6 summarizes this paper and gives an outlook to further work in this area.

2   Related Work

In this section related work in the field of smart grid reference architectures, privacy evaluation and assessment as well as automated assessment tools are presented. Often, privacy and security are used interchangeably. For the purpose of this paper we refer to privacy as legally accessing data but not using it for the intended purpose. Security, by contrast, would involve the illegal acquisition of data. In both cases, the well established and widely understood terminology from security assessment is used, i.e., *threat*, *attacker*, *vulnerability* and *countermeasure*.

2.1   Reference Models

Stakeholders in the smart grid come from historically different areas, including electrical engineering, computer science and economics. To ensure interoperability and to foster a common understanding, standardization organizations are rolling out reference models and road maps. In the US the NIST Framework and Roadmap for Smart Grid Interoperability Standards [6] and in the EU the Smart Grid Reference Architecture [7] were published. The European Smart Grid Architecture Model (SGAM) is based on the NIST Framework, but extends the model to better meet European requirements, such as distributed energy resources. In this paper we investigate use cases from the US. In particular we are focusing on use cases from the University of Southern California microgrid and we thoroughly discuss a typical DR use case. Investigations have, however, shown that for the purpose of this project all use cases from the US can be directly mapped to the European SGAM without the loss of information. Therefore we propose the utilization of the SGAM for two reasons: (i) the SGAM builds on the NIST model and allows to capture both, use cases from the US and the EU; and (ii) with the SGAM Toolbox Dänekas et al. [8] present a framework for modeling use cases based on the SGAM; in that way formally modeled use cases are the input for the evaluation.

2.2   Privacy

Privacy (and security) issues in the smart grid are addressed by standards in the US [9] and the EU [10]. Privacy, in specific, has no clear definition. According to a thorough analysis in [11], privacy can be defined as the right of an individual's control over personal information. More formally this is defined by [12] in a four dimensional privacy taxonomy. The dimensions are *purpose*, *visibility*, *granularity* and *retention*. The *purpose* dimension refers to the intended use of data, i.e., what personal information is released for. The purpose ranges from single, a specific use only, to any. *Visibility* refers to who has permitted access. The range is from owner to all/world. *Granularity* describes to what extent information is detailed. The *retention* dimension finally is the period for storage of data. In any case, privacy is assured if all these dimensions are communicated clearly and fully disclosed to data owners and the compliance to the principles is governed.

Hence, data is collected and processed for the intended purpose only, and the degree of visibility, granularity and retention is at the necessary minimum.

2.3   Assessment Tools

To measure the degree to which systems adhere to privacy requirements, approaches for automated qualitative assessments (resulting in statements of possible privacy impacts due to privacy critical actions or relationships) and quantitative assessments (resulting in a numeric value that determines the risk of privacy impacts) exist.

In [13], the authors present an approach towards ontology based risk assessment. The authors propose three ontologies, the *user environment ontology* capturing where users are working, i.e., software and hardware, the *project ontology* capturing concepts of project management, i.e., work packages and tasks and the *attack ontology* capturing possible attacks, e.g., non-authorized data access, virus distribution or spam emails. For a risk assessment, attacks (defined in the attack ontology) are matched with information available from the other ontologies. For a quantitative assessment, the annual loss expectancy is calculated by combining a set of harmful outcomes and the expected impact of such an outcome with the frequency of that outcome. This approach is designed for security issues and does not explicitly cover privacy assessments.

In [14,15] an ontology driven approach for privacy evaluation is presented. The aim of these papers is to integrate privacy in the design process. High-level privacy statements are matched to system specifications and implementation details. The proposed *privacy by design* process includes the following phases: identification of high-level privacy requirements, translation of abstract privacy requirements to formal privacy descriptions, realization of the requirements and modeling of the system and analyzing the system by matching formal privacy requirements to the formal system model. Contrary to our work this approach is not focused on use cases in the smart grid and therefore does not model systems based on a standardized reference architecture.

A workflow oriented security assessment is presented in [16]. This approach is not based on ontologies but on argument graphs. The presented framework uses *security goal, workflow and system description, attacker model* and *evidence* as an input. This information is aggregated in a discriminative set of argument graphs, each taking into account additional input. Nodes in the graph are aggregated using boolean expressions and the output is a quantitative assessment of the system. Instead of focusing on workflow analysis using graphs, we model systems as a whole in adherence to the standardized reference architecture using an ontology driven approach to integrate expert knowledge.

A considerably broader approach for an assessment tool that incorporates both, the balancing of privacy requirements and operational capabilities is presented in [17]. This work presents a graph based approach that allows the modeling of systems with respect to the operational requirements of certain nodes (e.g. metering at a certain frequency) and the impact of privacy restrictions on subsequent nodes. The authors further present an optimum balancing algorithm, i.e. to what extent restrictions gained from privacy enhancing technologies and the necessary operational requirements can be combined. However, this needs sufficient information on how privacy is impacted by certain use cases which is provided by this work.

3   Architecture

This section is dedicated to an architectural overview as well as a detailed discussion of the components. Figure 1 shows the principal components of the proposed architecture, including input and output. For a privacy assessment, the framework accepts two inputs, a use case UC modeled as a DFG in adherence to the SGAM and a set of threat patterns T. In order to qualitatively analyze this input the use case is mapped to individuals – i.e., instances of classes – of an ontology (sometimes referred to as the *assertion box, ABox* [18]). The corresponding class model (sometimes referred to as the *terminological box, TBox* [18]) is based on the SGAM. This qualitative analysis provides explicit and implicit information about the elements from the DFG: actors, components, information objects and their interrelation. The results of the qualitative assessment are the input for the subsequent quantitative analysis. The output of that analysis is finally a class c from a set of classes C that the use case is assigned to. A threat pattern t is used to describe potential threats, where $t \in T$ and a class c represents a subset of threats T^*. A class c describes how threat patterns and the qualitative results are combined, which is presented as a threat matrix as an output. Note that the terminology *threat matrix* is borrowed from security analysis and that the output is not a matrix in the mathematical sense. A threat matrix compares a set of threats and the risk for these threats. Formally, the classifier is defined as Assign UC to c_i if $t \in T_i^*, \forall t \in T, 1 \le i \le \{C\}$. A threat exploits a set of vulnerabilities and is mitigated by a set of countermeasures. Each threat pattern can be evaluated for itself or multiple patterns are combined to classes of threats. A vulnerability is any kind of privacy impact for any kind of stakeholder or actor. Threats are evaluated using the attack vector model which is adapted from security analysis and defined in detail later in this paper. In general, an attack is feasible, if given (i) an attacker; (ii) a privacy asset; and (iii) the resources to perform the attack. Hence, a receiver or collector of privacy critical data items is potentially able to access these assets and to use them in a way not corresponding to the original purpose. This is formally represented as ⟨data access, privacy asset, attack resources⟩.

3.1   Data Flow Graphs

In order to qualitatively and quantitatively assess the privacy impact of a use case a formalization is crucial. In this section we introduce the concept of Data Flow Graphs (DFG) for the smart grid based on a model-driven design approach originally presented in [8,19]. DFGs formally capture all aspects of use cases in the smart grid in adherence to the SGAM. They contain high-level business cases

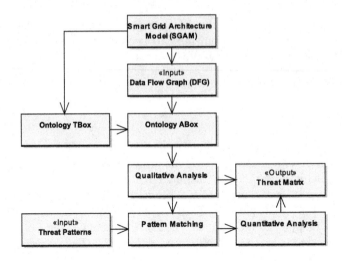

Fig. 1. Architecture overview showing input, output, components and principal information flows of the framework.

as well as detailed views of a system's characteristics such as encryption and protocols. DFGs are a powerful tool as they allow both, easy modeling and full adherence to the reference architecture. Furthermore, in the graph relationships between actors, as well as the transported information objects (IO) are modeled. Nodes in a graph represent business actors, system actors or components and edges represent data flows annotated with IOs. In accordance to the standard [7], DFGs consist of the following five layers:

1. Business Layer. In a DFG this layer is a high level description of the business case. Business actors, their common business goal and their business requirements are modeled.
2. Function Layer. The function layer details the business case by mapping business actors to system actors and by dividing the high level business goals in use cases and steps.
3. Information Layer. This layer describes information flows in detail. System actors communicate to each other through IOs. IOs are characterized by describing information attributes on a meta-level. An IO is one of the key data used for classification and is discussed in greater detail below.
4. Communication Layer. The communication layer is a more detailed view on communication taking into account network and protocol specifications.
5. Component Layer. In a DFG this layer contains concrete components. Therefore system actors are mapped to components and devices.

Each layer is a directed graph. Both, nodes and edges can have attributes. The semantics, however, are varying. For instance, where attributed edges in the business layer describe a business case, in the information layer concrete metadata of communication flows are captured. Even though implicitly covered in the model presented above, for automated evaluation we introduce two additional layers: Between business and function layer we include the *Business Actor to System Actor Mapping* and between communication and component layer the *System Actor to Component Mapping*. This allows to capture the complexity of use cases on different levels while still maintaining the cross-layer relationship between high-level business actors and their representation as components. These layers are directed graphs as well, with edges indicating the mapping. The mapping defines a one to many relationship from business actors to system actors and from system actors to components. In the European Smart Grid Reference Architecture with the SGAM Methodology an approach for mapping use cases to the reference model is suggested. DFGs build on this methodology focusing on actors and their interrelation. An implementation for modeling DFGs in UML is available as the *SGAM Toolbox*[1]. Data Flow Graphs contain explicit information (what is modeled) and implicit information (what can be concluded). Conclusions are drawn using ontology reasoning.

3.2 Ontology Design

The ontology driven approach for classification has been chosen for two main reasons: (i) ontologies are powerful for capturing domain knowledge explicitly; and (ii) through logic reasoning [18] ontologies are a source for implicit knowledge. The power of ontologies to formally capture knowledge and how to draw conclusions is discussed in [20]. The power of reasoning for gaining additional, implicit knowledge can easily be outlined with two examples: In a DFG, information objects may be sent from an actor A to an actor B and from there to another actor C. This is explicitly modeled in the DFG. A reasoner in an appropriate ontology, however, may conclude directly the transitivity, hence that actor A in fact sends information to actor C. Another example is concerned with compositions of data. An information object I_1 may contain sensitive data and it may be used by an actor D to compose another information object I_2 that is sent to a collecting actor E. It is not explicitly modeled in the DFG, but it can be concluded by the reasoner, that E receives an information object which is of type sensitive data since I_2 is a composition of I_1. The ontology we propose here is designed to capture all aspects of a DFG. The ontology is modeled in OWL[2] and class expressions are stated in Manchester Syntax[3]. Therefore, all components available for modeling DFGs are represented either directly or as an abstraction in the ontology (referred to as the *TBox*). The DFG is represented in the ontology as a set of individuals (referred to as the *ABox*). Figure 2 depicts the principal classes and relationships of the ontology and therefore the most relevant concepts for mapping a DFG to the ontology. This view shows the main classes and relationships for illustration purposes only; our current ontology comprises more than 60 classes, data properties and object properties. Crucial concepts represented immediately, include which actor sends or receives

---

[1] http://www.en-trust.at/downloads/sgam-toolbox/.
[2] http://www.w3.org/TR/owl-features/.
[3] http://www.w3.org/TR/owl2-manchester-syntax/.

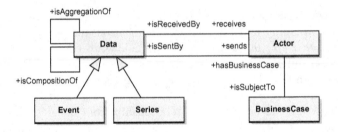

Fig. 2. Principal components of the ontology, showing a subset of the relationships between actor and data.

which data and IO and how these IOs are composed. Furthermore, a set of pre-classifiers is defined to determine implicit knowledge.

These classifiers are OWL classes using an equivalent class expression in Manchester Syntax. For instance, to determine if some aggregation consists of direct personal data, the following expression is used: `Data and isAggregationOf some DirectPersonalData`. To determine the multiplicity of the sending actor and if the data is a composition sent by many of such actors, more elaborate expressions can be phrased: `Data and isSentBy some Actor and Multiplicity value "n" and isCompositionOfMany some Data`.

3.3   Threat Patterns

In this paper we evaluate the privacy impact on customers, thus we identified the following list of typical high-level threats based on literature reviews [1,2,4]. These threats have been modified in order to be more representative for the use cases from the University of Southern California microgrid that are investigated in this paper. Subsequently, IOs that may cause these threats are determined.

Customer Presence at Home. This privacy concern is discussed in [1]. To potentially determine a person's presence at home, some device in the customer premises is needed. This device collects data at a certain frequency, high enough to have a resolution that allows to draw conclusions on the energy usage of specific devices. Furthermore, data collected from that device needs to be sent to another actor (i.e., a utility). At the utility an individual or a system needs to have access to the data in an appropriate resolution. Since we always assume that data is accessed legally, we do not focus on unallowed data access. Additionally, the total delay of the data transmission is of relevance. If data is collected and transmitted in almost real time the presence at home can be determined immediately. If data is available with a delay only, the analysis of past events and predictions might be possible. If this information is published, an attacker might exploit this vulnerability in order to break in the house.

Tracking Customer Position. This threat is especially interesting for electric vehicle charging. Assuming the customer has some identification towards the charging station, at least the location, a timestamp and the amount of energy consumed will be recorded for billing. Depending on the design of the infrastructure only little information will be sent to the operator or a very detailed profile of the customer is maintained. Here, the multiplicity of the actors is crucial and the fact that different actors have access to the same data. Attacks for this threat are described in [2], e.g., using information for targeted ads, for tracking movements to certain places or to infer the income based on recharges.

3.4   Pattern Matching

Actual classification is done in the pattern matching process. For each actor in the DFG and the ontology, respectively, the attack vector is determined, i.e., to which resources does an actor have access and what is the effort. If that shows feasible matching this is seen as a threat. It can be retrieved immediately from the ontology if an actor has access to a certain IO. This is done by evaluating actor and data object properties and by incorporating information from the pre-classifiers. Furthermore, relationships on the business layer and data properties such as encryption are taken into account. The following, discriminative set of classifiers is used to determine potential threats: first, for each information object the data provider and the data collector are determined (according to the terminology defined in [12]) and it is assessed who has access to the data. This yields a list of three-tuples in the form ⟨information object (IO), data provider (DP), data collector (DC)⟩. Then it is determined if an information object either contains sensitive or direct personal data (according to the terminology defined in [21]). This yields another three-tuple in the form ⟨information object (IO), sensitive (S), direct personal (DP)⟩. Finally it is determined if the attacker has actual data access, yielding one more three-tuples in the form ⟨information object (IO), data collector (DC), access (A)⟩. Data access depends on the relationship of actors, on data resolution, retention and encryption. Matching these tuples to each other results in the components of the attack vector, recalling ⟨data access, privacy asset, attack resources⟩ yields ⟨⟨IO, DP, DC⟩, ⟨IO, S, DP⟩, ⟨IO, DC, A⟩⟩. An exemplary attack vector for a DR use case where DR preferences are sent to the utility is ⟨⟨DR preferences, customer, utility⟩, ⟨DR preferences, false, false⟩, ⟨DR preferences, utility, true⟩⟩. This already provides thorough qualitative analysis. It is possible to determine which actor can potentially threaten the privacy of another actor. It is even possible to conclude how and where this might happen. However, for a quantitative assessment the risk for a particular threat is calculated. While a qualitative assessment is useful in supporting detailed system design decisions and evaluation, for a very first outline of the overall system characteristics, a quantitative value is much more expressive. Further, providing a numeric value for the system's privacy impact helps to easily compare and contrast proposed designs.

Risk is calculated as the product of the *probability of occurrence* (PO) and the *expected loss* (EL). For the set T^* a number of patterns $t_{v,1} \ldots t_{v,N}$ and $t_{c,1} \ldots t_{c,M}$, respectively is defined. A pattern therefore contains a set of conditions for vulnerabilities $t_{v,i}$ and countermeasures $t_{c,i}$. Conditions are SPARQL ASK queries[4] that return either *true* or *false* if the pattern applies or not. For brevity, t'_v denotes the number of vulnerabilities that apply, t'_c the number of countermeasures that apply and t_v and t_c denote the total number of vulnerabilities and countermeasures, respectively. In this paper we propose the following approach for determining values for the probability of occurrence $PO(t'_v, t'_c)$ and the expected loss $EL(t'_v, t'_c)$: $PO(t'_v, t'_c)$ is determined by defining a plane that satisfies the following conditions: $PO(t'_v = t_v, t'_c = 0) = 1$, $PO(t'_v = 0, t'_c = t_c) = 0$ and $PO(t'_v = 0, t'_c = 0) = \frac{1}{2}$. This yields $PO(t'_v, t'_c) = \frac{1}{2}(\frac{t'_v}{t_v} - \frac{t'_c}{t_c} + 1)$. A linear model is chosen due to its simplicity and might be extended by more complex approaches in future. A condition that is of type *vulnerability* increases $EL(t'_v, t'_c)$, a condition of type *countermeasure* decreases $EL(t'_v, t'_c)$. The value of $EL(t'_v, t'_c)$ is defined in the pattern. Risk R is finally defined by $R = PO(t'_v, t'_c)EL(t'_v, t'_c)$.

To feed in the results gained from the qualitative analysis, certain variables in the query can be bound to instances. For example, given the following fraction of a query (where usc denotes the namespace prefix for actors and IOs in the University of Southern California microgrid) to determine if *some* information object is sent by *some* business actor.

```
$io usc:isSentBy ?systemactor . $io usc:isReceivedBy ?systemactor .
?systemactor usc:isRealizationOf ?businessactor .
?businessactor a usc:BusinessActor
```

It is now possible to bind the variable $io to a concrete value as determined in the qualitative assessment, e.g., $io ← InformationObject.CustomerName. This allows to assess a particular impact on a particular information object or component/actor based on the previously calculated attack vectors.

We developed generic patterns for *typical* threats, i.e., such as the ones mentioned above. The framework is, however, not limited to this set of patterns and allows the definition of an arbitrary number of additional patterns to meet the individual needs of the application scenario. The output of the framework is a threat matrix contrasting the results from the qualitative analysis and from the quantitative risk assessment. For a UC, a threat matrix contains the attack vector and the assigned risk for the determined class c.

For illustrative purposes, the following listing shows an example pattern for *customer presence at home*. This includes the vulnerability *device in customer premises* (exemplary assigned an EL of 4) and the countermeasure *aggregation of data from multiple customers* (exemplary assigned an EL of -6).

---

[4] http://www.w3.org/TR/sparql11-query/.

```
<Pattern name="customer presence at home">
  <Vulnerability
    name="device in customer premises">
    <EL>4</EL>
    <Condition>
      ?device x:isRealizationOf $ba .
      $ba a x:BusinessActor .
      ?device x:Zone
      "Customer Premises"^^xsd:string
    </Condition>
  </Vulnerability>
  <Countermeasure
    name="aggregation of data from multiple
      customers">
    <EL>-6</EL>
    <Condition>
      $io x:manyAreAggregatedBy ?io2 .
      ?io2 x:isReceivedBy ?ba1 .
      $io x:isRecevivedBy ?ba2
      FILTER (?ba1 != ?ba2)
    </Condition>
  </Countermeasure>
</Pattern>
```

4 Evaluation

For evaluating the framework new, previously unused use cases are applied. The set of threat patterns and their impact on privacy is based on the aforementioned literature reviews. We are therefore using a representative set of use cases describing typical applications in the smart grid. This includes, but is not limited to, smart metering, electric vehicle charging and DR. In this section a real-life use case from the University of Southern California microgrid, and a real-life use case from the Salzburg Smart Grid Model Region are evaluated as an example. These use cases have been chosen as they are (i) simple enough to verify results based on literature reviews; and (ii) complex enough to have an interesting combination of actors and information flows. Evaluation is performed with a prototypical implementation that uses DFGs and threat patterns as an input and produces a threat matrix as an output.

4.1 Smart Metering

For the Salzburg Smart Grid Model Region use case we investigate a typical smart metering scenario as shown in Fig. 3. Smart metering is the basis for many advanced applications in the smart grid and therefore considered as a key enabling technology [22]. Today, smart metering is typically applied for network monitoring and billing. The use case is outlined as follows: once a smart meter is installed in a residential building meter values are collected at a fixed frequency.

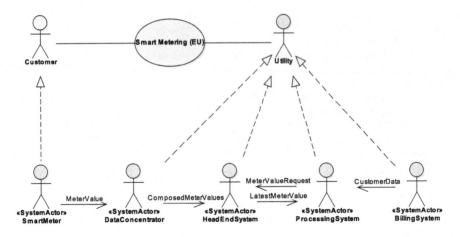

Fig. 3. Outline of the smart metering use case that is discussed for evaluation.

Due to regulatory provisions this is (e.g., in Austria and Germany) limited to one value each 15 min and 96 values per day, respectively. Data for one day is summarized in the smart meter and forwarded to the utility on the next day. Multiple smart meters are connected in a mash-like topology and data is sent to a data concentrator that (i) relays data from power line communication to IP; and (ii) collects data from the attached meter. Smart meter data is finally stored in a head-end system. For billing, meter data (energy consumption) is linked to additional data from the billing system, such as contract details, name, address and past payment behavior.

Actors. Business actors are the *user* and the *utility*. The user is mapped to the system actor *smart meter*. The utility is represented as *data concentrator, head-end system, billing system* and *processing system*. The latter is the component linking the data from the billing system to the data from the head-end system.

Information Objects. Meter values are sent at a fixed rate from the customer premises to the utility. The utility stores these values in the head end-system and the processing system finally combines both, data from the head-end system and data from the billing system.

Customer Presence at Home. When metering is done on a regular basis, it is easily detectable if a customer is present at home. The qualitative analysis shows that meter values are sent from the smart meter to the data concentrator and further to the head-end system. Storing in the head-end system is privacy critical, since data metered at a certain frequency is persisted. For this threat four vulnerabilities (device in customer premises, collecting data at a certain frequency, receiver has access to data, data retention is unlimited) and one countermeasure (aggregation of data from multiple customers) are identified, resulting in a *PO* of 0.9, and *EL* of 11.5 and a risk value of 10.35.

Identification of Customer Habits. While the intended use case for persisting meter data is billing, such data can be used to identify customer behavior, e.g., by running statistics and predicting future actions. For this threat eight vulnerabilities (device in customer premises, collecting data at a certain frequency, receiver has access to data, data retention is unlimited, composition of location and timestamp, different actors have access to the same data, location information with unlimited retention) and two countermeasures (aggregation of data from multiple customers, retention is for processing only) are identified, resulting in a *PO* of 0.75, an *EL* of 11.5 and a risk value of 8.63.

The model-driven assessment of the smart metering use case has shown that the risk of identifying customer habits is less than the risk of determining customer presence at home. This is due to the fact that determining presence is a yes/no decision whereas determining and predicting habits requires way more data and information.

4.2   Demand Response

For the University of Southern California microgrid use case, we are focusing on a DR scenario similar to the one described in [23]. This scenario is outlined in Fig. 4. A customer interested in DR creates an online profile stating on which DR actions the customer is interested to participate (e.g., turning down air condition). When the utilities want to curtail load with DR, a customer whose profile fits the current requirements is sent a text message to, e.g., turn down the air condition. This message is acknowledged by the customer and the utility further reads the meter values to track actual power reduction. Besides the data flows mentioned, this further involves the storing of the profile and the past behavior of the customer for a more accurate prediction. For modeling this use case as a DFG, the following actors and IOs are identified.

Actors. Business actors are the *user* and the *utility*. The user is mapped to the system actors *smart meter*, *device* and *portal*. DR requests are sent to the user device (e.g., a cell phone) and the user's DR preferences are set in the portal (e.g., a web service). The smart meter is used to measure actual curtailment. The utility is mapped to a *DR repository*, containing preferences for each user and past behavior, to a *prediction unit* predicting DR requests based on the preferences and a *control unit* to meter user feedback and actual curtailment.

Information Objects. Cross-domain/zone information flows include user preferences sent to the utilities, DR requests sent to the user from the utility and both, the user acknowledge/decline and the meter values sent back to the utility. Information flows within the utilities' premises are from the DR repository to the prediction unit and from the control unit to the DR repository. Given the threat patterns introduced in Sect. 3, we use our framework to determine the privacy impact of this use case which provides the following results.

Customer Presence at Home. The qualitative analysis shows that in the DR repository of the utility information about both, past customer behavior and

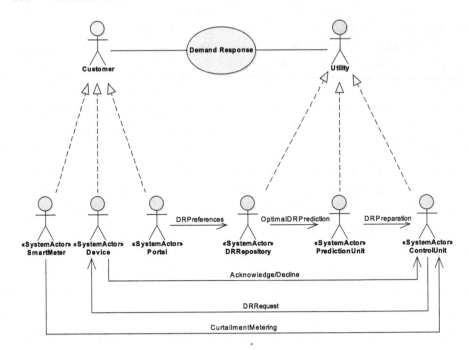

Fig. 4. Outline of the DR use case that is discussed for evaluation.

customer data is brought together, i.e., direct personal data is composed with a detailed history of a person's actions. Furthermore, the customer's acknowledge/decline and the measured curtailment reveal if a customer (i) responded to the DR request; and (ii) actually participated in DR; both is a indication for the presence at home. For this threat we identified four vulnerabilities (device in customer premises, collecting data at a certain frequency, receiver has access to data, data retention is unlimited) and one countermeasure (aggregation of data from multiple customers), resulting in a *PO* of 0.9, an *EL* of 11.5 and a risk value of 10.35.

Tracking Customer Position. In our case, this threat might apply in two different scenarios: First, this threat is immediate if the acknowledge/decline response to DR requests contains the customer position (e.g., if sent by a cell phone or other mobile device). This does not only show the customers past and present position, but also if the customer is able to remotely control devices in his premises. Second, when the customer is represented by an additional component *electric vehicle charging station*. Assuming that DR requests are also sent with respect to the charging behavior. Based on the amount of energy the customer is willing to DR it might be possible to estimate the consumption of the electric vehicle and subsequently the traveled distance. For this threat we identified two vulnerabilities (composition of location and timestamp, different actors have access to the same data) and one countermeasure (aggregation of data from multiple customers), resulting in a *PO* of 0.66, an *EL* of 5 and a risk value of 3.33.

The mode-driven assessment of the DR use case has shown that the risk of tracking customer position is low compared to the risk of determining customer presence at home. This result stems from the fact that there apply a number of vulnerabilities with high expected loss value, hence a device in the customer premises, data collected at a certain frequency, receiver has access to data and unlimited data retention. For the risk of detecting the customer presence at home, the same value applies as for the smart metering itself. This is due to the fact that smart meter data is used as a basis for demand response.

5   Recommender System

Having a framework for assessing the privacy impact of a use case in the smart grid is a powerful foundation for building a recommender system. The objective of such a recommender system is to provide users with the ability to decide on the usage of certain application and services in the smart grid based on the privacy impact of these applications and services. We therefore adapt the policy decision point (PDP) and policy enforcement point (PEP) patterns for a recommender system as originally presented in [24]. This is primarily targeting users in order to allow them having full control over information flows, but also the utilities and the vendors of third party applications.

The principal PDP-PEP architecture is standardized as Extensible Access Control Markup Language (XACML) in [25]. This architecture has already been applied to the smart grid by Jung et al. in [26]. The recommender system we present here enhances this approach by enabling an automated assessment of applications and use cases, respectively.

In general, a PDP is a component that evaluates access requests and issues some authorization. The PDP therefore provides some mechanisms to authenticate users, usually by prompting credentials such as username and password. The PDP then checks in a repository (policy store) if a certain user is granted access to a certain resource. The assessment framework presented in the previous sections is used as a PDP in order to allow privacy-aware data retrieval in the smart grid. The scenario at hand is as follows: a user wants to access a new application or service in the smart grid. This application or service has a certain privacy impact that has been assessed with this framework upon registration (*Registration of Application*). Additionally, the application or service is governed by a PEP. The PEP redirects the user to a PDP that displays to the user a list of privacy implications associated with this particular application or service. The user is then requested to confirm the intention to use the application or service. If the user accepts, the PEP grants access (*Accessing Applications*). For this system, we propose a traffic light-styled display of privacy implications (red: high risk, yellow: medium risk, green: no or low risk) with the option to show the full, detailed analysis.

Registration of Application:

1. A vendor submits a formal application description (DFG) to the recommender system.
2. The recommender system performs the model-based privacy assessment; this yields a set of qualitative metrics (attack vectors) that are stored in the PDP.

Accessing Applications:

1. A user requests access to a new application registered at the recommender system.
2. The PEP of this application checks if the user has already allowed access.
3. If *no*, the user is redirected to the PDP and the qualitative assessment is performed based on the user's role (i.e., which business actor corresponds the user to for variably binding and business actor and information object) and the user allows or denies access.
4. If *yes*, the user is forwarded to the application.

In our prototypical implementation as presented in [24], Java 1.7 Servlets running on Apache Tomcat 7 represent PDP and PEP, respectively. A user request for an application is guarded by a PEP and forwarded to the PDP, including information about the intended application and the sending party. The PDP performs an ontology driven privacy assessment for the particular use case with a predefined set of threat patterns and displays the result to the user. The result shown includes (i) a summary for the overall privacy impact (traffic light: high, medium, no or low) in appropriate colors for immediate recognizability; and (ii) an optional detailed view showing the full threat matrix. The user is requested to either continue and allow access or cancel. If the user decides to continue, the browser is forwarded to the application. In case the user cancels, one is directed back to the PEP which displays that access will not be granted. For the prototypical implementation, the set of applications is given by the use cases defined above. As the focus is on demonstrating the PDP-PEP pattern for ontology-driven privacy assessment there is no actual implementation of the use cases, i.e., no application that actually performs demand response or the like. In practical use the formal use case description will be provided by either third-parties or the providers of the application themselves.

6   Conclusion and Future Work

In this paper we introduced both, a framework for the model-driven privacy assessment in the smart grid and an advanced recommender system based on that framework. The framework itself builds on an ontology driven approach matching threat patterns to use cases that are modeled in adherence to standardized reference architectures. The approach presented here builds on meta-information and high-level data flows. It has been shown how to utilize this framework to successfully assess the privacy impact on use cases in early design time. Exemplary threats and exemplary use cases draw on insights from the University of Southern California microgrid. Further we proposed a recommender system based on the PDP-PEP pattern. This system utilizes our privacy assessment framework in order to provide users the option to allow or deny access to applications and services based on their privacy impact. Future work will include the rolling out of our recommender system to a real-world setting.

Acknowledgements. The financial support of the Josef Ressel Center by the Austrian Federal Ministry of Economy, Family and Youth and the Austrian National Foundation for Research, Technology and Development is gratefully acknowledged. Funding by the Austrian Marshall Plan Foundation is gratefully acknowledged. The authors would like to thank Norbert Egger for his contribution to the prototypical implementation. Funding by the Federal State of Salzburg is gratefully acknowledged.

This material is based upon work supported by the United States Department of Energy under Award Number number DE-OE0000192, and the Los Angeles Department of Water and Power (LA DWP). The views and opinions of authors expressed herein do not necessarily state or reflect those of the United States Government or any agency thereof, the LA DWP, nor any of their employees.

References

1. Cavoukian, A., Polonetsky, J., Wolf, C.: Smartprivacy for the smart grid: embedding privacy into the design of electricity conservation. Identity Inf. Soc. **3**, 275–294 (2010)
2. Langer, L., Skopik, F., Kienesberger, G., Li, Q.: Privacy issues of smart e-mobility. In: 39th Annual Conference of the Industrial Electronics Society, IECON 2013, pp. 6682–6687. IEEE (2013)
3. McDaniel, P., McLaughlin, S.: Security and privacy challenges in the smart grid. IEEE Secur. Priv. **7**, 75–77 (2009)
4. Simmhan, Y., Kumbhare, A., Cao, B., Prasanna, V.: An analysis of security and privacy issues in smart grid software architectures on clouds. In: IEEE International Conference on Cloud Computing (CLOUD 2011), pp. 582–589. IEEE (2011)
5. Boehm, B.: A view of 20th and 21st century software engineering. In: Proceedings of the 28th International Conference on Software Engineering, ICSE 2006, pp. 12–29. ACM, New York (2006)
6. National Institute of Standards and Technology: NIST Framework and Roadmap for Smart Grid Interoperability Standards, Release 2.0. Technical Report NIST Special Publication 1108R2. National Institute of Standards and Technology (2012)
7. CEN, Cenelec and ETSI: Smart Grid Reference Architecture. Technical report, CEN/Cenelec/ETSI Smart Grid Coordination Group Std. (2012)
8. Dänekas, C., Neureiter, C., Rohjans, S., Uslar, M., Engel, D.: Towards a model-driven-architecture process for smart grid projects. In: Benghozi, P.-J., Krob, D., Lonjon, A., Panetto, H. (eds.) DED & M 2014. AISC, vol. 261, pp. 47–58. Springer, Heidelberg (2014)
9. National Institute of Standards and Technology: Guidelines for smart grid cyber security, vol. 2, privacy and the smart grid. Technical report, The Smart Grid Interoperability Panel - Cyber Security Working Group (2010)

10. CEN, Cenelec and ETSI: Smart Grid Information Security. Technical report, CEN/Cenelec/ETSI Smart Grid Coordination Group Std. (2012)
11. Wicker, S., Schrader, D.: Privacy-aware design principles for information networks. Proc. IEEE **99**, 330–350 (2011)
12. Barker, K., Askari, M., Banerjee, M., Ghazinour, K., Mackas, B., Majedi, M., Pun, S., Williams, A.: A data privacy taxonomy. In: Sexton, A.P. (ed.) BNCOD 26. LNCS, vol. 5588, pp. 42–54. Springer, Heidelberg (2009)
13. Ahmed, M., Anjomshoaa, A., Nguyen, T., Tjoa, A.: Towards an ontology-based risk assessment in collaborative environment using the semanticlife. In: Proceedings of the Second International Conference on Availability, Reliability and Security, ARES 2007. IEEE Computer Society, Washington, D.C., pp. 400–407 (2007)
14. Kost, M., Freytag, J.C., Kargl, F., Kung, A.: Privacy verification using ontologies. In: Proceedings of the 2011 Sixth International Conference on Availability, Reliability and Security, ARES 2011, pp. 627–632. IEEE Computer Society, Washington, D.C. (2011)
15. Kost, M., Freytag, J.C.: Privacy analysis using ontologies. In: Proceedings of the Second ACM Conference on Data and Application Security and Privacy, CODASPY 2012, San Antonio, Texas, USA, pp. 205–2016. ACM (2012)
16. Chen, B., Kalbarczyk, Z., Nicol, D., Sanders, W., Tan, R., Temple, W., Tippenhauer, N., Vu, A., Yau, D.: Go with the flow: toward workflow-oriented security assessment. In: Proceedings of New Security Paradigm Workshop (NSPW), Banff, Canada (2013)
17. Knirsch, F., Engel, D., Frincu, M., Prasanna, V.: Model-based assessment for balancing privacy requirements and operational capabilities in the smart grid. In: Proceedings of the 6th Conference on Innovative Smart Grid Technologies (ISGT 2015), 2015 IEEE Power & Energy Society, Washington, D.C., USA, pp. 1–5 (2015)
18. Shearer, R., Motik, B., Horrocks, I.: Hermit: a highly-efficient owl reasoner. In: Dolbear, C., Ruttenberg, A., Sattler, U. (eds.) OWLED, vol. 432. CEUR Workshop Proceedings. CEUR-WS.org (2008)
19. Neureiter, C., Eibl, G., Veichtlbauer, A., Engel, D.: Towards a framework for engineering smart-grid-speficic privacy requirements. In: Proceedings of IEEE IECON 2013, Special Session on Energy Informatics, Vienna, Austria. IEEE (2013)
20. Guarino, N., Oberle, D., Staab, S.: What is an ontology? In: Staab, S., Studer, R. (eds.) Handbook on Ontologies. International Handbooks on Information Systems, 2nd edn, pp. 1–17. Springer, Heidelberg (2009)
21. The European Parliament and the Council: Official Journal L 281, 23/11/1995 P. 0031–0050 - Directive 95/46/EC of the European Parliament and of the Council of 24 October 1995. Online (1995)
22. Simmhan, Y., Zhou, Q., Prasanna, V.: Semantic information integration for smart grid applications. In: Kim, J.H., Lee, M.J. (eds.) Green IT: Technologies and Applications, pp. 361–380. Springer, Heidelberg (2011)
23. Simmhan, Y., Zhou, Q., Prasanna, V.: Semantic information integration for smart grid applications. In: Kim, J.H., Lee, M.J. (eds.) Green IT: Technologies and Applications, vol. 77, pp. 361–380. Springer, Heidelberg (2011)
24. Knirsch, F.: Model-driven Privacy Assessment in the Smart Grid. Master's thesis, Salzburg University of Applied Sciences (2014)
25. Rissanen, E.: eXtensible Access Control Markup Language (XACML) Version 3.0 (2013). http://docs.oasis-open.org/xacml/3.0/xacml-3.0-core-spec-os-en.pdf
26. Jung, M., Hofer, T., Dbelt, S., Kienesberger, G., Judex, F., Kastner, W.: Access control for a smart grid SOA. In: Proceedings of the 7th IEEE Conference for Internet Technology and Secured Transactions, London, UK, pp. 281–287. IEEE (2012)

ViSPE: A Graphical Policy Editor for XACML

Henrik Nergaard$^{(\boxtimes)}$, Nils Ulltveit-Moe, and Terje Gjøsæter

Institute of Information and Communication Technology, University of Agder,
Jon Lilletuns vei 9, 4879 Grimstad, Norway
{henrin10,nils.ulltveit-moe,terje.gjosater}@uia.no

Abstract. In this paper we present the Visual Security Policy Editor (ViSPE), a policy-maker-friendly graphical editor for the eXtensible Access Control Markup Language (XACML). The editor is based on the programming language Scratch and implemented in Smalltalk. It uses a graphical block-based syntax for declaring access control polices that simplifies many of the cumbersome and verbose parts of XACML. Using a graphical language allows the editor to aid the policy-maker in building polices by providing visual feedback and by grouping blocks and operators that fit together and also indicating which blocks that stick together. It simplifies building policies while still maintaining the basic structure and logic of XACML.

Keywords: Access control · XACML · Editor · Smalltalk

1 Introduction

The eXtensible Access Control Markup Language (XACML) is a declarative access control policy language, standardised by OASIS, that is implemented in XML [1]. The XACML Standard defines a large set of XML elements and attributes, it is very verbose, and has high expressive power, which creates a high usage threshold for users that are not familiar with it or other XML based languages. Writing these polices can be difficult, especially for larger policies when the complexity increases, and user errors and typos can easily happen. XML does not have a user friendly representation, especially when the number of elements increases. Manual reading and error correction of bigger XML files can be a tedious and complicated task. The complexity in writing and correcting XACML policies may be part of the reason why simpler and less expressive authorisation standards (e.g. OAuth, RBAC or simple access control lists) may be preferred in practical implementations, or even that users decide to roll their own authorisation solution, with the possible security risks this may cause.

When creating a policy based on XACML, the creator has to have knowledge from both the standardization of XACML as well as general XML behaviour. Problematic areas in XACML include the length of XACML attributes, correct handling of long URLs, and a vast amount of functions that must be used correctly, which is not always trivial for users. Without help from proper tools,

© Springer International Publishing Switzerland 2015
O. Camp et al. (Eds.): ICISSP 2015, CCIS 576, pp. 107–121, 2015.
DOI: 10.1007/978-3-319-27668-7_7

creating large policies can involve much work. Our solution is to design and develop a user-friendly editor that helps in creating these XACML polices.

The rest of the article is organised as follows: Sect. 2 covers general background and motivation. Section 3 covers the design criteria, goals, and implementation of the graphical editor for designing XACML policies. In Sect. 4, the benefits and limitations of the proposed editor is discussed. Section 5 contains a summary of the article. Finally Sect. 6 contains plans for future work on ViSPE.

2   Background and Motivation

The Visual Security Policy Editor (ViSPE) for XACML policies is implemented based on the Scratch programming environment [2,3], on the Pharo Smalltalk engine [4]. It aims at providing a policy-maker-friendly policy description language for designing XACML authorisation policies. It is also a design objective that it shall be able to design XACML-based anonymisation policies for XML documents [5,6]. Scratch is a programming language for children created by the Lifelong Kindergarten research group at Massachusetts Institute of Technology's Media LAB [2,3]. It is a graphical language which defines a set of programming constructs which can be put together as puzzle pieces in order to define a computer program [2]. The language enforces that only blocks that fit logically together according to the language syntax will stick together.

We believe that a high-level policy language editor for policy makers is needed, to avoid much of the underlying distraction and syntactic complexity of XACML. The two examples below illustrate this. Figure 1 shows all the complexity and intricacies of an XACML policy written in XML. The XACML has been simplified somewhat by denoting the XACML namespace as *&xacml;* and the XML Schema namespace as *&xs;*. This is a simple XACML policy example[1] that applies for requests to a server called *SampleServer*, with a rule that matches a login action and contains an XACML Condition stating that the Subject only is allowed to log in between 09:00 and 17:00.

Figure 2 shows the same policy implemented using our XACML policy editor ViSPE. The syntactic blocks used by the editor is able to hide much of the complexity involved in writing XACML statements by providing features such as:

- Managing XACML identities and XML schema data types.
- Automatically matching attribute designators to the context they are in and the data type they belong to.
- Automatically inferring some XML elements, for example the *Condition* clause.
- Performing run-time type checking operations, ensuring that only sensible XML elements with correct attributes can be put together.

---

[1] The policy example was inspired by http://www.oasis-open.org/committees/download.php/2713/Brief_Introduction_to_XACML.html.

```
<PolicySet xmlns="&xacml;policy"
 xmlns:xsi="http://www.w3.org/2001/XMLSchema-instance"
 xmlns:xs="http://www.w3.org/2001/XMLSchema"
 xmlns:gml="http://www.opengis.net/gml"
 xsi:schemaLocation="&xacml;policy cs-xacml-schema-policy-01.xsd"
 PolicySetId="MyPolicySet"
 PolicyCombiningAlgId="&xacml;&algorithm;deny-overrides">
 <Target />
 <Policy PolicyId="SamplePolicy"
  RuleCombiningAlgId="&xacml;&algorithm;permit-overrides">
 <Target> <Resources> <Resource>
    <ResourceMatch MatchID="&xacml;function:string-equal">
     <AttributeValue DataType="&xs;#string">
       SampleServer
     </AttributeValue>
     <ResourceAttributeDesignator DataType="&xs;#string"
       AttributeId="&xacml;resource:resource-id" />
     </ResourceMatch>
    </Resource> </Resources> </Target>
  <Rule RuleId="LoginRule" Effect="Permit">
   <Target> <Actions> <Action>
      <ActionMatch MatchID="&xacml;function:string-equal">
       <AttributeValue DataType="&xs;#string">
          login
       </AttributeValue>
      <ActionAttributeDesignator DataType="&xs;#string"
       AttributeId="&xacml;action:action-id" />
     </ActionMatch>
   </Action> </Actions> </Target>
  <Condition>
   <Apply FunctionId="&xacml;function:and">
    <Apply FunctionId="&xacml;function:time-greater-than-or-equal">
     <Apply FunctionId="&xacml;function:time-one-and-only">
      <EnvironmentAttributeDesignator
        DataType="&xs;#time"
        AttributeId="&xacml;environment:current-time" />
      </Apply>
      <AttributeValue DataType="&xs;#time">T9H</AttributeValue>
     </Apply>
     <Apply FunctionId="&xacml;function:time-less-than-or-equal">
      <Apply FunctionId="&xacml;function:time-one-and-only">
       <EnvironmentAttributeDesignator
         DataType="&xs;#time"
         AttributeId="&xacml;environment:current-time" />
      </Apply>
      <AttributeValue DataType="&xs;#time">T17H</AttributeValue>
     </Apply>
    </Apply>
   </Condition>
  </Rule>
  <Rule RuleId="FinalRule" Effect="Deny">
   <Target />
  </Rule>
 </Policy>
</PolicySet>
```

Fig. 1. Simple XACML policy generated by ViSPE.

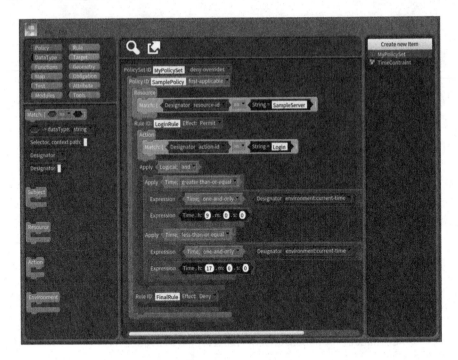

Fig. 2. Simple policy made using ViSPE.

Still the question remains - why write another XACML policy editor, and not reuse and extend one of the existing XACML policy editors? A basic requirement for us is that the policy editor would need to be Open Source, since we want it to be freely available and possible to adapt to a user's specific needs.

One example of an open source policy editor for XACML is the UMU-XACML editor[2]. This editor is made by the University of Murica in Spain. The editor is written in Java and essentially manages a DOM tree with XACML nodes, and provides a user interface with sensible default values or choices for each type of DOM nodes in the XACML document. The editor supports folding down elements within a given policy in order to view parts of the DOM tree. The editor does not yet support unfolding everything, which makes it cumbersome to get an overview over anything but very small policies. The folding mechanism is problematic from a usability perspective, since the policy-maker does not get an overview over the entire policy.

Another problem with this approach, is that the details of each XACML element is shown in a separate window, which means that it is not possible for a policy-maker to get an overview over how a given policy works without reading the generated XACML. Furthermore, some choices are missing, for example for choosing functions. In total, UMU-XACML does not reduce the overall complexity in writing XACML policies much. UMU-XACML will in other words aid the

---

[2] UMU-XACML-Editor: http://umu-xacmleditor.sourceforge.net.

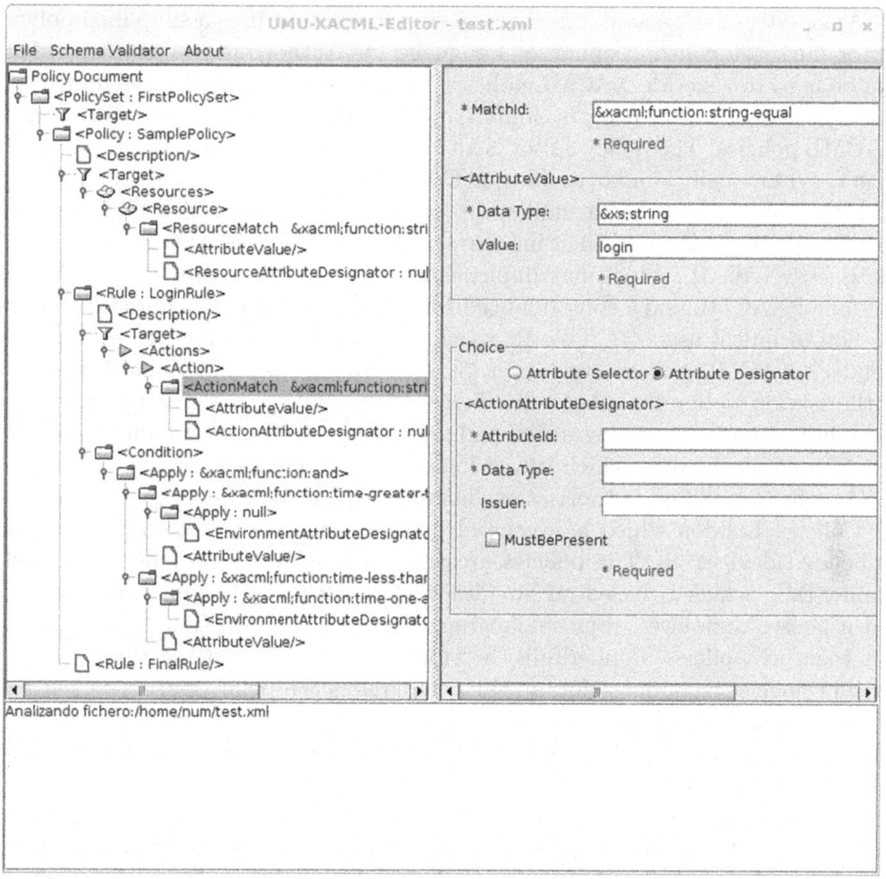

Fig. 3. Simple policy using UMU XACML editor.

user in creating an XACML policy, but it has some severe usability issues that makes it undesirable as a design base for our policy editor (Fig. 3).

The WSO2 Identity Server[3] is a complete identity management solution that has a web based user interface for designing XACML policies. This interface is from a structural perspective quite similar to UMU XACML, but provides web based forms for generating different policy templates (simple, basic or standard), as well as having a separate policy set editor. This approach has similar deficiencies as the UMU XACML editor since it is difficult to get an overview over the policies without reading the generated XACML. Our approach aims on the other hand at giving the policy maker all necessary information in order to understand the policy in an easily readable high-level graphic language, instead of using a program that creates a forms-based user interface for generating XACML.

---

[3] WSO2 Identity Server: https://docs.wso2.com/display/IS450/Creating+an+XACML+Policy.

Axiomatics has created a freeware policy editor that uses a simplified policy editor language called Axiomatics Language for Authorization (ALFA), which can be used to generate XACML policies. This approach aims at achieving similar objectives as our project, by simplifying the policy language used to generate XACML policies. The policy editor is an Eclipse plugin that provides a language that is syntactically similar to Java or C#[4].

Others have also taken a similar approach, by defining user-friendly domain-specific languages for implementing parts of the XACML syntax. One such example is easyXACML, which has implemented an XACML editor for the *target* section of XACML and a constraints editor using their simplified notation aimed for non-technical users [7]. This approach is in some ways similar to ALFA and Ponder2 XACML policy integration [8], by defining domain-specific high-level authorisation policy languages. We believe our solution achieves much of the same objective by providing a rich and simple graphical programming environment based on Scratch, which is well known for being easy to use.

Another simplified authorisation language is Ponder2, developed at Imperial College, London which is a general purpose authorisation environment for embedded devices [9]. The policies are written in a high-level language called PonderTalk, which is based on Smalltalk. Ponder2 is a powerful environment, but it lacks a high-level graphical language that can aid policy-makers on how to put together policies. PonderTalk therefore has a higher starting threshold for writing policies than our solution, since it requires the policy-makers to learn a subset of Smalltalk as well as how to write the policies in PonderTalk. Another disadvantage is that Ponder2 cannot generate XACML policies, which is required by our use cases [5].

Our solution could in principle be extended to achieve the same benefits as PonderTalk, by supporting a message passing interface [9], since our solution also is based on Smalltalk. This is another observation that went in favour of using Scratch as design base. However adding a message passing interface like this would mean evolving away from the core XACML standard.

A major requirement of the policy editor, in addition to writing general XACML policies, is being able to support writing anonymisation policies for XML documents [5]. This means that Ponder2 is not a suitable design base for us.

This overview over different XACML editors shows that there is a need for a good XACML editor that is able to provide a simplified policy development language for policy-makers. All existing environments have their disadvantages with respect to usability and other issues; many DOM-tree-based XML editors require you to edit sub-tree-objects by zooming in; clicking on them to open them up and show the details, without allowing the user to see the big picture with all details at the same time. Our solution avoids this problem by providing all information available for the user in the simplified graphical language, so that there is no need to zoom in or out of the policy.

---

[4] Axiomatics Language for Authorization (ALFA) http://www.axiomatics.com/axiomatics-alfa-plugin-for-eclipse.html.

There are many language workbenches and tools for creating editors - both textual and graphical, but from a usability perspective even text editors with language assistance, are too unstructured for XML in general and in particular for such a highly structured language as XACML. On the other hand, creating a diagram-like graphical syntax for XACML using graphical editor tool-kits like GMF[5] would be an option, but diagrams tend to take a lot of space and it is easy to lose the overview in a similar way as with DOM-tree-based editors.

But why choose Scratch of all things - a programming language designed for children? We wanted a highly structured design that was radically different from existing Java/Eclipse based editors.

Other possible design bases exist, for example MIT App Inventor for Android. This is a similar block programming language based on Scratch which can be used for designing mobile apps [10]. App Inventor was considered being too tied to the underlying Android operating system and was therefore rejected.

There are also other blocks based programming languages, for example UML [11], Ladder [12] or Lego Mindstorm [13]. However Scratch is considered one of the early models of such languages with the necessary functionality which is open source and was therefore chosen. We did not base the editor on Scratch 2.0, to avoid dependencies to Flash, and ended up using a version of Scratch 1.3 ported to the Pharo Smalltalk engine called Phratch[6]. The Pharo Smalltalk environment[7] was chosen instead of Squeak to get a more modern look and feel on the development environment than the venerable Smalltalk-80 user interface.

3   An Editor for XACML

3.1   Design

The underlying idea is to use the same approach as Scratch has done with its environment, but using the blocks to express XACML elements. The pure XACML can then be hidden behind the scenes and a simplified representation is used to create and express policies. Simplifications are done by using blocks for elements and their arguments for the attributes. The policies are then built by placing and stacking blocks onto each other forming a functional policy. Using this representation of graphical blocks and arguments enables a type-what-you-need based design, letting the user focus on the important policy logic and not the XACML XML syntax. Another useful feature with using graphical elements is that the possibility for user error due to misspellings and syntax errors is reduced. The arguments and blocks can have constraints in them, enabling only blocks that are applicable to fit.

The main goal for the editor is to generate correct XACML according to the XACML 2.0 Standard [1]. Support for generating XACML 3.0 is left as future work. This implies also that the editor should be able to express the whole or at least the most frequently used parts of the standard.

---

[5] Graphical Modelling Framework, http://www.eclipse.org/modeling/gmp/.

[6] Phratch: http://www.phratch.com/.

[7] Pharo: http://pharo.org.

3.2   Implementation Platform

Our Editor implementation is based on Phratch, an editor for graphical programming based on Scratch [2,3]. Phratch uses the Pharo Smalltalk environment [4], which is portable across most common operating systems. An advantage by using Smalltalk, is that this is an agile development environment suitable for rapid prototyping. This means that we quickly can test out ideas and modify the functionality if it does not work out as well as expected. Implementing the editor was done by building on a subset of Phratch. The shapes used for blocks and arguments is similar for the ViSPE as it is from Phratch, since they represent a similar top down structure as the original XACML would have with its nested elements.

3.3   User Interface

The user interface consists of three core parts; a block palette, a build area, and a management list, as shown from left to right in Fig. 2.

In the top of the block palette is a list of the different categories that blocks are distributed in, while the rest of it presents the available graphical blocks for the category selected. Blocks from the palette can be dragged over to the build area to form the graphical policy.

The management list shows the graphical polices currently active in the editor, and presents the selected policy in the build area. This enables the policy maker to work with multiple polices, and also gives the ability to split them up into different parts which can be useful for large polices with multiple *Policy* and *PolicySet* elements.

In the build area, blocks can be placed anywhere such that a part of the policy can easily be formed before placing it into the policy itself. This also makes it possible to have certain parts that might be used on a later occasion present together with the policy. However only the blocks that are placed into the starting block will be part of the generated policy.

Every new policy starts out with one fixed top level block, used as the starting point for the policy, and can either be a policy-set, or a single policy element.

3.4   Graphical Policy Shapes

For expressing the selection of elements and attributes from XACML, our block syntax uses three different graphical shapes, illustrated in Fig. 4. The first two block shapes are used for expressing XACML elements, while the last one is a

Fig. 4. Example of the different block shapes available.

block for special attributes. Each of these shapes have text embedded in them that is meant to closely resemble their XACML equivalent part.

Attributes for a specific element is also embedded into the block, each attribute has a prefix text combined with an appropriate input field. The most basic of these inputs is a textural or numeric field where the user provides its value. Numerical input fields are differentiated from text fields by providing a more circular shape, illustrated in the *Time* attribute block in Fig. 5. For attributes that only have a fixed number of valid values, an embedded list is provided that presents the user with the allowed choices, and the current selected choice is shown in the block. There is also a special version of the list field that instead of presenting a list of options, opens a dialogue with a custom tailored widget for providing the valid attribute value. An example of such a widget is for the *Date* attribute block shown in Fig. 4, here the list it replaced by a calendar widget, ensuring that only valid dates can be used for this attribute.

For attributes where a simple input is not enough, an attribute block is used. These blocks give the opportunity to add more context to the attribute. An example use for attribute blocks is for expressing the *data-type* attribute, where the block provides the data type as a prefix text, with an appropriate input field for the value itself, such as the *Date* block from Fig. 4. Elements that use such an attribute block has an embedded slot where this can be placed.

Some of the attribute blocks are also used to add more optional information to other attribute blocks. An example of this is the time data type value that might be negative, and also have a Coordinated Universal Time (UTC) component. To express this using the graphical blocks, the *Time* attribute block is placed into a *UTC* block that is placed into a *Negative* block, illustrated in Fig. 5.

Input fields can constrain the input allowed to be placed into them, for example text input fields can use regular expression when accepting new inputs, while numerical fields have the option to only accept values of a certain range.

Some of the list fields can modify the options that are available according to the context they are in, an example of this is the *Designator* attribute block which only shows attribute designators for a specific attribute category if placed inside that category element, otherwise it shows the full selection for all the attribute categories. Placing attribute blocks into their place-holder is also constrained such that only the valid attribute blocks will be allowed to take the place-holders place.

When placing a new block into an existing block in the build area, visual feedback will indicate if that block can fit where the user wants it to be. Figure 6 shows what this visual indication looks like for both element and attribute blocks. If a block cannot be placed in the element or attribute slot due to the rules

Fig. 5. Example of nested attribute blocks.

Fig. 6. Example of the visual placement indicator feedback in action.

and constraints, then no indication is shown, and it will not be placed into the accepting block. Many of the attribute slots is colour coded with the same colour as the attribute blocks that are allowed to be placed into them. For example a black attribute slot means that only attribute blocks in that are in the *DataType* category can be placed there.

3.5 XACML XML Generation

XML can be generated from the graphical policy by using the buttons provided above it. The output can either be shown in a dialogue box that opens inside the editor, or saved directly into a file with name and location chosen by the user.

All the elements that are enclosed by the starting outermost element provided by the policy script are included when generating the policy.

Some of the elements defined in XACML has an outer encapsulation without any attributes. These elements add unnecessary depth and verbosity, but are useful for the XML parsing. Our graphical syntax does not need these outer encapsulations. When generating the XACML XML this outer encapsulation is automatically added for elements that requires it.

An example of this encapsulation is for the different attribute category elements that needs to be encapsulated first by a parent element, and then by a target element. Figure 7 shows the Action element block and the added XACML encapsulation.

During generation, the policy also checks for errors that can occur, and stops the process and notifies the user. The most common error checking is

```
<Target>
  <Actions>
    <Action>
      ...
    </Action>
  </Actions>
</Target>
```

Fig. 7. Example of automatically added element encapsulation.

for attributes, and it check that text inputs, and slots are not empty. There is also some error checking in the element composition, however there is some more work needed to cover all possibilities. The generated XML is also formatted during generation to give a more readable output, such as adding indenting to each new line according to the current depth of nested elements.

3.6   Additional Features

Some combinations of policy elements might occur often in a policy, but only with slight variations. For example, adding a time constraint for several rules where only the time might be different from each rule. XACML offers some support for dealing with recurring parts using the *VariableDefinition* element where parts of the condition sub-elements can be placed, and later referred to with the use of the *VariableReference* element when both of them has the same identifier. However, this approach only works for parts that are fully static, meaning that it cannot be used for generalising parts that has some variation in them. Our approach to this has been to add support for modularisation. This enables any collection of blocks to be placed in their own script, that can then be merged into a single block usable by the policies. These modules do not only support static declaration of attributes, but also dynamic ones. Providing these dynamic attributes is done by replacing input fields from elements in a module script with place-holders. When all the fields have been defined in a module, it can be merged into one single block where the place-holder variables define the embedded attributes. The newly generated block is then available under the *Module* category of the editor, and can be used as any other block.

An example of how the modules work is presented in Fig. 8. Here, the time constraint from the policy in Fig. 2 is placed into its own module script.

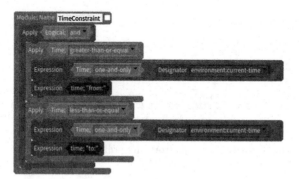

Fig. 8. Modularisation example for a time constraint condition.

The merged block from this module is illustrated in Fig. 9. The embedded attribute slots for this block only accepts an attribute block with the time data type, since this is what the place-holder blocks were defined as. Our module

Fig. 9. The merged block made from the module in Fig. 8.

system makes it simple to forge lightweight yet powerful standalone blocks using a subset of the already present blocks.

4   Discussion

Our approach has the advantage over existing XACML tools by focusing on the meaning and attributes of the policy, and not the XML syntax of XACML. ViSPE manages to remove many of the verbose parts from XACML, and bring the focus to the core policy itself.

Generating the graphical XACML policy into XML is quite fast. Using the policy presented in Fig. 2, we have simulated how the generation scales as policies become larger. The simulation was done by duplicating the policy inside the top element, and appending it to the bottom inside of the top element. Each iteration was run 400 times before appending the next policy. The result is presented in Fig. 10, and shows the average time in milliseconds it took to generate N amount of stacked policies.

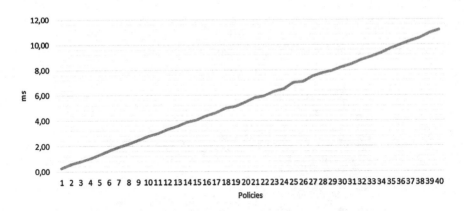

Fig. 10. N stacked policies from the policy presented in Fig. 2.

ViSPE can currently express almost all the elements and attributes from the XACML 2.0 standard. The elements and attributes that are not yet available is the ones used for self-made policy or rule-combining algorithms, and are less frequently used. This means that the editor is fully capable of creating most polices. The attribute slot and list field ensures that a wrong input cannot be added to them. Specific types of number and string literals have constraints that ensure that only a valid input can be typed. The stacking and nesting of blocks does however not yet have all the constraints needed to cover all possibilities. This means that it still may be possible for users not knowing the rules for XACML elements to put together non-functional policies. It is probably not possible to avoid all fault scenarios, however improving the constraints handling is ongoing work where improvements can be added when common fault scenarios are being detected and mitigated.

Our approach simplifies several XACML concepts significantly, as we have described earlier, which means that overall it should be much easier for policy-makers to create XACML policies with ViSPE than writing such policies using existing tools. An example of this is the policy presented in Figure, here ViSPE uses a total of 31 blocks to generate 3053 characters where only 63 them is typed by the policy maker. User-testing experiments proving that the usability is significantly improved is however left as future work. In this paper, we let the qualitative arguments for increased usability, based on the heritage from Scratch, speak for themselves.

5   Summary

We have designed, implemented, and tested an editor capable of generating XACML 2.0 from a graphical blocks-based representation. Our approach enables the user to focus more on the important details and logic of the policy and not on the complex syntax of XACML, or correct XML formatting. It allows policy makers to focus on creating the correct policies, and does not require a significant amount of programming experience. Policies created by the editor are represented in a simplified policy language that is quite close to XACML, and can be exported to XACML code. The blocks uses colour identification, and visual feedback to show the correct placement of elements and attributes in the policy. This reduces the learning curve for implementing XACML policies significantly compared to existing XACML editors, while still keeping core parts of the XACML structure and syntactic elements. Providing a simplified syntax based on Scratch both improves the maintainability and makes it easier to support an agile policy development strategy under dynamically changing environments. ViSPE also gives the policy maker the ability to take a subset of the policy and generalise it into one single block. This enables commonly used parts to be abstracted away, presenting a more simplified version that has the flexibility needed for reuse.

6   Future Work

Investigating the usability with regards to users familiar and non-familiar with XACML, is something we would like to do in the future. Users who can write XACML could test the editor by creating large complex policies, and non-technical users creating smaller, simpler policies. The criteria for such a study should include evaluating the time used versus size and complexity of the policy, syntax errors, and logical errors.

XACML 3.0 support is also left as future work, however we have considered this syntax when implementing some of the simplifications in the graphic language. Some more work is left on covering the last portion of elements and attributes from the XACML 2.0 standard.

Adding additional validation and analytical mechanisms into the editor could be beneficial. Such mechanisms could provide useful information about policies, for example when policies themselves or some of their rules contradict each other. Furthermore, it could be beneficial for the editor to have the ability of also creating the request context schema as graphical blocks, and uses these for testing different request towards a created policy. It would then also be possible to use some of the underlying Scratch framework to visually see the blocks evaluated down into the response.

Another useful feature that could be added is higher level visualizations of the policy, an example of this would be to see a tree structure from the top level policy Set down to specific rules in a policy where each layer shows their concrete attributes, so one can easily get an overview over where different attributes are invoked.

Another possible future improvement, is implementing support for location-based XACML policies based on GeoXACML [14]. This could make it possible to integrate map data, for example from OpenStreetMap, into the policy editor, which would allow for defining geographical authorisation constraints on the policies. Further elaboration of such a scenario may be supporting location-based dynamic access control policies for moving objects. This may be useful for designing access control policies for vehicles, boats or other objects moving in a 2D plane, which could be simulated using existing functionality in Scratch. Support for expressing the RBAC profile of XACML [15], is another possibility for extending the policy editor, for example based on the work in [16–18].

Acknowledgements. This project was sponsored as a summer internship at the University of Agder. The project has also been sponsored by the FP7 EU projects:

PRECYSE - Protection, prevention and reaction to cyberattacks to critical infrastructures, contract number FP7-SEC-2012-1-285181 (http://www.precyse.eu);

SEMIAH - Scalable Energy Management Infrastructure for Aggregation of Households, contract number ICT-2013.6.1-619560 (http://semiah.eu).

References

1. Moses, T.: eXtensible Access Control Markup Language (XACML) Version 2.0. OASIS Standard (2005)
2. Malan, D.J., Leitner, H.H.: Scratch for budding computer scientists. In: Proceedings of the 38th SIGCSE Technical Symposium on Computer Science Education. SIGCSE 2007, pp. 223–227, New York, NY, USA. ACM (2007)

3. Resnick, M., Maloney, J., Monroy-Hernández, A., Rusk, N., Eastmond, E., Brennan, K., Millner, A., Rosenbaum, E., Silver, J., Silverman, B., et al.: Scratch: programming for all. Commun. ACM **52**(11), 60–67 (2009)

4. Bera, C., Denker, M.: Towards a flexible Pharo compiler. In: Lagadec, L., Plantec, A. (eds.) IWST. Annecy, France, ESUG (2013)

5. Ulltveit-Moe, N., Oleshchuk, V.: A novel policy-driven reversible anonymisation scheme for xml-based services. Inf. Syst. **48**, 164–178 (2015)

6. Ulltveit-Moe, N., Oleshchuk, V.: Decision-cache based XACML authorisation and anonymisation for XML documents. Comput. Stand. Interfaces **34**(6), 527–534 (2012)

7. Stepien, B., Felty, A., Matwin, S.: A non-technical xacml target editor for dynamic access control systems. In: 2014 International Conference on Collaboration Technologies and Systems (CTS), pp. 150–157. IEEE (2014)

8. Zhao, H., Lobo, J., Bellovin, S.: An algebra for integration and analysis of ponder2 policies. IEEE Workshop Policies Distrib. Syst. Netw. **2008**, 74–77 (2008)

9. Twidle, K., Dulay, N., Lupu, E., Sloman, M.: Ponder2: a policy system for autonomous pervasive environments. In: Fifth International Conference on Autonomic and Autonomous Systems, 2009, ICAS 2009, pp. 330–335 (2009)

10. Roy, K.: App inventor for android: report from a summer camp. In: Proceedings of the 43rd ACM Technical Symposium on Computer Science Education, SIGCSE 2012, pp. 283–288, New York, NY, USA. ACM (2012)

11. Fowler, M.: UML Distilled: A Brief Guide to the Standard Object Modeling Language. Addison-Wesley Professional, Boston (2004)

12. Hammond, T., Davis, R.: LADDER, a sketching language for user interface developers. Comput. Graph. **29**(4), 518–532 (2005)

13. Ferrari, M., Ferrari, G., Clague, K., Brown, J., Hempel, R.: LEGO Mindstorm Masterpieces: Building and Programming Advanced Robots. Syngress, Rockland (2003)

14. Matheus, A., Herrmann, J.: Geospatial extensible access control markup language (GeoXACML). Open Geospatial Consortium Inc. (2008)

15. Anderson, A.: Core and hierarchical role based access control (RBAC) profile of XACML v2.0. OASIS Standard (2005)

16. Ulltveit-Moe, N., Oleshchuk, V.: Enforcing mobile security with location-aware role-based access control. Security and Communication Networks, pp. 172–183 (2013)

17. Ulltveit-Moe, N., Oleshchuk, V.: Mobile security with location-aware role-based access control. In: Prasad, R., Farkas, K., Schmidt, A.U., Lioy, A., Russello, G., Luccio, F.L. (eds.) MobiSec 2011. LNICST, vol. 94, pp. 172–183. Springer, Heidelberg (2012)

18. Bonatti, P., Galdi, C., Torres, D.: ERBAC: event-driven RBAC. In: Proceedings of the 18th ACM Symposium on Access Control Models and Technologies, SACMAT 2013, pp. 125–136, New York, NY, USA. ACM (2013)

Supporting Streaming Data Anonymization with Expressions of User Privacy Preferences

Aderonke Busayo Sakpere$^{(\boxtimes)}$ and Anne V.D.M. Kayem

Department of Computer Science, University of Cape Town, Cape Town, South Africa
olfade001@myuct.ac.za, akayem@cs.uct.ac.za

Abstract. Mining crime reports in real-time is useful in improving the response time of law enforcement authorities in addressing crime. However, limitations on computational processing power and in-house mining expertise make this challenging, particularly so for law enforcement agencies in technology constrained environments. Outsourcing crime data mining offers a cost-effective alternative strategy. Yet outsourcing crime data raises the issue of user privacy. Therefore encouraging user participation in crime reporting schemes is conditional on providing strong guarantees of personal data protection. Cryptographic approaches make for time consuming query result generation, so the preferred approach is to anonymize the data. Mining real-time crime data as opposed to static data facilitates fast intervention. To achieve this goal, Sakpere and Kayem presented a preliminary solution based on the notion of buffering. Buffering improves on information loss significantly in comparison with previous solutions. In this paper, we extend the Sakpere and Kayem result to support user privacy expressions. We achieve this by integrating a three-tiered user-defined privacy preference model in data stream process. The three-tiered model offers a simple and generic approach to classifying the data without impacting negatively on information loss. Results from our proof-of-concept implementation indicate that incorporating user privacy preferences reduces the rate of information loss due to misclassification.

Keywords: Data anonymity · Streaming data · Crime reporting · Information loss

1 Introduction

Law enforcement agencies in resource constrained environments.[1] generally lack the "on-the-ground" expertise and resources required to mine crime big data streams. A cost-effective solution is to transfer the task of mining the crime data streams to a third party data miner/analyst. Mining crime reports in real-time as opposed to in static form can be helpful in providing fast interventions in addressing crime. A further advantage is predictions of future crime or disaster occurrences to track the criminals or suspects in a relatively short period.

---

[1] These are environments that are characterized by low computational and processing resources. Examples emerge in disaster scenarios and remote areas.

© Springer International Publishing Switzerland 2015
O. Camp et al. (Eds.): ICISSP 2015, CCIS 576, pp. 122–136, 2015.
DOI: 10.1007/978-3-319-27668-7_8

1.1   Motivation and Problem Statement

Applying k-anonymity on data streams faces three drawbacks in relation to minimizing delay and incorporating user's privacy preferences during anonymization.

Firstly, existing data stream anonymization algorithms do not take user privacy preferences into consideration. K-anonymity uses the same privacy level (i.e. k-value) for all individuals in the data set. The use of the same privacy level for all users is unrealistic in real-life because individuals tend to have varying privacy protection requirements [12,13]. Furthermore, the use of the same privacy preference level for all users implies that individual privacy needs are misrepresented.

Secondly, existing data stream anonymization algorithms apply a delay constraint on each tuple in the buffered stream [5,6,14]. Buffering incurs high information loss levels in terms of delay in cases of intermittent streaming data flows. This is because anonymization is typically triggered on the basis of the number of records (tuples) in the buffer as opposed to the time-sensitivity of the data.

Thirdly, anonymization of intermittent or slow data streams results in high information loss or suppression as is the case in the crime reporting scenario. However, the focus of many of the existing data stream anonymization algorithms is on fast data streams and as a result overlooking the rate at which data arrives in the stream when determining an optimal buffer size. The buffer size and rate of arrival of the streaming crime data affects information loss with respect to delay and the levels of privacy offered by the anonymization scheme.

1.2   Contribution

In this paper, we offer two contributions. Firstly, we propose an approach to minimizing delay while a record waits to be anonymize in the buffer. Secondly, we augment our streaming data anonymization scheme by supporting anonymization of data stream with user-defined privacy preferences.

In order to minimize delay, we model our buffer as a time-based tumbling sliding window that is constrained by delay as opposed to record count as it is the case in other solutions because of the time-sensitive nature of crime data. Afterwards, we develop a solution to adaptively re-adjust the size of sliding window based on an arrival rate of data that follows a Poisson process.

In order to ensure that privacy controls are enforced in a balanced way i.e. there is no excessive privacy control or insufficient privacy measure, we supported our adaptive buffer resizing scheme with three-tiered user-defined privacy preference (low, neutral (medium) and high) model. In order to see how this can be integrated in real-life, we carried out a survey in a campus setting in a technology resource constrained environment. We modeled and analyzed the data gathered from our survey using association rules in order to automatically deduce features that determine a user's privacy preference in an automated way. Lastly, we came up with an appropriate k-value to be used for a user's anonymization when there is insufficient or excessive privacy enforcement in comparison to the user's need.

Firstly, we carried out a real-life survey in our do main of interest (crime data) in order to determine if the usage and integration of three-tiered user-privacy into k-anonymity is practicable in real-life. Secondly, we came up with association rules in order to determine factors that influence users privacy preference. As a further step, we integrated the association rules into the k-anonymity technique in order to further aid determination of an appropriate k-value to be used for anonymization process.

1.3   Outline

The rest of the paper is structured as follows. In Sect. 2, we present related work highlighting the weaknesses of existing data stream anonymization and user-defined privacy preferences. Section 3, presents a review of our previous work that addressed the buffering problem and we further improve on how to incorporate user privacy preferences. In Sect. 4, we present results from our proof-of-concept implementation and conclude in Sect. 5.

2   Related Work

Sakpere and Kayem [8], presented an adaptive buffer resizing scheme to minimize information loss (delay) during streaming data anonymization was proposed. The buffer is modeled as a time-based sliding window whose size is dynamically re-adjusted based on an arrival rate of data that follows a Poisson process. Information loss in terms of numbers of data records is minimized by selectively suppress data records from a sliding window. Depending on the time sensitivity, such suppressed records are either included in a subsequent sliding window or inserted into a reusable anonymity cluster. Results from our prototype implementation demonstrate that our proposed scheme is privacy preserving and incurs an information loss in terms of delayed records of 1.95 % in comparison to other schemes that incur a 12.7 % rate. However, Sakpere and Kayem's, as well as previous solutions do not consider user privacy preferences during anonymization of streaming data which has the drawback of offering insufficient or excessive protection with respect to user needs.

To address the issue of incorporating user's personal privacy preferences into k-anonymity, Aggrawal and Yu [11], Gedik and Liu [13] allow a user to select an integer, i, (where $1 \leqslant i \leqslant n$) to indicate his/her preferred k-value. A drawback of this is that it might be difficult for users to set a realistic k-value in real-life especially in a Crime Reporting System where users might be under shock. Also, setting a realistic k-value implies that users must understand how k-anonymity works.

An equally novel approach in achieving personalized anonymization using the concept of k-anonymity is the work of Xiao and Yufei [12]. In their work, a user is required to specify the degree of privacy protection for his/her sensitive values. Their solution assumes that each sensitive attribute has a classification tree and each record owner specifies a guarding node in the tree. Guarding nodes depend on user personal privacy preferences and indicate how users want their sensitive values to be represented. A major drawback of their approach is that a guarding node requires that a hierarchy-tree be defined on sensitive attribute. Another major drawback is that in real-life, it is unclear how individual record owners would set their guarding node [11].

We therefore note that the issue of incorporating user privacy preferences to cope with anonymization of streaming data in a manner that is usable in real-life is yet to be studied. This study is necessary in order to generate reliable anonymized reported crime data that meets users need.

3   User-Defined Privacy Preference in Adaptive Buffer Re-sizing Scheme

In this section we present the integration of user-defined privacy preferences into the adaptive buffer resizing scheme. However, we will like to briefly recap how we adaptively reduce buffer size in our previous work [8].

3.1   Adaptive Buffer Resizing Scheme

As mentioned in our introduction section, the buffer size and rate of arrival of the streaming crime data impacts on the accuracy in terms of minimizing information loss and reliability in terms of privacy enforcement of the anonymization scheme. In order to minimize the percentage of information loss (in terms of delay) during the streaming data anonymization process, we use a time-based tumbling sliding window to adjust the size of the buffer dynamically with respect to the arrival rate of the data.

As illustrated in Fig. 1, a "sliding window" or "buffer", sw_i, is a subset of the data stream, DS where DS $= \{sw_1, sw_2, sw_3,..., sw_m\}$ implies that the data stream consists of m sliding windows. The sliding windows obey a total ordering such that for $i < j$, sw_j precedes sw_i. Each sliding window, sw_i only exists for a specific period of time T and consists of a finite and varying number of records, n.

3.2   Streaming Data as a Poisson Process

We model the flow rate of the data stream as a Poisson process because the arrival rate of data in the stream can be viewed as a series of events occurring within a fixed time interval and with a known average rate that is independent of the time of occurrence of the last event [10]. The Poisson distribution is a discrete probability distribution that measures the probability of having a given number of records occurring in the stream within a fixed time and/or space interval provided that these records arrive are each with a known average rate and are each independent of the last event occurrence. So, this occurrence is a good distribution for estimating streaming data reporting rates. In the Poisson distribution, only one parameter needs to be known, namely rate at which the

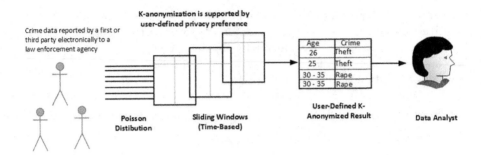

Fig. 1. Overview of buffer resizing process.

events occur which in our scenario would be the rate at which crime reporting occurs.

Considering that the data stream, DS follows a Poisson process with an arrival rate of events $\lambda > 0$, then we can say that for a sliding window sw_i the probability mass function is given by:

$$f\left(\text{sw}_i, \lambda\right) = \Pr\left(\text{DS} = \text{sw}_i\right) = \frac{\lambda^{\text{sw}_i} e^{-\lambda}}{\text{sw}_i!} \tag{1}$$

where e is the base of the natural logarithm (i.e. $e = 2.71828$) and sw_i is the size of the i_{th} sliding window under evaluation for anonymization.

3.3   Buffer Sizing

Our adaptive buffer re-sizing scheme relies on a streaming data flow rate that obeys the Poisson distribution model described above and works as follows. First we begin by setting the size of the buffer to an initial preset threshold value. Given the time-sensitivity of the data, we use a time value, T that is bounded between t_l and t_u. When the time threshold, T, is attained, the k-anonymization algorithm is applied to the data that was collected during this period. All records that are not anonymizable in the current data set are suppressed and based on the closeness of the suppressed records to their expiry deadlines, we either include the records in the next sliding window or incorporate the records into any of existing reusable clusters that has the smallest distance from the record(s).

In order to decide whether to include a suppressed record in the next sliding window sw_{i+1}, we first compute the average remaining time that the suppressed records have left before they expire. We denote this time as T_E and obtain a value for T_E by subtracting the average time for which the records have been stored in the buffer from the size of the current sliding window sw_i. Next, in order to determine the minimum number of records needed to minimize information loss from expired records in the data stream that will compose the next sliding window sw_{i+1}, we first compute an estimated time-bound for $\text{sw}_{i+1}!$ by adding T_E to the time T_A that was used to anonymize the data in sw_i. We then compute the minimum number of records required adding T_E to T_A and incorporating the value into Eq. 1 to obtain an expected data stream flow rate λ_{i+1} as follows:

$$f\left(\text{sw}_{i+1}, \lambda_{i+1}\right) = \Pr\left(\text{DS} = \text{sw}_{i+1}\right) = \frac{\lambda^{\text{sw}_{i+1}} e^{-\lambda}}{\text{sw}_{i+1}!} \tag{2}$$

where $\text{sw}_{i+1} = T_E + T_A$. From the values of λ_{i+1} and $(T_E + T_A)$ respectively we can easily obtain a value for the minimum number of records n needed for sw_{i+1}.

We must now decide what to do with the suppressed records. As mentioned before, we can either include a suppressed record in the new sliding window sw_{i+1} or based on its distance include the record in a reusable cluster of existing anoymized data. In the first case, for each suppressed record, we compare the remaining time T_R that the record has before it expires. We do this as follows, if $T_R \geq T_E + T_A$ then the affected suppressed record gets included in sw_{i+1}. Otherwise, if $T_R < T_E + T_A$ then the record concerned gets incorporated into an appropriate reusable cluster.

Finally, in order to decide which reusable cluster to include a suppressed record in, we choose the reusable cluster that has the least distance from the suppressed record. When only one reusable cluster exists, we simply add the suppressed value to the cluster. If we have several clusters to select from the one with the lowest distance is chosen. Lastly, when anonymization is not possible and there is no existing reusable cluster into which the suppressed records can be included we create a new reusable cluster.

From the discussion in this section, our framework for the Buffer Re-sizing anonymization of data streams can be summarized as follows [8]:

Algorithm 1. SWET (i,K).

1: **for** each sliding window sw_i, i:1 ...m **do**
2:     **if** $((sw_i == 1) \| (SuppRec == \phi))$ **then**
3:         $sw_{iExistTime} \leftarrow T$
4:     **else**
5:         $sw_{iExistTime} \leftarrow RSWET(T_R, T_A, i, SuppRec)$
6:     **end if**
7:     $T_A \leftarrow$ Anonymization Processing Time
8:     $SuppRec \leftarrow$ Suppressed Records
9:     $T_R \leftarrow$ Remaining Time of Suppressed Records
10:     Update Reusable Cluster (RC)
11: **end for**

3.4 Integration of User-Defined Privacy Preference into Adaptive Buffer-Resizing

As earlier stated in our introduction that the use of k-anonymity for data streaming anonymization uses a generic approach to enforce privacy preservation for all

Algorithm 2. RSWET($T_R, T_A, i, SuppRec$).

1: **Sort**: Sort T_R in ascending order and group by unanonymizable cluster
2: **for** j:1 ...$|SuppRec|$ **do**
3:    **if** T_{R_j} - $T_A < T_l$ **then**
4:        Anonymize $SuppRec_j$ using RC
5:        Delete $SuppRec_j$
6:    **else**
7:        Calculate arrival rate, λ, of $SuppRec_j$ in the sliding window, sw_i
8:        Find the Probability, P, of successful anonymization in sw_i
9:    **end if**
10:   **if** P or $\lambda > \delta$ **then**
11:       $ExistTime_i \leftarrow T_{R_j} - T_A$
12:       Add $SuppRec$ to sw_i
13:       **break**
14:   **else**
15:       anonymize $SuppRec_j$ using RC
16:       delete $SuppRec_j$ from $SuppRec$
17:   **end if**
18: **end for**
19: **if** P or λ for all suppressed records $< \delta$ **then**
20:    $ExistTime_i \leftarrow T$
21: **end if**
22: return $ExistTime_i$

---

users without catering for their concrete needs. The consequence of this is that insufficient protection might be provided to a subset of people while excessive privacy control is provided to another subset. In order to ensure a user's data protection meets her need we attempted to support data stream anonymization with user's privacy preference.

Existing literature [7] on personalized-privacy shows that in real-life, users view their privacy preferences as either High, Intermediate and Low. A high privacy level indicates an extreme privacy consciousness whereas a low privacy level depicts a lower privacy consciousness. Therefore, neutral privacy level is intermediate. We also carried out a real-life survey on personalized-privacy and result shows that in real-life, users find it easy to recognize their privacy setting if given three-preferences. The user study approach was used for the survey through questionnaire and interview. All the collected survey data comprised of 26 subjects and eight categorical variables: Sex, Age group, Present education level/Occupation, Highest education qualification (HEQ), Victim of crime, Crime experienced, Preferred privacy level (PPL) and Reason for choice of privacy (RCP). Figure 2 shows a summary of the data obtained during our analysis.

We integrate our three-tier level privacy preference into k-anonymity in the adaptive buffer resizing scheme by starting data streaming anonymization with k-anonymity principle/scheme. K-anonymization schemes classify records into different buckets such that each record in a bucket is indistinguishable from at least *k-1* records [2].

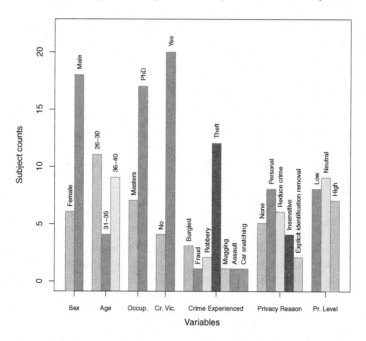

Fig. 2. Histogram illustrating the distribution of subjects over the different categories of variables surveyed in the primary study of privacy level preference.

Our basis for starting anonymization with the principles of k-anonymity schemes is because according to Sweeney, an optimal privacy is reached if a subset contains at least k data set [1,2]. However, it is still possible that a subset can contain records greater than or lesser than k. If a subset is lesser than k, then records in such subsets are not sufficiently protected and if a subset contains greater than k records then excessive privacy control is enforced. Therefore, the integration of user-defined privacy preference into adaptive buffer resizing during k-anonymization is to ensure that no subset contains lesser than or greater than k-records.

To address the shortcomings of a generic privacy enforcement in k-anonymity, we define three different levels of protection for users and incorporate them into adaptive buffer resizing scheme.

We begin by starting anonymization of all tuples using the principles of k-anonymity. Next, we search for subsets that contain lesser than k-records and attempt to anonymize records in the subset using user-defined privacy preference. For example, if a user's privacy preference is medium and his/her record is in a subset that contains lesser than k records, then we attempt to use a mid k-value to carry out anonymization for such records. Finally, we Search for subsets that contain greater than k-records and attempt to anonymize records in the subset using user-defined privacy preference. For example, if a user's privacy preference is low and his/her record is in a subset that contains greater than k records, then we attempt to use a low k-value (obtained by simply removing every explicit identifier) to carry out anonymization for such records.

4   Implementation and Results

We divide this section into two. The first section focuses results on minimizing delay before anonymization while the second section addresses privacy preservation guided by user requirements. Both experiments were performed on an Intel Core i5-3210 2.50Ghz computer with 4GB of physical memory. The operating system used was Ubuntu 12.10.

4.1   Buffering

The proposed adaptive buffering framework was implemented by extending the existing CSE 467[2] k-anonymization implementation. To depict streaming data, we used the file input stream functions in java, that reads data in real-time from an external source/excel file into sliding window. MySQL database storage was used to depict our sliding window. We assume that only a single data is read from the external file into the buffer at each instant in time.

We synthetically generated a realistic crime data set that follows the structure of the Cry-Help App using a random generator software[3]. The CryHelp App is a simple crime reporting application developed for mobile phones running the Android Operating System. Figure 3 shows some screenshots from the CryHelp App. The app was developed in conjunction with the University of Cape Town Campus Protection Service (CPS). The app enables users to send crime reports[4].

As a baseline case, for evaluating our proposed adaptive buffering scheme we implemented the proactive-FAANST and passive-FAANST. These algorithms are a good comparison benchmark because they are the current state-of-the-art streaming data anonymization that reduce information loss with minimum delay [14]. The proactive-FAANST decides if an unanonymizable record will expire if included in the next sliding window while passive-FAANST searches for unanonymizable records that have expired. A major drawback of these two variants is that there is no way of deciding whether or not unanonymizable records would be anonymizable during the next sliding window. In our experiment, the proactive-FAANST and passive-FAANST solutions also use the reusable cluster concept as well but do not allow for overlapping of sliding windows, which our implementation does, nor do they model the flow rate of reported crime data as a Poisson process.

Our experiments were conducted to measure the following:

1. Information loss in terms of delay

---

[2] http://code.google.com/p/cse467phase3/source%20/browse/trunk/src/Samarati. java?r=64.

[3] http://www.mockaroo.com.

[4] Further details about the app can be found in http://cryhelp.cs.uct.ac.za/download.

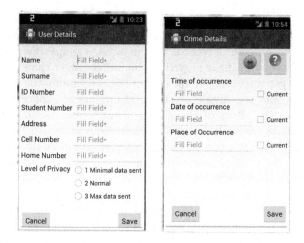

Fig. 3. Screenshots from CryHelp app.

2. Information gain obtained from modelling the flow rate of the data as a Poisson process

Effect of Privacy Levels (k-anonymity value) on Information Loss (delay).

As a heuristic, the choice of $k >= 2$ and $t_l = 2000$ ms and $t_u = 5000$ ms, is guided by values that are used in published experimentation results [14]. Figure 4 shows the effect of k-anonymity level on information loss with respect to delay (the number of expired records).

The main goal of our adaptive buffering solution is to reduce information loss (delay) (i.e. to lower the number of expired tuples). Figure 4 depicts that

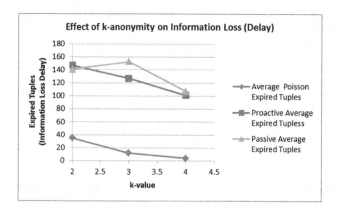

Fig. 4. Performance comparison: information loss with respect to privacy levels (expressed by the K-value).

our solution is successful in achieving its main goal and the information loss (delay) in our solution is lower than passive and proactive solutions. In order to determine the total number of records that expired, a simple query was executed to retrieve all records that have stayed in the buffer longer than the upper limit threshold, t_u. To get the average expired records, we sum up the expired records in all the experiments and divide by the total number of experiments.

Figure 4 shows the effect of the sliding window and k-anonymity level on information loss with respect to delay. In general, our approach shows that there are fewer expired tuples when compared to passive and proactive solutions. This is because before the Poisson probability prediction model transfers suppressed records to another sliding window, it checks for possibility of anonymization of the records. For other solutions, there is no mechanism in place to check the likelihood of the anonymizability of a suppressed record before allowing it to go to the next sliding window/round. As a result, such tuples may be sent to other rounds/sliding windows and eventually expire.

The main goal of our solution is to reduce information loss (delay)(i.e. to lower the number of expired tuples). Figure 4 depicts that our solution is successful in achieving its main goal and the information loss (delay) in our solution is lower than passive and proactive solutions. In general, our approach shows that there are fewer expired tuples when compared to passive-FAANST and proactive-FAANST solutions. This is because before our Poisson prediction transfers suppressed records to another sliding window, it checks for possibility of its anonymization. In other solutions, there is no mechanism in place to check the likelihood of the anonymizability of a suppressed record before allowing it to go to the next sliding window/round. As a result, such tuples get sent to other rounds/sliding windows and has high tendency to eventually expire.

Effect of Poisson Probability Value δ on Information Loss (Record).

To calculate information loss with respect to records i.e. deviation of anonymized data from its initial form, we used the formula in Eq. 3 as it is in [3]. We adopted this metric because it is a benchmark in many data stream anonymization schemes [5,6,14].

$$\text{InfoLoss} = \frac{M_P - 1}{M - 1} \tag{3}$$

M_p is number of leaf nodes in the subtree at node P and M is the total number of leaf nodes in the generalization tree. We calculate the information loss of a Sliding Window, $SW_i = \{R_1, R_2, R_3,..., R_n\}$ as follows:

$$\frac{1}{n} \sum_{i=1}^{n} \text{InfoLoss}(R_i) \tag{4}$$

The total information loss of a data stream is simply calculated by averaging the information loss of all sliding windows in it.

Figure 5 shows the effect of Poisson probability value, δ, on information loss (record). The figure shows that a higher value of δ results in higher information loss. This is because if the probability that a suppressed record will be

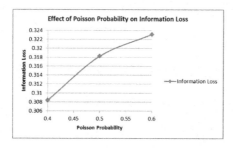

Fig. 5. Effect of poisson probability on information loss (record).

unanonymizable falls below δ such a record will be suppressed if there is no suitable reusable cluster. Suppressed records incur the highest rate of information loss. As a result, the higher the value of δ, the higher the chance of suppressed records and subsequently higher information loss. The result is based on the k-anonymity value of 2 and maximum suppression of 5 per sliding window. Time-based sliding window varies from 2000 ms to 5000 ms.

4.2   User-Defined Privacy Preference

We integrated our three-tier user-defined privacy preference into k-anonymity in data streaming anonymization by starting with a general k-value into a more specific or personalized k-value. As a heuristic, the choice of a general k value is guided by values used in published experimentation results [14].

As earlier stated, k-anonymity uses a generic approach to enforce privacy preservation for all users without catering for their concrete needs. The outcome of this is that insufficient protection might be provided to a subset of people, while excessive privacy control is provided to another subset. Therefore, our experiment is geared towards ensuring that there is a balanced protection by taking user's privacy preference into consideration.

Reduction of Excessive Privacy Control. Results from experiment as shown in Fig. 6, shows that integration of our approach to k-anonymity in comparison to other approaches ensure that excessive privacy control is reduced while at the same time guiding against insufficient protection. Our three-personalised approach has 16.15 % rate of excessive privacy control while Gedik- Personalised model and non-personalised has 63.08 % and 23.08 % rate of excessive privacy control respectively.

The reason our approach performed better than Gedik and non-personalized privacy is because we first used a general k-value and then attempt to personalize when there is excessive privacy control in comparison to user's preference. The result of our three-tier personalized result also shows that the higher the k-value, the higher the rate of excessive privacy control. This is because as k-value increases anonymization and privacy quality increases too. Hence more records

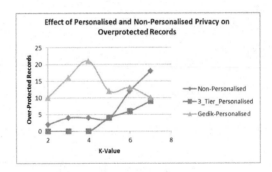

Fig. 6. Effect of personalised and non-personalised privacy on excessive privacy control.

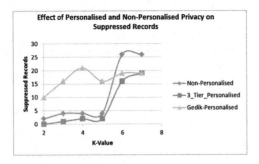

Fig. 7. Impact of the personalized and non-personalized privacy scheme on minimizing number of suppressed records.

have the chance of been suppressed which in-turn leads to excessive privacy control.

Record Suppression. One of the goals of a good anonymization scheme is to ensure that information loss is minimal. Records suppression usually leads to a high information loss. The use of personalized privacy scheme minimizes total number of suppressed records and as a result reduces information loss while the use of non-personalized privacy scheme leads to high number of suppressed records.

Figure 7 shows the effect of personalized and non-personalized privacy on suppressed records. Our result shows that our three-tier personalized privacy has lower rate of suppressed records which is 26 % when compared to Gedik-personalized privacy that has 77.7 % and non-personalized Privacy that has 51 %. This is because our three-tiered personalized privacy model considers suppressed records and attempts to reduce information loss by using user privacy prefer-ences. In order to also measure the effect of k-values on suppressed records, we set k-value to values between 2 and 7. The result also shows that the higher the k-value, the higher the number of suppressed records which is to be expected since high k-values imply a high anonymization degree.

5   Conclusions

We began this paper with an overview of the problem scenario which emerges in developing nations where the lack of data analytics expertise within a law enforcement agency makes the need to have a third party data analytics provider intervene to aid in fast crime report analysis. In addition, we highlighted the fact that the growing need to make the processed information available to field officers requires a mechanism for capturing crime reports in real-time and transferring these reports to the third-party service provider. While solutions in the literature that are hinged on cryptography have been shown to be successful in protecting data in outsourced scenarios from unauthorized access including that of "honest-but-curious" service providers, we noted that querying encrypted streaming data is a time consuming process and that k-anonymization technique is a more practical approach to data privacy preservation in this case.

Anonymizing streaming data in a crime reporting context however, can have strong real-time requirements and therefore information loss can lead to faulty or misguided conclusions on the part of the data analytics service provider. Therefore, streaming data anonymization algorithms (schemes) need to be supported by good buffering mechanisms. Our proposed approach uses the concept of modelling the flow rate of reported crime streaming data as a Poisson process that guides the sizing of a time-based sliding window buffer. The data collected in the buffer is subjected to k-anonymization to ensure privacy of the data. Results from our prototype implementation demonstrate that in addition to ensuring privacy of the data our proposed scheme outperforms other with an information loss rate of 1.95 % in comparison to 12.7 % on varying the privacy level of crime report data records. However, the generic paradigm approach to privacy enforcement in the k-anonymity model needs to be refined in order to cater for individual's need. Therefore, we refined our model to integrate users privacy preference into the k-anonymity model while attempting to reduce delays incurred as a result of buffering. The results show that the use of personalized privacy preferences ensure that protection is enforced in a balanced way by a 23.08 % information loss rate in comparison to non-personalized techniques that have an average balanced protection and incur loss rates of 63.08 %.

References

1. Sweeney, L.: k-anonymity: a model for protecting privacy. Int. J. Uncertainty Fuzziness Knowl. Based Syst. **10**(05), 557–570 (2002)
2. Sweeney, L.: Achieving k-anonymity privacy protection using generalization and suppression. Int. J. Uncertainty Fuzziness Knowl. Based Syst. **10**(05), 571–588 (2002)

3. Iyengar, V.S.: Transforming data to satisfy privacy constraints. In: Proceedings of the Eighth ACM SIGKDD International Conference on Knowledge Discovery and Data Mining, pp. 279–288. ACM (2002)

4. Kabir, M.E., Wang, H., Bertino, E.: Efficient systematic clustering method for k-anonymization. Acta Informatica **48**(1), 51–66 (2011)

5. Cao, J., Carminati, B., Ferrari, E., Tan, K.L.: Castle: continuously anonymizing data streams. IEEE Trans. Dependable Secure Comput. **8**(3), 337–352 (2011)

6. Guo, K., Zhang, Q.: Fast clustering-based anonymization approaches with time constraints for data streams. Knowledge-Based Systems, Elsevier (2013, in press)

7. Sakpere, A.B.: User-defined privacy preferences for k-anonymization in electronic crime reporting systems for developing nations. In: Doctoral Consortium, pp. 13–18 (2015). doi:10.5220/0005364700130018

8. Sakpere, A.B., Anne, V.D.M.K., Marchetti-Mercer, M.C.: Adaptive buffer resizing for efficient anonymization of streaming data with minimal information loss. In: Proceedings of the 1st International Conference on Information Systems Security and Privacy, pp. 191–201 (2015). doi:10.5220/0005288901910201

9. Stone, C.: Crime, justice, and growth in South Africa: toward a plausible contribution from criminal justice to economic growth. John F. Kennedy School of Government Working Paper No. RWP06-038(2006)

10. Li, S.: Fuzzy optimization and decision making. Poisson Process with Fuzzy Rates, pp. 289–305. Kluwer Academic Publishers, Hingham (2010)

11. Aggarwal, C.C., Yu, P.S. (eds.): TA General Survey of Privacy-preserving Data Mining Models and Algorithms. Springer, Heidelberg (2008)

12. Xiao, X., Tao, Y.: Personalized privacy preservation. In: Proceedings of the 2006 ACM SIGMOD International Conference on Management of Data. ACM (2006)

13. Gedik, B., Liu, L.: Protecting location privacy with personalized k-anonymity: architecture and algorithms. IEEE Trans. Mob. Comput. **7**(1), 1–18 (2008)

14. Zakerzadeh, H., Osborn, S.L.: FAANST: Fast Anonymizing Algorithm for Numerical Streaming DaTa. In: Garcia-Alfaro, J.; Navarro-Arribas, G., Cavalli, A., Leneutre, J. (eds.) DPM 2010 and SETOP 2010. LNCS, vol. 6514, pp. 36–50. Springer, Heidelberg (2011)

Mobile Systems Security

An Efficient Anonymous Authenticated Key Agreement Protocol for Vehicular Ad-Hoc Networks Based on Ring Signatures and the Elliptic Curve Integrated Encryption Scheme

Carsten Büttner[1]([✉]) and Sorin A. Huss[2]

[1] Adam Opel AG, Advanced Technology, Rüsselsheim am Main, Germany
carsten.buettner@de.opel.com
[2] Integrated Circuits and Systems Lab,
Technische Universitt Darmstadt, Darmstadt, Germany
huss@iss.tu-darmstadt.de

Abstract. Privacy in Vehicular Ad-hoc NETworks (VANETs) is one of the most important issues in order to successfully attract users to this new technology. In a common VANET use case two vehicles using the same application frequently need to exchange confidential application-related data. When it comes to a confidential data exchange, both vehicles need to authenticate each other and to agree on an encryption key. The new protocol proposed in this paper satisfies these requirements and, in addition, preserves the privacy of the vehicles. After execution of the protocol neither any vehicle in the communication range nor even the communication partners can reveal the identity of any of the communicating vehicles. To achieve this important goal we rely on the standardized Elliptic Curve Integrated Encryption Scheme (ECIES) and on ring signatures. We demonstrate how the advocated protocol can be used within GeoNetworking messages and evaluate its characteristics regarding the privacy of the participating vehicles. The presented results clearly show that the number of necessary pseudonyms for each vehicle may be reduced considerably when compared to a sole ECIES usage while still maintaining the privacy of the vehicles.

Keywords: Anonymous authentication · Vehicular Ad-hoc NETworks · Key agreement · Ring signatures · ECIES

1 Introduction

For safety reasons vehicles in Vehicular Ad-hoc NETworks (VANETs) use broadcast over ITS-G5 to inform other vehicles in the communication range about their current status, including position, heading, and speed. All safety messages are digitally signed to prove the integrity of the message and eligibility of the

O. Camp et al. (Eds.): ICISSP 2015, CCIS 576, pp. 139–159, 2015.
DOI: 10.1007/978-3-319-27668-7_9

sender. Since every participant shall receive and interpret these messages as fast as possible, they are in general not encrypted. Besides this safety relevant communication, there are other applications available where the data exchanged between vehicles is confidential and therefore needs to be encrypted.

Consider as an example a service provider that collects data about potholes on roads in a certain area. Vehicles thus record data about potholes and report it to the service provider, which subsequently offers the data to other service providers or local administrations. However, the data sent to the service provider contains privacy related data such as the location of the pothole and a coarse time, when it was detected. If all vehicles would simply sent their detected data to the service provider, then this entity may create movement profiles of the vehicles out of the reported data. In order to preserve the privacy of its users and to advertise the privacy considerations, the service provider decides to implement a privacy preserving mechanism. This mechanism requires that the vehicles exchange their collected data between each other prior uploading. When using this mechanism the vehicles report pothole locations detected by other vehicles too. Therefore, the service provider can no longer determine where a specific vehicle was driving at the given point in time and can no longer create movement profiles of this vehicle. The provider may decide to use the ETSI ITS-G5 network to exchange the data between the vehicles, because it is free of charge. In addition, the provider enforces an encrypted data exchange policy, so no attacker can record and sell the collected data next to the service provider. The exchange of the encrypted data shall also be privacy preserving.

In general, there are three basic problems to be considered, when confidential data is being exchanged between vehicles: (i) How does a vehicle ensure whether the other vehicle is eligible to receive confidential data? (ii) How do vehicles exchange the key for encrypting their communication data? (iii) How can the first two problems be solved while preserving the privacy of the vehicles?

For safety-related communications in VANETs each vehicle uses a pseudonym to sign all messages. To ensure the privacy of the vehicle the pseudonym is changed on a regular basis, so that two pseudonyms cannot be linked to the same vehicle. Of course, a vehicle might simply use an own set of pseudonyms for each application by encoding the application into the pseudonym and exploit well-known key agreement protocols like the Elliptic Curve Integrated Encryption Scheme (ECIES) as standardized in [15] to authenticate against each other and finally to agree on an encryption key. However, the vehicle then needs to change its pseudonym for the application at hand at the same time as the one intended for safety-related communication to prevent linking of pseudonyms. This introduces a cost overhead both for additional secure storage of the private keys and for the data transmission aimed to obtain new pseudonyms. Therefore, we propose in the sequel a novel protocol that solves all three outlined problems and at the same time reduces the number of necessary pseudonyms in comparison to exploiting ECIES only. In order to do so we pick up the concept of k-anonymity [19], combine ring signatures [17] with the ECIES scheme, and evaluate the resulting protocol with respect to the privacy of the vehicles.

The rest of this paper is organized as follows: In Sect. 2 we discuss the term of application-specific pseudonyms. The state of the art of anonymous authenticated key agreement protocols is reviewed in Sect. 3. We then introduce the new anonymous authentication scheme in Sect. 4. The evaluation of this protocol is presented in Sect. 5. Finally, we conclude the paper in Sect. 6.

2   Application-Specific Pseudonyms

Each vehicle participating in a VANET is equipped with a set of certificates to sign safety messages. These certificates are named pseudonyms, since they do not leak the identity and therefore preserve the privacy of the vehicle. In this paper we assume that each application such as the outlined pothole detection service issues its own pseudonyms, thus proving that the owner of the corresponding private key is eligible to run the application. So, only vehicles equipped with a valid pseudonym can get access to it. We name such pseudonyms *application-specific pseudonyms*.

An unique identifier is assigned to each application in order to determine which pseudonym belongs to which application. In case that this identifier is also part of the pseudonym, the application can check, whether the pseudonym is eligible to use the service. Pseudonyms used in VANETs contain an ITS Application ID [11], which may be exploited for this purpose.

3   Related Work

The IEEE Standard 1609.2 for Wireless Access in Vehicular Environments [15] uses the hybrid encryption scheme ECIES to encrypt messages between vehicles. In ECIES both parties agree on a key to encrypt and exchange an AES key. This AES key is later on used to encrypt the exchanged data. However, since it is necessary that the vehicles change all their identities each time the safety pseudonym changes, one set of pseudonyms with the same size as the one for safety messages would be necessary for each single application to prevent linking pseudonyms. We reduce the considerable size of the sets necessary for each application by combining ECIES with ring signatures.

Ring signatures based on RSA and Rabin's signature scheme have been introduced in [17]. In order to create a signature, the signer takes in addition to his own private key the public key of n other entities to sign the message. To verify the message, the public key of the signer and the n public keys of the other entities are necessary. The verifier of a ring signature cannot distinguish who of the $n + 1$ entities actually signed the message because the probability of each signer results in $1/(n + 1)$. The authors of [16] propose ring signatures for anonymous routing in wireless ad-hoc networks, but they did not evaluate related ring building strategies nor the size of the protocol nor multiple own pseudonyms. In [14] the authors advocate ring signatures in mobile ad-hoc networks for authentication of neighbor nodes. They did investigate ring building strategies, but most of their strategies require either a central server or the nodes have to be a-priori aware of the pseudonyms of all other nodes. In addition, these authors only considered the case where each node has just one pseudonym and elaborated a general formula to calculate the transmission overhead, but they did not evaluate their suggestion.

Secret Handshakes [2,5] are used to identify secretly if two parties belong to the same group. Even if the handshake fails, both parties cannot retrieve the group of the opposite. Accordingly, a third party is never able to retrieve the affiliation of a participant to a group. To reach unlinkability between different handshakes, an unique pseudonym has to be used for each handshake. Otherwise an attacker may eventually link different handshakes to a specific participant. This method is similar to the usage of ECIES in VANETs with regular pseudonym changes. However, we aim to significantly reduce the amount of required pseudonyms compared to this method.

Group Signatures [6] allow a member of a group to create a signature on behalf of the group. The verifiers can only prove that the signature was created by a member of the group but not by whom. Unfortunately, group signatures are not suitable for the envisaged scenario, because each time a user leaves the group, new credentials have to be distributed to all group members. This property obstructs in our case the scalability of the approach because of the high probability that multiple vehicles leave the group every day. Moreover, we cannot assume that all vehicles are quipped with mobile communication devices to obtain on time the required information from the central entity.

An Anonymous Credential [4] is a set of attributes issued by a trustworthy entity. An user can prove a subset of her attributes to a verifier without revealing her identity, whereas several proofs cannot be linked. Again, Anonymous Credentials are not suitable in our case, because they require a regular connection to a central entity to get revocation information. As before, we cannot assume that all vehicles are linked to a central entity, because we cannot assume that all vehicles are equipped with a mobile communication. In addition, proofs of attributes do not establish an encryption key and show a high computational complexity.

Matchmaking Protocols [1] are intended to authenticate two members of the same group without revealing their group to others. However, this scheme does not hide the identity of the members, it hides only the group they are a member of. In contrast, we need to hide the identity of the members and not of the group.

The authors of [12] propose to use Physical Unclonable Functions (PUFs) to generate the private keys of the pseudonyms. This may well reduce the amount of necessary secure storage for the private keys of the pseudonyms. However, we aim to directly reduce the number of necessary pseudonyms. This also diminishes the amount of necessary secure storage, because less keys have to be stored, but also reduces the number of keys to be generated, of certificates to be issued by the infrastructure, and the amount of data to be transmitted to the vehicle. The advocated protocol can be used to reduce the overall number of necessary pseudonyms and, in addition, PUFs may be exploited to decrease the amount of necessary secure storage.

K-anonymity as defined in [19] provides a metric to measure the anonymity of a subject, where k denotes the number of subjects it is indistinguishable from. This metric will be exploited in the sequel for the envisaged scenario.

4   Anonymous Authentication

In this section we first specify the requirements of the proposed anonymous authenticated key agreement protocol and then present it in detail. We also characterize possible attacks and comment on the protocol parameters considered so far.

An anonymous authenticated key agreement protocol allows two parties, who are members of the same group, to establish a confidential communication. To achieve this goal, both parties have to agree on a session key to encrypt the exchanged messages. The identity of the other party is unknown at the beginning of the protocol and both parties are not willing to expose for privacy reasons their application-specific identity to anyone. In addition, it shall be possible to revoke access for single parties and only members of the same group shall be able to agree on the session key. The protocol shall fail, if one party is not a member of the group. Not eligible parties shall gain as few information as possible about the other party. We only consider single-hop connections, because multi-hop connections are difficult to maintain in VANETs due to frequent topology changes.

4.1   Protocol

The advocated key agreement protocol takes the approach proposed by the authors of this paper in [3] as a foundation and relies on both the ECIES scheme and ring signatures. Such a signature is intended to sign the transmitted ECIES parameters. By combining ECIES with ring signatures, the vehicles agree on a symmetric encryption key as standardized in [15] and bind this key to a specific application with the help of a ring signature created with application-specific pseudonyms. This generic approach has the advantage that the vehicles can use the safety identities already known to each other for ECIES and hide the application-specific identity by means of ring signatures. So, it is no longer possible to identify the entity which actually created the signature. The only information to be derived points to the set of pseudonyms present in the ring. Therefore, the application-specific pseudonyms can be reused after a pseudonym change without any link to safety pseudonyms. As a consequence, less application-specific pseudonyms are necessary. We exercise the ring signature scheme based on elliptic curves as proposed in [16]. We favor this scheme, since elliptic curves provide the same security level with a much shorter signature length compared to RSA. In addition, we propose a second version of the protocol, where the pseudonyms of the ring signature are encrypted together with the signature. We denote these protocol versions as non-encrypted and encrypted, respectively.

We introduce the following notation for the description of the protocol: *Service Announcement* denotes a service announcement according to [10]. V, C, and T are defined according to [15]: V is the public key of the sender, the parameter C is the symmetric AES key K encrypted by ECIES, while T denotes the authentication tag of ECIES. The pseudonym of entity X is denoted as $Cert_X$. The ring signature consists of n different pseudonyms $Cert_{Xn}$, where one is an application-specific pseudonym of the respective signer and the others are the collected application-specific pseudonyms. The values x_{Xn} are necessary to validate the ring signature. The actual ring signature is denoted as σ. When Y is encrypted with the encryption key K, it is denoted as $E_K(Y)$.

The non-encrypted version of the protocol is defined as follows and is discussed in the sequel.

(1) A → *: *ServiceAnnouncement*

(2) B → A: $V, C, T, Cert_{B1}, ..., Cert_{Bn}, x_{B1}, ..., x_{Bn}, E_K(\sigma)$

(3) A → B: $Cert_{A1}, ..., Cert_{An}, x_{A1}, ..., x_{An}, E_K(\sigma)$

In Step 1 Alice (A) announces that she offers a service that uses the anonymous authenticated key agreement protocol.

Assuming Bob (B) receives the service announcement from Alice and wants to use this service, he first generates an AES key K as payload for ECIES and calculates V, C, and T according to the ECIES scheme. Then he selects $n - 1$ pseudonyms from his collected pool and one of his own pseudonyms in order to calculate the ring signature σ over V, C, and T. Then, he encrypts σ with the symmetric key K. Finally, he sends V, C, T, the ring signature, and everything necessary for validation to Alice (Step 2).

After reception Alice decrypts the AES key K according to the ECIES scheme and applies it to decrypt σ before validating the ring signature. In case that the validation was successful, she selects both one of her own pseudonyms and $n - 1$ collected pseudonyms. With this set of pseudonyms she calculates a ring signature σ over V, C, and T and encrypts it with K. Then she sends the ring signature and everything necessary to validate it to Bob (Step 3).

When Bob receives the ring signature from Alice, he decrypts σ and validates the ring signature. If the validation was successful, he starts the confidential communication with Alice. After the execution of the protocol, Alice and Bob know that the other party is authorized to use the service. In addition, both are in possession of the same encryption key K still without knowing the application-specific identity of the other party.

The encrypted version of the protocol differs in Steps 2 and 3. The difference to the non-encrypted one is that not only σ is encrypted, but additionally all necessary data to validate the ring signature. This version is defined as follows.

(2′) B → A: $V, C, T, E_K(Cert_{B1}, ..., Cert_{Bn}, x_{B1}, ..., x_{Bn}, \sigma)$

(3′) A → B: $E_K(Cert_{A1}, ..., Cert_{An}, x_{A1}, ..., x_{An}, \sigma)$

Given that the other party and a potential attacker already know the pseudonym used for safety messages, the identity applied to execute the ECIES scheme does not give an attacker any new knowledge. These safety pseudonyms should be changed on a regular basis and not be reused. Therefore, they cannot be exploited to track anything. The goal of an attacker is to determine the application-specific pseudonym of a vehicle, since this will be reused in different ring signatures and may therefore be used to link different safety identities of the vehicles. This may be achieved, when a vehicle exploits the same application-specific pseudonym twice, but with different pseudonyms for safety communication in VANETs. Then, an attacker can link the two safety pseudonyms, because they are used in combination with the same application-specific pseudonym.

Thus, please consider the case that Alice applies the safety pseudonym $Cert_{S1}$ and application-specific pseudonym $Cert_{A1}$ at the same time. Then, she changes her safety pseudonym to $Cert_{S2}$, while still using the application-specific pseudonym $Cert_{A1}$. An attacker now may link $Cert_{S1}$ and $Cert_{S2}$ because they were exploited with the same application-specific pseudonym.

We assume that each vehicle may have multiple valid application-specific pseudonyms at a time. So, the vehicles are in the position to change their application-specific pseudonym they use for building the ring signature regularly with their pseudonyms for safety relevant communication to avoid being tracked by means of the pseudonyms not being changed.

Multiple pseudonyms confuse an attacker considerably, since each vehicle features multiple identities and these identities may easily be used at the same time in ring signatures of different vehicles. We evaluate the impact of multiple parallel pseudonyms in Sect. 5.

For the outlined protocol we stick for compatibility purposes to the same pseudonym format already existing in VANETs to sign safety messages, however we bind them to a specific application. We also exploit elliptic curve cryptography and ECIES, which is already standardized for safety communication. Therefore, this protocol fits very well in the present VANET environment.

It is quite simple to exclude a vehicle from successfully executing the protocol by revoking its application-specific pseudonyms. The revocation may be done in the same way as for safety pseudonyms.

4.2   Message Format

To address the receiving vehicle, the actual protocol payload needs to be encapsulated in a network protocol. Due to the high mobility in VANETs, GeoNetworking [7] is used to address the receivers of a message. When using GeoNetworking, the vehicles define an area wherein the message is relevant and the message is then distributed within this area. For safety applications the receiver is not a single vehicle, but all vehicles in the destination area. However, it is also possible to address a single vehicle as the receiver of a message. Due to the ad-hoc characteristics of the network even in this case the geographic region of the vehicle is necessary too. In order to address a single vehicle, it needs a so called GeoNetworking address.

GeoMessaging messages are structured according to [7] as follows. They always start with a Basic Header for general information followed by a Secured Package. The Secured Package contains all immutable content of the message and can be split into Header Fields, Payload Fields, and Trailer Fields. The

Header Fields contain security related information. The Payload Fields can be separated into a Common Header for general immutable content, an Extended Header for the definition of the origin and destination, and the actual payload of the message. The Extended Header can be for example a Geographically-Scoped Broadcast (GBC) packet header to address all vehicles in a geographic region or a Geographically-Scoped Unicast (GUC) packet header to address a single vehicle. The Trailer Fields contain basically a signature over the complete secured packet. The structure of the GeoNetworking message is depicted in Fig. 1.

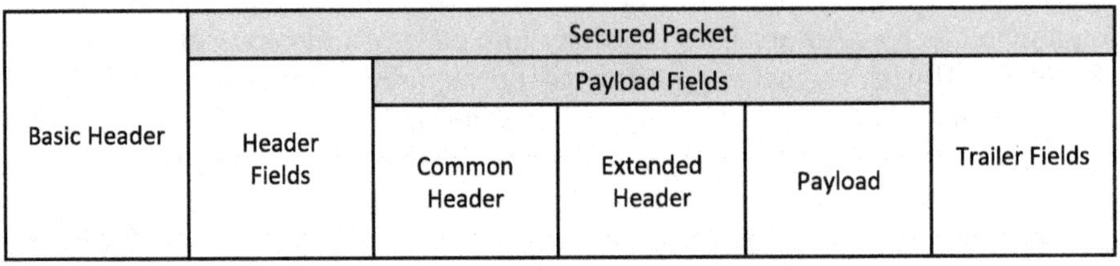

		Secured Packet				
		Payload Fields				
Basic Header	Header Fields	Common Header	Extended Header	Payload		Trailer Fields

Fig. 1. GeoNetworking message format.

For the proposed protocol GUC messages are most suitable, because the exchanged messages are only relevant for a single receiving vehicle. Therefore the Extended Header will be a GUC packet header. The format of the service announcement message (Step 1) is sent via broadcast to all vehicles in proximity and already standardized in [10]. Due to this reason, we will discuss in the sequel the used format only for the subsequent messages.

The Basic Header consists of a version number, the type of the next header (Secured Package), the remaining lifetime of the message, and the remaining hop limit. The contents of the Header Fields are defined by profiles. A profile defines the header fields to be included from a list of all possible fields. The corresponding standard [11] defines a generic profile, one for CAM messages, and one for DENM messages. However, none of these profiles are suitable for the advocated protocol. Therefore, we defined a dedicated profile. It consists of the generation time of the message aimed to detect replay attacks and a signer info, which is the pseudonym for safety relevant communication of the sender to check the authenticity of the message. This profile is used for all messages of the outlined protocol. The encrypted messages exchanged subsequently can use this profile too. The Common Header defines the next header (in our case the GUC-Header), the traffic class of the message, the length of the payload, the maximum hop limit, and whether the station is mobile or not. The GUC package header is responsible for the addressing of the recipient and contains a sequence number, information about the source like its GeoNetworking address and position, and the GeoNetworking address, position and timestamp of the last known position of the receiver. The payload is the data denoted in the protocol Steps 2 and 3, respectively. The Trailer Fields contain a signature over the content of the Secured Package

The overhead introduced by GeoNetworking is considered in the evaluation of the message size of the protocol in Sect. 5.1.

4.3 Attacker

Capabilities. We distinguish between *passive* and *active attackers*. A passive attacker can only listen to and record exchanged messages, while active attackers can also replay and send messages under a forged identity. We consider four types of active attackers that differ in their access to pseudonyms as detailed in Table 1. The least powerful attacker has no access to any valid pseudonyms. Another attacker has only access to pseudonyms for safety relevant communication. The third one has only access to application-specific pseudonyms, while the most powerful attacker is an insider and has access to both pseudonym types.

Table 1 compares the encrypted and non-encrypted version of the protocol regarding the information the different attacker types can yield. We consider the size of the ring and the pseudonyms used by Alice and Bob as critical. When the attacker can get the respective information, it is denoted as X, otherwise as O.

Table 1. Capabilities of attackers.

Attacker	Protocol	Ring size	Alice	Bob
Passive	Non-Encrypted	X	X	X
	Encrypted	X	O	O
Active without pseudonyms	Non-Encrypted	X	X	X
	Encrypted	X	O	O
Active with safety pseudonyms	Non-Encrypted	X	X	X
	Encrypted	X	O	X
Active with application pseudonyms	Non-Encrypted	X	X	X
	Encrypted	X	O	O
Active with safety and application pseudonyms	Non-Encrypted	X	X	X
	Encrypted	X	X	X

Regardless of the used version of the protocol, all attackers can calculate the current ring size from the message size. When the non-encrypted version is used, all attackers can get the pseudonyms used by Alice and Bob, since they are transmitted in plain text. Therefore, only the capabilities of the attackers regarding the encrypted version of the protocol are discussed in the sequel.

The passive attacker cannot get the pseudonyms of Alice and Bob when the encrypted version is used, since they are encrypted and the attacker cannot derive the encryption key K just by listening to the exchanged messages.

Without access to valid pseudonyms, an active attacker is not able to successfully inject any message, since all of them are either signed or encrypted. If the attacker replays the first message, she cannot encrypt the second or reply a valid third message, since she does not know and cannot calculate the encryption key. If she replays the second message, she is not in the position to decrypt the pseudonyms used by Bob in Step 3, since she does not know and cannot calculate the encryption key. Therefore, all active attackers are not able to get any information by replaying messages.

An active attacker with access to pseudonyms for safety relevant communication may generate and send the first messages. If she sends the first message, she cannot replay with the third step, because she has no application-specific pseudonym available in order to generate a valid ring signature. However, she can decrypt the pseudonyms used by Alice in Step 2 by calculating the encryption key K and therefore can get the pseudonyms used by Alice. The attacker is also not able to generate a valid second message, since a valid application-specific pseudonym is necessary for this purpose.

An active attacker, who has only access to application-specific pseudonyms, cannot generate and send a valid service announcement, because it is signed with a pseudonym for safety relevant communication. The same holds for the second message.

If an active attacker has access to both a pseudonym for safety relevant communications and to an application-specific pseudonym, she is now in the position to send and to answer to all messages of the protocol and therefore gets the pseudonyms used by Alice and Bob.

This analysis shows, that only the most powerful active attacker is able to unveil the identities used by Alice and Bob when the encrypted version of the protocol is being applied. However, lots of sophisticated work will be necessary to implement this type of attacker in practice, since the private keys of the pseudonyms are in general stored on a hardware security module (HSM) inside the vehicle. Of course, if the HSM fails and an attacker is thus able to extract the private keys, she can get both the valid safety and the application-specific pseudonyms and send valid fake messages. However, then the attacker may also extract only the private keys of the safety pseudonyms and link them directly or send valid fake safety messages. In general, it is possible to detect and to revoke the affected vehicle, which works well with the proposed protocol. However, failed HSMs are a general problem in VANETs and we will therefore not address it in more detail in this paper.

Behavior. In this section we discuss the behavior of the considered attacker. This attacker is a passive one aiming at the non-encrypted version of the protocol. This attacker type is sufficient, because even the most powerful attacker aiming at the encrypted version cannot gain more information. The attacker tries to identify the application-specific pseudonym of a vehicle from the ones used in the ring signature. The behavior of the attacker can be characterized by three stages.

```
 1: // Count pseudonym usage
 2: Create hashmap hm for pseudonym usage
 3: for each colected message m do
 4:     for each used pseudonym p in m do
 5:         if hm.contains(p) then
 6:             hm.put(p, hm.get(p) + 1)
 7:         else
 8:             hm.put(p, 1)
 9:         end if
10:     end for
11: end for
12: // Select relevant pseudonyms
13: Create list relevantPseudonyms
14: for each pseudonym p in hm do
15:     if p > DaysObserving/PseudonymPoolSize then
16:         relevantPseudonyms.add(p)
17:     end if
18: end for
```

Fig. 2. Pseudonym filtering algorithm used by the passive attacker.

In the first stage the attacker just records the exchanged messages.

After recording, the attacker counts how often each pseudonym has been applied. Then, she selects the relevant pseudonyms, which are used at least $DaysObserving/PseudonymPoolSize$ times, where $DaysObserving$ denotes the number of days the attacker recorded the messages and $PseudonymPoolSize$ the number of own pseudonyms each vehicle has at the same time, respectively. Thus, only pseudonyms used regularly are considered. The filtered ones might be introduced to the communication by vehicles driving only once the observed street. The pseudocode for this second stage is shown in Fig. 2.

The the third and last stage starts with the identification of unambiguous pseudonyms and is shown as pseudocode in Fig. 3. A pseudonym is unambiguous, if it is the only relevant pseudonym of a ring. Therefore, this pseudonym must be the identity of the vehicle. Afterwards, these unambiguous pseudonyms are deleted from all rings of the other vehicles on this day. By 'delete' we mean that it is now clear that this pseudonym does not belong to the vehicle and we therefore do no longer need to consider it in the respective rings.

If each vehicle applies an own ring size, unambiguous pseudonyms are also deleted from the vehicles using a different ring size in other days. By 'own ring size' we mean that not all vehicles use the same number of pseudonyms to construct their ring signature. We may delete these pseudonyms, because we know the ring size of the vehicle owning the pseudonym is different.

If any pseudonyms were deleted, the attacker tries to identify new unambiguous pseudonyms, otherwise the attacker is finished. Now the attacker has reduced the ring size of the vehicles by excluding pseudonyms, which cannot be the identities of the vehicles. We evaluate in Sect. 5.2 by how much the attacker

```
 1: do
 2:     reduced = false
 3:     // Identify unambiguous pseudonyms
 4:     Create list unambiguousPseudonyms
 5:     for each collected message m do
 6:         for each pseudonym p in m do
 7:             if m.relevantPseudonyms == 1 then
 8:                 unambiguousPseudonyms.add(p)
 9:             end if
10:         end for
11:     end for
12:     // Reduce ring sizes
13:     for each collected message m do
14:         for each pseudonym p in m do
15:             if p ∈ unambiguousPseudonyms ∧
16:                 m.day == unambiguousPseudonyms.get(p).day then
17:                 m.delete(p)
18:                 reduced = true
19:             end if
20:         end for
21:     end for
22:     // Handle different ring sizes
23:     if differentRingSizes then
24:         for each collected message m do
25:             for each pseudonym p in m do
26:                 if p ∈ unambiguousPseudonyms ∧ p.ringSize! = m.ringSize then
27:                     m.delete(p)
28:                     reduced = true
29:                 end if
30:             end for
31:         end for
32:     end if
33: while reduced == true
```

Fig. 3. Ring size reduction algorithm used by the passive attacker.

can reduce the ring size and therefore the k-anonymity value in presence of various parameters.

4.4 Considered Parameters

The anonymity of the vehicles is influenced by various parameters when they use the proposed anonymous authentication protocol. We considered the following parameters in the subsequent simulation runs.

Ring Size: The number of pseudonyms present in the ring signature. Unless explicitly mentioned, we used the maximum possible ring size of 10 according to Fig. 4.

Fraction of One Time Vehicles: These vehicles use a set of pseudonyms in their ring that is completely unknown to the other vehicles. They shall reflect that most vehicles drive the same route each day, but there are always vehicles that normally do not take this route in rush-hour, e.g., trucks. Unless explicitly mentioned, we consider 30 % of such one time vehicles.

Standard Deviation of the Starting Times: The starting times of the vehicles are assumed to be normally distributed. The standard deviation has an influence on the potential communication partners. Unless explicitly stated we use a standard deviation of 5 min.

Ring Building Strategy: When ring signatures are in place, a vehicle is one of n possible signers. It is important to apply a good ring building strategy, because a poor strategy can lead to revealing of most or even all of the non-signers, so the anonymity of the signer may decrease significantly. In the following we propose some appropriate strategies to build a ring. We evaluate these strategies later on in Sect. 5.

All: The vehicles collect and save all pseudonyms they receive from other vehicles. When the vehicles need to build a new ring, they randomly select the required number of pseudonyms from their pools.

SameDirection: Vehicles using this strategy collect and save all pseudonyms they receive from other vehicles driving in the same direction. The basic idea behind this method is that vehicles in rush-hour drive every day at approximately the same time in the same direction. Therefore, an attacker cannot delete the pseudonyms of the vehicles driving each day in the opposite direction from the ring. The same ring building method as for "All" is applied.

SameDirectionLastX: This strategy is similar to "SameDirection". The main difference is that the vehicles discard pseudonyms they met more than X days ago. The reason for this is that each day the vehicles collect pseudonyms of one time vehicles they never met before and unlikely meet again. If a vehicle uses such pseudonyms in its ring, an attacker can identify and remove them to get the identity of the victim vehicle. This can be done because they are less used than other pseudonyms. When limiting the number of pseudonyms by the number of previous days, the influence of these vehicles decreases. Unless explicitly mentioned, we use this ring building strategy.

SameDirectionLastXDifferentSizes: This strategy works like "SameDirectionLastX", but each vehicle applies an own ring size. This strategy is evaluated later on to assess the influence of different ring sizes on the anonymity of the vehicles.

Number of Own Pseudonyms: The number of own pseudonyms a vehicle has at the same time. Each time a ring is being build, the vehicle randomly selects one. Unless explicitly stated, we exploit 10 simultaneous pseudonyms.

Duration of the Attack: The duration denotes the number of days the attacker listens to the exchanged messages. Unless explicitly mentioned, we consider an attack duration of 30 days.

Number of Previous Days: This parameter denotes the number of days a vehicle stores the collected pseudonyms in the strategies *SameDirectionLastX* and *SameDirectionLastXDifferentSizes*.

5   Evaluation

5.1   Ring Size

The ring size denotes the number of pseudonyms used in the ring signature. It is obvious that the k-anonymity of the vehicle increases with the ring size. Since we want the maximum possible anonymity for the vehicles, we try to make the ring as large as possible, but we also have to avoid at the same time any fragmentation at the MAC layer [8].

To determine the maximum feasible message size, we measured the size of the largest message in the protocol. In this implementation we exploited the elliptic curve ring signature scheme proposed in [16] with curve P-256 and ECIES as described in [15]. For the pseudonym size we took 161 bytes, which is the size of a pseudonym certificate of the Pilot PKI of the Car-2-Car Communication Consortium[1]. We also took advantage of elliptic curve point compression [20] to minimize the size of the messages.

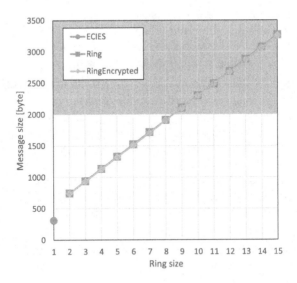

Fig. 4. Size of the largest message as a function of ring size: Size of largest message.

The size of the largest message as a function of the ring sizes as well as for ECIES without ring signatures is shown in Fig. 4. The darker area indicates the

---

[1] www.car-2-car.org.

Maximum Transmission Unit (MTU), which is expected to be larger than 2.000 bytes [9]. ECIES without the ring signatures has the lowest message size at an anonymity of 1. For ring signatures the message size increases linearly with the ring size. Due to the fixed size of the secured GeoNetworking packet headers and trailers (240 bytes), V (33 bytes), C (16 bytes), and T (20 bytes) the size of the message increases with every ring member by the size of a $Cert$ (161 bytes) and an x (32 bytes), which are in total 193 bytes. The graph indicates that depending on the MTU ring signatures with 9 or more members are the ones with the maximum anonymity in VANETs, when fragmentation at the MAC layer shall be avoided. We demonstrate in the following that a ring signature with 10 members is sufficient for the protocol and use case presented in order to preserve the privacy of the vehicles while reducing the number of necessary pseudonyms.

Messages of this size are much larger than safety messages. However, they are sent at a much lower frequency: Safety messages are sent up to 10 times a second, whereas the messages in the proposed protocol for the envisaged use case will be sent only a few times per hour. The messages are also sent on a different channel as the safety messages and do not have critical time constraints like safety messages. The envisaged channel is expected to be also used for Internet browsing, video streaming, or software updates.

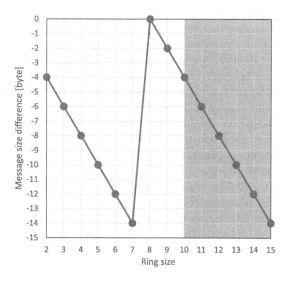

Fig. 5. Message size as a function of ring size: Size difference of encrypted and plain message.

Figure 5 shows the difference of the largest message of the encrypted and non-encrypted version in bytes. The negative values indicate that the encrypted version of the protocol has a smaller message size. When the non-encrypted version is applied only the signature is encrypted. It has a length of 33 byte and is therefore stored in three AES blocks of 16 bytes each, where the last block is padded with 15 bytes. In the encrypted version of the protocol more data is encrypted, whereby less padding bytes are used and therefore the overall message size is reduced. The darker area indicates the ring size when the MTU is in operation.

5.2   Simulation

Setup. For we exploited the VSimRTI tool set [18]. As simulation scenario we selected the motorway A60 south of Rüsselsheim, Germany. At each junction of the motorway one RSU is placed, which is assumed to be under control of an attacker, who can record all messages exchanged in the communication range. The vehicles enter the simulation area at two points: One in the east for the vehicles driving westbound and one in the west of the map for vehicles driving eastbound.

Normally the same vehicles drive the same way every day during rush-hour. Because these are ideal conditions for an attacker to link pseudonyms used at different days, we evaluated the privacy protocol under this condition. According to the traffic density categorization in [13] we applied a high density of vehicles in one and a low density in the other direction. Three classes of vehicles are considered in the simulation: The fast ones have a maximum speed of 130 km/h, the regular ones a maximum speed of 110 km/h, and the slow ones of 80 km/h. The different vehicle classes are equally distributed. The vehicles only drive the maximum speed if the traffic conditions allow it. They also overtake only if there is space to do so. Ten percent of the vehicles are equipped with an application software that uses the proposed anonymous key agreement protocol.

The envisaged simulation duration is 60 min. Since it takes some time until the simulation is adjusted, we cut 10 min both at the beginning and at the end of the simulation. Due to the long simulation duration, we decided to run the simulation without a specific ring building strategy. Instead, we log which vehicles establish a session key to map the ring building strategies afterwards on the vehicles. To evaluate more than 50 days, we randomly select as much simulation results as necessary from the pool of all 50 simulation runs and map the recurring vehicles afterwards into the simulation results.

The elaborated results show that every day each vehicle executes the protocol at least once in the communication range of each RSU. Thus, an attacker needs only one RSU under her control to get the rings of all passing vehicles. The attacker would also not get any benefit by having control over some of the vehicles, because it is not possible to get more information in this way.

Influence of the Considered Parameters

Ring Size: The k-anonymity of the vehicles, calculated according to [19], increases linearly with the ring size from 7.0, when a ring size of 10 is used, up to 10.3 when a ring size of 15 is being considered.

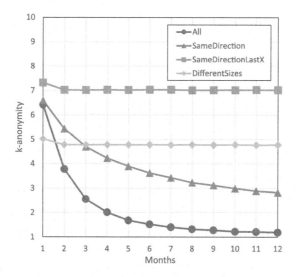

Fig. 6. Impact of ring building strategies.

Fraction of One Time Vehicles: The k-anonymity of the vehicle increases from 4.7, when 55 % of the vehicles are one time vehicles, up to 8.6, when only 11 % of the vehicles in the simulation appear only once. The reason for this is that there are more new pseudonyms in the simulations, which are considered by the vehicles during ring building.

Standard Deviation of the Starting Times: An increase or decrease of the standard deviation of the starting times had no notable influence on the anonymity of the vehicles.

Ring Building Strategy: The influence of the ring building strategy to the k-anonymity is shown in Fig. 6. The x-axis displays the month in which the attacker analyzes the messages since the start of pseudonyms usage. Month 1 is therefore the analysis of the first month and so on.

The k-anonymity value decreases over time from 6.4 in the first month down to 1.2 in the twelfth month, when the strategy "All" is in operation. The average k-anonymity value when using the "SameDirection" strategy is 6.6 in the first month and steadily decreases over time down to 2.8 after twelve months. When using the "SameDirectionLastX" strategy, the vehicles have a constant k-anonymity of 7.0 from the second month on. For the strategy "SameDirection-LastXDifferentSizes" the k-anonymity value drops from 7.0 to 4.8 compared to the case when the same sizes are used after the first month.

These results show that all vehicles should use the same ring size to keep the k-anonymity at a high level. If only pseudonyms received in the last X days are considered, then the k-anonymity of the vehicles does not decrease over time.

Number of Previous Days: To get the optimal number of previous days, we ran simulations with different day values for the various pseudonym pool sizes.

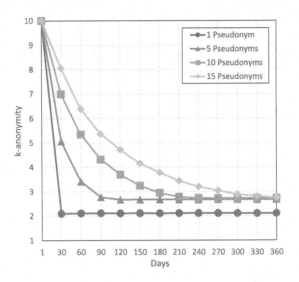

Fig. 7. Impact of pseudonym pool size.

Based on the outcome of these runs, we selected the most appropriate numbers of days.

Number of Own Pseudonyms and Duration of the Attack: Figure 7 illustrates the average k-anonymity of the vehicles for different numbers of own pseudonyms as a function of the number of days an attacker records the exchanged messages. It shows that the k-anonymity value decreases with the number of days an attacker listens to the exchanged messages. In addition, the k-anonymity value increases with the number of own pseudonyms. Depending on the assumed attack duration, either more pseudonyms have to be used or the pseudonyms have to be renewed more often in order to maintain a certain level of anonymity.

If an service provider aims to, for example, at an average k-anonymity of at least 5 for its users, the vehicles might use a new set of 5 pseudonyms every 30 days, a set of 10 pseudonyms every 60 days or a set of 15 pseudonyms every 90 days. This sums up to 60 pseudonyms per year. If we compare this value to the safety pseudonyms, where the pseudonym is to be changed at least with every trip, we can easily see that the proposed protocol reduces the number of necessary pseudonyms considerably.

A higher average anonymity of the vehicle increases the individual anonymity of the vehicles too. However, some vehicles might be still identifiable. Figure 8 visualizes the number of vehicles featuring at least a certain k-anonymity value in the case of using the same set of pseudonyms for 90 days.

The average k-anonymity for vehicles using 5 parallel pseudonyms is 2.8 for 90 days of usage (see Fig. 7). When using this setup, 16 % of all vehicles are identifiable as visible from Fig. 8. Only 9 % of the vehicles are indistinguishable

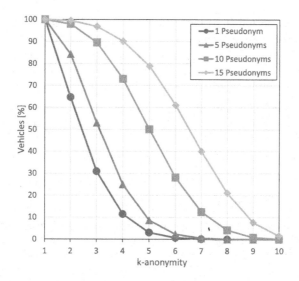

Fig. 8. K-anonymity for various pseudonym pool sizes after 90 days of usage.

from 5 or more identities. For 15 parallel pseudonyms the average k-anonymity is 5.4. Only 0.5 % of all vehicles are now identifiable while 79 % of the vehicles are indistinguishable from 5 or more identities.

6   Conclusion

In this work we proposed a novel anonymous authenticated key agreement protocol which combines ECIES with ring signatures. Based on this protocol we elaborated recommendations for an appropriate ring size for the communication between vehicles in a VANET.

We showed how the protocol can work with the standardized GeoNetworking messages aimed to address vehicles.

We demonstrated that the anonymity of the vehicles increases significantly when a good ring building strategy is applied. We also outlined that the number of pseudonyms each vehicle uses at the same time and the duration of the attack do have a clear influence on the anonymity level of the vehicles. In comparison to safety-related communication less pseudonyms for each vehicle over time are necessary to maintain a high level of anonymity, because they can be reused without the risk of being linked by an attacker. Therefore, the amount of pseudonyms, which have to be assigned to the vehicles, is significantly reduced. This both saves storage space and communication overhead and thus helps to reduce costs.

The proposed protocol is not restricted to VANET use cases, but it is especially well-suited for VANETs, because in such a context it is both expensive and some times rather difficult to obtain new pseudonyms. In addition, the well-known pseudonyms for safety-related communication can be reused by binding them to specific applications.

In the next future we plan to implement the outlined protocol into real vehicles and to take measurements to validate the presented simulation results.

Acknowledgement. This work was funded within the project CONVERGE by the German Federal Ministries of Education and Research as well as Economic Affairs and Energy.

References

1. Baldwin, R., Gramlich, W.: Cryptographic protocol for trustable match making. In: Proceedings of the IEEE Symposium on Security and Privacy (1985)
2. Balfanz, D., Durfee, G., Shankar, N., Smetters, D., Staddon, J., Wong, H.C.: Secret handshakes from pairing-based key agreements. In: Proceedings of the Symposium on Security and Privacy (2003)
3. Büttner, C., Huss, S.A.: A novel anonymous authenticated key agreement protocol for vehicular ad hoc networks. In: Proceedings of the 1st International Conference on Information Systems Security and Privacy, ICISSP (2015)
4. Camenisch, J.L., Lysyanskaya, A.: An efficient system for non-transferable anonymous credentials with optional anonymity revocation. In: Pfitzmann, B. (ed.) EUROCRYPT 2001. LNCS, vol. 2045, pp. 93–118. Springer, Heidelberg (2001)
5. Castelluccia, C., Jarecki, S., Tsudik, G.: Secret handshakes from CA-oblivious encryption. In: Lee, P.J. (ed.) ASIACRYPT 2004. LNCS, vol. 3329, pp. 293–307. Springer, Heidelberg (2004)
6. Chaum, D., van Heyst, E.: Group signatures. In: Davies, D.W. (ed.) EUROCRYPT 1991. LNCS, vol. 547, pp. 257–265. Springer, Heidelberg (1991)
7. ETSI EN 302 636-4-1: Intelligent Transport Systems (ITS); Vehicular Communications; GeoNetworking; Part 4: Geographical addressing and forwarding for point-to-point and point-to-multipoint communications; Sub-part 1: Media-Independent Functionality (2013)
8. ETSI ES 202 663: Intelligent Transport Systems (ITS); European profile standard for the physical and medium access control layer of Intelligent Transport Systems operating in the 5 GHz frequency band (2009)
9. ETSI TS 102 636-6-1: Intelligent Transport Systems (ITS); Vehicular Communications; GeoNetworking; Part 6: Internet Integration; Sub-part 1: Transmission of IPv6 Packets over GeoNetworking Protocols (2011)
10. ETSI TS 102 890–2: Intelligent Transport Systems (ITS); Facilities Layer Function, Part 2: Services Announcement (2010)
11. ETSI TS 103 097: Intelligent Transport Systems (ITS); Security; Security header and certificate formats (2013)
12. Feiri, M., Petit, J., Kargl, F.: Efficient and secure storage of private keys for pseudonymous vehicular communication. In: Proceedings of the 2013 ACM Workshop on Security, Privacy and Dependability for Cyber Vehicles, CyCAR 2013 (2013)
13. Forschungsgesellschaft für Straßen- und Verkehrswesen: Handbuch für die Bemessung von Straßenverkehrsanlagen (HBS) (2005)

14. Freudiger, J., Raya, M., Hubaux, J.-P.: Self-organized anonymous authentication in mobile ad hoc networks. In: Chen, Y., Dimitriou, T.D., Zhou, J. (eds.) SecureComm 2009. LNICST, vol. 19, pp. 350–372. Springer, Heidelberg (2009)
15. IEEE 1609.2: Standard for Wireless Access in Vehicular Environments - Security Services for Applications and Management Messages, IEEE Standard 1609.2 (2013)
16. Lin, X., Lu, R., Zhu, H., Ho, P.H., Shen, X., Cao, Z.: ASRPAKE: an anonymous secure routing protocol with authenticated key exchange for wireless ad hoc networks. In: Proceedings of the IEEE International Conference on Communications, ICC. IEEE (2007)
17. Rivest, R.L., Shamir, A., Tauman, Y.: How to leak a secret. In: Boyd, C. (ed.) ASIACRYPT 2001. LNCS, vol. 2248, p. 552. Springer, Heidelberg (2001)
18. Schünemann, B.: V2X simulation runtime infrastructure VSimRTI: an assessment tool to design smart traffic management systems. Comput. Netw. **55**, 3189–3198 (2011)
19. Sweeney, L.: k-anonymity: a model for protecting privacy. Int. J. Uncertainty Fuzziness Knowl. Based Syst. **10**, 557–570 (2002)
20. Vanstone, S.A., Mullin, R.C., Agnew, G.B.: Elliptic curve encryption systems. Patent, US 6141420 (2000)

Implicit Authentication for Smartphone Security

Wei-Han Lee$^{(\boxtimes)}$ and Ruby B. Lee

Princeton Architecture Lab for Multimedia and Security (PALMS),
Department of Electrical Engineering, Princeton University,
Princeton, NJ, USA
{weihanl,rblee}@princeton.edu
http://www.springer.com/lncs

Abstract. Common authentication methods based on passwords, or fingerprints in smartphones, depend on user participation. They do not protect against the threat of an attacker getting hold of the phone after the user has been authenticated. Using a victim's smartphone, the attacker can launch impersonation attacks, which threaten the data that can be accessed from the smartphone and also the security of other users in the network. In this paper, we propose an implicit authentication method using the sensors already built into smartphones. We utilize machine learning algorithms for smartphones to continuously and implicitly authenticate the current user. We compare two typical machine learning methods, SVM and KRR, for authenticating the user. We show that our method achieves high performance (more than 90 % authentication accuracy) and high efficiency. Our method needs less than 10 s to train the model and 20 s to detect an abnormal user. We also show that the combination of more sensors provides better accuracy. Furthermore, our method enables adjusting the security level by changing the sampling rate.

Keywords: Smartphone · Security · Authentication · Support Vector Machine (SVM) · Sensors · Accelerometer · Orientation sensor · Magnetometer · Android

1   Introduction

In recent years, the use of mobile devices like smartphones and tablets has increased dramatically. Smartphones are becoming an important means for accessing various online services, such as online social networks, email and cloud computing. Many applications and websites allow users to store their information, including passwords and other security-critical information. Users also save various contacts, photos, schedules, email, messages and other personal information in their smartphones. They do not want personal and sensitive information to be leaked to others without their permission. However, the smartphone is easily stolen, and the attacker can have access to the personal information stored in the smartphone. Furthermore, the attacker can steal the victim's identity and

© Springer International Publishing Switzerland 2015
O. Camp et al. (Eds.): ICISSP 2015, CCIS 576, pp. 160–176, 2015.
DOI: 10.1007/978-3-319-27668-7_10

launch impersonation attacks in networks, which could threaten the victim's sensitive information like his bank account and confidential data stored in the cloud, as well as the security of networks, especially online social networks. Therefore, providing reliable access control of the information stored on smartphones, or accessible through smartphones, is very important. But, first, it is essential to be able to authenticate the legitimate user of the smartphone, and distinguish him or her from other unauthorized users. It is also important to continue to authenticate a user, since his smartphone may be taken over by an attacker after the legitimate user has been authenticated.

Passwords are currently the most common form of authentication. However, they suffer from several weaknesses. Passwords are vulnerable to attacks because they are easily guessed. They suffer from social engineering attacks, like phishing, pretexting, etc. The usability issue is also a serious factor, since users do not like to have to enter, and reenter, passwords or pins. A study [1] shows that 64 % of users do not use passwords or pins as an authentication mechanism on their smartphones. Hence, this paper proposes a means of implicit and continuous authentication, beyond the initial authentication by password, pin or biometric (e.g., fingerprint).

Implicit authentication does not rely on the direct involvement of the user, but is closely related to his/her biometric behavior, habits or living environment. We propose a form of implicit authentication realized by building the user's profile based on measurements from various sensors already present in a typical smartphone. Specifically, sensor measurements within the smartphones can reflect users' behavior patterns and environment characteristics. The recent development and integration of sensor technologies in smartphones, and advances in modeling user behavior create new opportunities for better smartphone security.

In this paper, we propose a multi-sensor-based system to achieve continuous and implicit authentication for smartphone users. The system leverages data collected by three sensors: accelerometer, orientation sensor, and magnetometer, in a smartphone, and then trains a user's profile using the SVM machine learning technique. The system continuously authenticates the current user without interrupting user-smartphone interactions. The smartphone's security system is alerted once abnormal usage is detected by our implicit authentication mechanism, so that access to sensitive information can be shut down or restricted appropriately, and further checking and remediation actions can be taken. Our authentication mechanism can adaptively update a user's profile every day considering that the user's pattern may change slightly with time. Our experimental results on two different data sets show the effectiveness of our proposed idea. It only takes less than 10 s to train the model everyday and 20 s to detect abnormal usage of the smartphone, while achieving high accuracy (90 %, up to 95 %).

We arrived at our three-sensor solution by first testing the performance on a single-sensor-based system, considering each of the accelerometer, the orientation sensor and the magnetometer. We found that the authentication accuracy for measurements from the orientation sensor alone is worse than that of the accelerometer alone or the magnetometer alone. Then, we test a two-sensor-based system, using pairwise combinations from these three sensors. This showed that the combination of multiple sensors can improve the accuracy of the resulting authentication. We then combined the measurements from all three sensors, and showed that while there was a slight performance improvement, this incremental improvement is much less than going from one to two sensors, and the authentication accuracy is already 90 %, reaching 95 %. We also show that our method allows the users to adjust their security levels by changing the sampling rate of the collected data. Furthermore, we compare our method with another popular machine learning method, kernel ridge regression (KRR), and show that our proposed method outperforms KRR.

The main contributions of our paper are summarized below:

- We propose a multi-sensor-based system to achieve continuous and implicit authentication, which is accurate, efficient and flexible.
- We compare our three-sensor-based method with single-sensor and twosensor-based methods on two real data sets. Our three-sensor-based method is shown to have the best performance.
- We also analyze the balance between the authentication accuracy and the training time. We give a reasonable trade-off with respect to the sampling rate and the data size, that is practical and meaningful in the real world environment of commodity smartphone users.
- We compare our SVM method with a method based on KRR, and show that our SVM method outperforms the KRR method.

Table 1. Sensors enabled in some popular smartphones.

Sensor	Nexus 5	iphone 5s	Galaxy S5
accelerometer	Yes	Yes	Yes
gyroscope	Yes	Yes	Yes
magnetic field	Yes	Yes	Yes
light	Yes	Yes	Yes
proximity	Yes	Yes	Yes
pressure	Yes	No	Yes
orientation	Yes	No	No
temperature	No	No	No
GPS	Yes	Yes	Yes
Network	Yes	Yes	Yes
MIC	Yes	Yes	Yes
camera	Yes	Yes	Yes

Table 2. Sensor measurements, common usage and whether applications need the user's permission to access measurements.

Sensor	Description	Common use	Permission
accelerometer	Measures the acceleration force on all three physical axes	Motion detection	No
orientation	Measures degrees of rotation on all three physical axes	Rotation detection	No
magnetometer	Measures the geomagnetic field for all three physical axes	compass	No
gyroscope	Measures a device's rate of rotation on all three physical axes	Rotation detection	No
light	Measures the ambient light level	Environment detection	No
proximity	Measures the proximity of an object relative to the view screen	Phone position during a call	No
pressure	Measures the ambient air pressure	Environment detection	No
temperature	Measures the ambient temperature	Environment detection	No
GPS	Positioning	Positioning	Yes
network	Provide user connection to internet	Connectivity, location, surfing patterns	Yes
microphone	Record voice	Speech recognition	Yes
camera	Record image	Face recognition	Yes

2 Background

2.1 Smartphone Inputs and Sensors

A unique feature of a smartphone is that it is equipped with a lot of sensors. Table 1 lists some common sensors in some of the most popular smartphones. Table 2 lists the sensors' functionality, description of the measurements made, what it can be used for in terms of user or smartphone authentication, and whether Android permissions are required to read the sensor's measurements.

Smartphone sensor information include measurements from an accelerometer, orientation sensor, magnetometer, gyroscope, ambient light, proximity sensor, barometric pressure and temperature. Other more privacy sensitive inputs include a user's location as measured by his GPS location, WLAN, cell tower ID and Bluetooth connections. Also privacy sensitive are audio and video inputs like the microphone and camera. These privacy sensitive inputs require Android permissions. The contacts, running apps, apps' network communication patterns, browsing history, screen on/off state, battery status and so on, can also help to characterize a user. Since we would like to perform implicit authentication, we prefer those sensors that do not require explicit Android permissions, and are commonly available on smartphones.

2.2 Related Work

Table 3 summarizes and compares our work with past work on sensor-based authentication.

With the increasing development of mobile sensing technology, collecting many measurements through sensors in smartphones is now becoming not only

Table 3. Comparison of our three-sensor SVM method with state-of-the-art research in implicit authentication (if the information is given in the paper cited, otherwise it is shown as n.a. (not available)). FP is false positive rate and FN is false negative rate. train means the time for training the model and test means the time for detecting the abnormal usage. The script column shows whether a user has to follow a script. If a script is required, we can not achieve implicit authentication without user participation.

	Devices	Sensors	Method	Accuracy	Detecting time	Script
Our method	Nexus 5 Android	orientation, magnetometer, accelerometer	SVM	90.23 %	train:6.07s test:20s	No
Kayacik et al. [2]	Android	light, orientation, magnetometer, accelerometer	temporal &spatial model	n.a.	train: n.a. test:$\geq$122s	No
Zhu et al. [3]	Nexus S	orientation, magnetometer, accelerometer	n-gram language model	71.3 %	n.a.	Yes
Buthpitiya et al. [4]	n.a.	GPS	n-gram model on location	86.6 %	train:n.a. test:$\geq$30 min	No
Trojahn et al. [5]	HTC Desire	screen	keystroke &hand-writing	FP:11 % FN:16 %	n.a.	Yes
Li et al. [6]	Motorola Droid	screen	sliding pattern	95.7 %	train: n.a. test:0.648s	Yes
Nickel et al. [7]	Motorola Milestone	accelerometer	K-NN	FP:4 % FN:22 %	train:1.5 min test:30s	Yes

possible, but quite easy through, for example, Android sensor APIs. Mobile sensing applications, such as the CMU MobiSens [8], run as a service in the background and can constantly collect sensors' information from smartphones. Sensors can be either hard sensors (e.g., accelerometers) that are physicallysensing devices or soft sensors that record information of a phone's running status (e.g., screen on/off).

Continuous authentication on smartphones is likely to become an interesting new research area, given the easily accessible data today in smartphones.

In [2], a lightweight, and temporally &spatially aware user behavior model is proposed for authentication based on both hard and soft sensors. They considered four different attacks (uninformed outsider, uninformed insider, informed outsider and informed insider) and showed that even the informed insider can be detected in 717 s. However, they did not quantitatively show the accuracy of their method. In comparison, our method not only clearly shows high accuracy performance but also requires much less detection time (e.g., we only need 20 s to detect an abnormal user while training the profiles for less than 10 s.)

SenSec [3] constantly collects data from the accelerometer, orientation sensor and magnetometer, to construct the gesture model while the user is using the device. SenSec is shown to achieve an accuracy of 75 % in identifying users and 71.3 % in detecting the non-owners. However, they ask users to follow a script, i.e., a specific series of actions, for authentication. In comparison, we do not need users to follow a specific script while still getting better authentication accuracy, higher than 90 %.

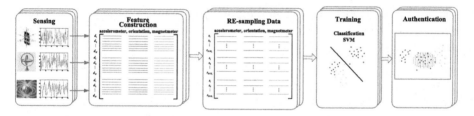

Fig. 1. In our method, we first construct a vector at each sample time by using sensors' data. For example, our three-sensor-based method uses 9 values from the accelerometer, magnetometer and orientation sensor in a smartphone. After that, we re-sample the data collected from the sensors. Then, we train the re-sampled data with the SVM technique to get a user's profile. Based on the user's profile, we can do the implicit authentication.

In [4], an n-gram geo-based model is proposed for modeling a user's mobility pattern. They use the GPS sensor to demonstrate that the system can detect abnormal activities (e.g., a phone being stolen) by analyzing a user's location history, and the accuracy they achieve is 86.6 %. However, they just utilize a single sensor for authentication, which largely limits their performance. By exploiting multiple sensors, our method achieves better accuracy.

Biometric-based systems have also been used to achieve continuous and unobservable authentication for smartphones [5–7]. However, they ask users to follow a script for authentication. In comparison, we do not need users to follow a specific script while still getting good authentication accuracy. [5] developed a mixture of a keystroke-based and a handwriting-based method to realize authentication through the screen sensor. Their approach has 11 % false acceptance rate and 16 % false rejection rate. [6] proposed another biometric method to do authentication for smartphones. They exploited five basic movements (sliding up, down, right, left and tapping) and the related combinations as the user's features, to perform authentication. An accelerometer-based biometric gait recognition to authenticate smartphones using k-NN algorithm was proposed in [7]. Their work is based on the assumption that different people have different walking patterns. Their process only takes 30 s. However, their approach asks the users to follow a script, where they just record the data when the user is walking. In comparison, we do not need the user to follow any script, which means that we can provide continuous protection without user interaction, while their approach can only guarantee security for walking users.

The fact that sensors reflect an individual's behavior and environment can be used for authentication as well as for new attacks. [9] proposed an attack to infer a user's input on a telephone key pad from measurements of the orientation sensor. They used the accelerometer to detect when the user is using a smartphone, and predicted the PIN through the use of orientation sensor measurements.

Sensors also reflect environmental information, which can be used to reveal some sensitive information. By using measurements from an accelerometer on a smartphone to record the vibrations from a nearby keyboard [10], the authors could decode the context. In [11], the authors show that the gyroscope can record the vibration of acoustic signals, and such information can be used to derive the credit card number.

3 Key Ideas

Some past work only consider one sensor for authentication [4–7]. We will show that the authentication accuracy can be improved by taking other sensors into consideration. We propose a multi-sensor-based technology with a machine learning method for implicit authentication, which only takes a short time to detect the abnormal user, but also needs less than 10 s to retrain the user's profile. First, we collect the data from the selected sensors. Then, we use the SVM technique as the classification algorithm to differentiate the usage patterns of various users and authenticate the user of the smartphone.

Our methodology can be extended to other sensors in a straight-forward manner. Figure 1 shows our methodology, and the key ideas are presented below.

3.1 Sensor Selection

There are a lot of sensors built into smartphones nowadays as shown in Tables 1 and 2. With smartphones becoming more connected with our daily lives, a lot of personal information can be stored in the sensors. The goal is to choose a small set of sensors that can accurately represent a user's characteristics. In this paper, we experiment with three sensors that are commonly found in smartphones: accelerometers, orientation sensors and magnetometers. They also represent different information about the user's behavior and environment: the accelerometer can detect coarse-grained motion of a user like how he walks [7], the orientation sensor can detect fine-grained motion of a user like how he holds a smartphone [9], and the magnetometer measurements can perhaps be useful in representing his environment. Furthermore, these sensors do not need the user's permission to be used in Android applications (Table 2), which is useful for continuous monitoring for implicit authentication.

Also, our method using these three sensors does not need the user to perform a sequence of actions dictated by a script hence facilitating implicit authentication. Note that our method is not limited to these three sensors, but can be easily generalized to different selections of hard or soft sensors, or to incorporate more sensors.

3.2 Data Sets and Re-sampling

We use two data sets, a new one which we collected locally by ourselves which we call the PU data set, and another data set which we obtained from the authors of a published paper [2], which we call the GCU data set.

The PU data set is collected from 4 graduate students in Princeton University in 2014 based on the smartphone, Google Nexus 5 with Android 4.4. It contains sensor data from the accelerometer, orientation sensor and magnetometer with a sampling rate of 5 Hz. The duration of the data collected is approximately 5 days for each user.

Our pseudo code for implicit data collection in Android smartphones is given in Listing 1. Our application contains two parts. The first part is an Activity, which is a user interface on the screen. The second part is a Service, which is running in the background to collect data. Each sensor measurement consists of three values, so we construct a vector from these nine values from three sensors. We use different sampling rates as a factor in our experiments, to construct data points.

We use the second data set, called the GCU dataset version 2 [2], for comparison. This is collected from 4 users consisting of staff and students of Glasgow Caledonian University. The data was collected in 2014 from Android devices and contains sensor data from wifi networks, cell towers, application use, light and sound levels, acceleration, rotation, magnetic field and device system statistics. The duration of the data collected is approximately 3 weeks. For better comparison with our PU data set, we only use the data collected from the accelerometer, orientation sensor and magnetometer.

Listing 1. Pseudo code for PU dataset collection using Android smartphones.

```
1   In Activity.java
2   protected onCreate(Bundle Instance){
3     register a BroadcastReceiver;
4     set ContentViews and Buttons on the screen;
5   }
6   private start_button = new Button.OnClickListener() {
7     start Service.java to collect and record data;
8   }
9   private stop_button = new Button.OnClickListener() {
10    stop Service.java;
11  }
12  In Service.java
13  private onStart(Intent intent, int startId) {
14    get Sensor Service ss;
15  for (Sensor s : sensors) {
16    ss register a sensorEventListener s;
17  }
18  private sensorEventListener = new SensorEventListener() {
19    public onSensorChanged(SensorEvent event) {
20      case Sensor.TYPE_ACCELEROMETER:{
21        record data with time stamp in memory.
22        send data to Activity.java and show on the screen.
23      }
24      case Sensor.TYPE_ORIENTATION:{
25        record data with time stamp in memory.
26        send data to Activity.java and show on the screen.
27      }
28      case Sensor.TYPE_MAGNETIC_FIELD:{
29        record data with time stamp in memory.
30        send data to Activity.java and show on the screen.
31      }
32    }
33  }
```

The sensor measurements originally obtained are too large to process directly. Hence, we use a re-sampling process to not only reduce the computational complexity but also reduce the effect of noise by averaging the data points. For example, if we want to reduce the data set by 5 times, we average 5 contiguous data points into one data point. In Sect. 4, we will show that the time for training a user's profile can be significantly reduced by re-sampling.

3.3   Support Vector Machines

The classification method used by prior work typical did not give very accurate results. Hence, we propose the use of the SVM technique for better authentication accuracy.

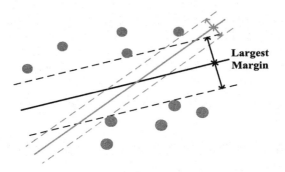

Fig. 2. Illustrating SVM. The purpose of SVM is to find the largest margin separating two groups of data. The black dotted lines represent the largest margin, whereas the green dotted lines do not give the largest margin (Color figure online).

Support Vector Machines (SVMs) are state-of-the-art large margin classifiers, which represent a class of supervised machine learning algorithms first introduced by [12]. SVMs have recently gained popularity for human activity recognition on smartphones [13]. In this section, we provide a brief review of the related theory of SVMs [12,14].

After obtaining the features from sensors, we use SVM as the classification algorithm in the system. The training data is represented as $\mathcal{D} = \{(\boldsymbol{x}_i, \boldsymbol{y}_i) \in \mathcal{X} \times \mathcal{Y} : i = 1, 2, \ldots, n\}$ for n data-label pairs. For binary classification, the data space is $\mathcal{X} = \mathbb{R}^d$ and the label set is $\mathcal{Y} = \{-1, +1\}$. The predictor $\boldsymbol{w}$ is $\mathcal{X} \to \mathcal{Y}$. The objective function is $J(\boldsymbol{w}, \mathcal{D})$. The SVM finds a hyperplane in the training inputs to separate two different data sets such that the margin is maximized. Figure 2 illustrates the concept of SVM classification. A margin is the distance from the hyperplane to a boundary data point. The boundary point is called a support vector and there may exist many support vectors. The most popular method of training such a linear classifier is by solving a regularized convex optimization problem:

$$\boldsymbol{w}^* = \mathrm{argmin}_{\boldsymbol{w} \in \mathbb{R}^d} \frac{\lambda}{2} \|\boldsymbol{w}\|^2 + \frac{1}{n} \sum_{i=1}^n l\left(\boldsymbol{w}, \boldsymbol{x}_i, y_i\right) \tag{1}$$

where

$$l\left(\boldsymbol{w}, x, y\right) = \max\left(1 - y\boldsymbol{w}^T\boldsymbol{x}, 0\right) \qquad (2)$$

The margin is $\frac{2}{\|w\|}$ in SVM. So, Eq. 1 minimizes the reciprocal of the margin (first part) and the misclassification loss (second part). The loss function in SVM is the Hinge loss (Eq. 2) [15].

Sometimes, we need to map the original data points to a higher dimensional space by using a kernel function so as to make training inputs easier to separate. In our classification, we label the smartphone owner's data as positive and all the other users' data as negative. Then, we exploit such a model to do authentication. Ideally, only the user who is the owner of the smartphone is authenticated, and any other user is not authenticated. In our experiments, we selected LIBSVM [16] to implement the SVM. The input of our experiment is n positive points from the legitimate user and n negative data points from randomly selected n other users. The output is the user's profile for the legitimate user.

3.4   Kernel Ridge Regression

For comparison, we utilize another popular classification method, kernel ridge regression (KRR) [17], to train the user's model. The KRR is a regularized least square method for classification and regression. It is similar to an SVM, except that a different objective is being optimized, which does not put emphasis on points close to the decision boundary. The solution depends on all the training examples instead of a subset of support vectors. The classifier is obtained by solving an optimization problem:

$$\boldsymbol{w}^* = \operatorname{argmin}_{\boldsymbol{w} \in \mathbb{R}^d} \rho\|\boldsymbol{w}\|^2 + \frac{1}{n}\sum_{i=1}^{n}\left(\boldsymbol{w}^T\boldsymbol{x} - y\right)^2 \qquad (3)$$

An advantage of kernel ridge regression is that the optimization solution has an analytic solution, which can be solved efficiently. The solution of KRR is as follows [18]:

$$\boldsymbol{w}^* = [\boldsymbol{S} + \rho\boldsymbol{I}]^{-1}\boldsymbol{X}\boldsymbol{y} \qquad (4)$$

4   Experimental Results

Figure 1 shows the steps in our experiments. The following are some settings in our experiments:

- We use both the PU data set and the GCU data set.
- We use accelerometer, magnetometer and orientation sensors (can be extended to other sensors).
- We re-sample the data by averaging the original data, with the sampling rate changing from 1 s to 20 min.
- Each data is a 9-dimensional vector (three values for each sensor). We use SVM to train the data to obtain a user's profile.

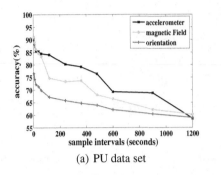 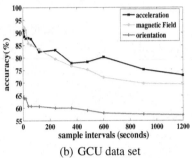

(a) PU data set   (b) GCU data set

Fig. 3. Authentication accuracy for single sensor system in (a) the PU data set, and (b) the GCU data set. Higher sampling rates give better accuracy for each sensor. The accelerometer and magnetometer have better performance than the orientation sensor. The reason is that both of them record a user's longer term characteristics, where the accelerometer somehow represents a user's walking style and the magnetometer records a user's general environment. However, the orientation sensor represents how the user holds a smartphone, which is more variable.

- We label one user's data as positive and the other users' data as negative, and randomly pick equivalent data from both positive and negative sets.
- We experiment with data from one sensor, a pair of two sensors, and all three sensors to train the user's profile. We show that multi-sensor-based authentication indeed improves the authentication accuracy.
- In our experiments, we use 10-fold cross validation, which means that the size of training data over the size of training data and testing data is 1/10.

4.1 Single-Sensor Authentication

From Fig. 3, we observe the single-sensor-based system in both the PU data set and the GCU data set. First, we find that the accuracy increases with faster sampling rate because we use more detailed information from each sensor. Second, an interesting finding is that the accelerometer and the magnetometer have much better accuracy performance than the orientation sensor, especially for the GCU data set. We think this is because they both represent a user's longer-term patterns of movement (as measured by the accelerometer) and his general environment (as measured by the magnetometer). The orientation sensor represents how the user holds a smartphone [9], which may be more variable. Therefore, the accelerometer and magnetometer have better authentication accuracy. The difference is more marked in the GCU data set, but the overall relative accuracy of the three sensors is the same in both data sets. The accuracy is below 90 % even for fast sampling rates like 10 s (see also Table 4).

4.2 Two-Sensor Authentication

Figure 4 shows that for all pairwise combinations, accuracy increases with faster sampling rate. The combination of data from two sensors indeed gives better

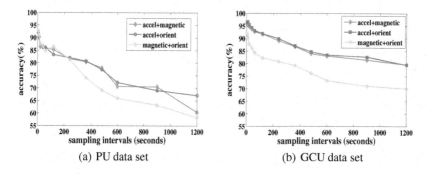

(a) PU data set   (b) GCU data set

Fig. 4. Authentication accuracy with SVM for a combination of two sensors, for (a) the PU data set, and (b) the GCU data set. The higher sampling rate gives better accuracy for each sensor.

authentication accuracy than using a single sensor (see Table 4). The average improvement from one sensor to two sensors is 7.4 % in PU data set (14.6 % in GCU data set) when the sampling rate is 20 s. Another interesting finding is that using a combination of magnetometer and orientation sensors is worse than the other two pairs which include an accelerometer. In fact, the combination of magnetometer and orientation sensors is not necessarily better than using just the accelerometer (see also Table 4). Therefore, choosing good sensors is very important. Also, using higher sampling rate gives better accuracy.

4.3 Three-Sensor Authentication

Now, we compare the three-sensor-based system with one and two sensor-based authentication experiments. From Fig. 5 and Table 4, we observe that the three-sensor results give the best authentication accuracy, as represented by the top line with triangles in both data sets, seen more clearly as the highest value in each column in Table 4. Again, we find that the accuracy increases with faster sampling rates because we use more detailed information from each sensor.

4.4 Training Time vs. Sampling Rate

In the rest of the evaluations below, we use the three-sensor-based system, since it has the best authentication accuracy.

From Fig. 5 and Table 4, when the sampling rate is higher than 4 min (samples every 240 s or less), the accuracy in the PU data set is better than 80 %, while that in the GCU data set is better than 90 %. The average improvement from two sensors to three sensors is 3.3 % in PU data set (4.4 % in GCU data set) when the sampling rate is 20 s. Furthermore, when the sampling rate is higher than 20 s, the accuracy in the PU data set is better than 90 %, while that in the GCU data set is better than 95 %.

Figure 6 and Table 5 shows that a higher sampling rate (smaller sampling interval) needs more time to train a user's profile. The time exponentially

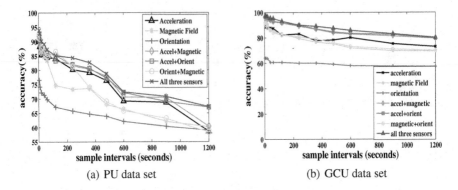

(a) PU data set   (b) GCU data set

Fig. 5. Authentication accuracy for single sensors, two sensors and three sensors, for the PU data set and the GCU data set. The higher sampling rate has better accuracy for each combination of sensors. Two sensors give better accuracy than using a single sensor, and three sensors further improves the accuracy.

increases with the increase of the sampling rate. It is a trade-off between security and convenience. However, the good news is that when the sampling interval is about 20 s, it only needs less than 10 s in the PU data set (and roughly 1 s in the GCU data set) to train a user's profile, but the accuracy is higher than 90 % (and 95 % in the GCU data set), as seen from Table 4. It means that a user only needs to spend less than 10 s to train a new model to do the implicit authentication for the whole day in the PU data set and only 1 second for the GCU data set.

These findings validate the effectiveness of our method and its feasibility for real-world applications. Furthermore, our method can be customized for users. They can change their security level by changing the sampling rate of the sensors in their smartphones.

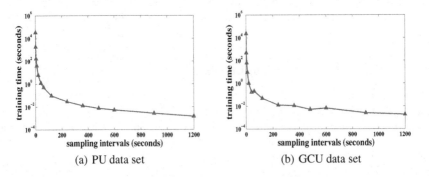

(a) PU data set   (b) GCU data set

Fig. 6. (a),(b) Represent respectively the time for training a user's profile by using the SVM algorithm for three-sensors-based system in the PU data set and the GCU data set.

Table 4. The accuracy (%) vs. sampling rate in both PU data set and GCU data set for all combinations of 1, 2 or 3 sensors.

Sampling rate (s)	5	10	20	40	60	120	240	360	480	600	900	1200
acc(PU)	90.1	88.3	85.4	85.3	84.5	84.0	80.2	79.2	76.4	69.2	68.8	58.6
mag(PU)	91.0	88.9	86.2	84.6	83.4	74.7	73.3	73.7	68.0	66.4	62.2	60.2
ori(PU)	76.5	74.2	72.2	71.3	69.8	67.1	65.8	64.7	63.9	62.1	60.4	59.0
acc+mag(PU)	92.0	90.0	86.4	86.6	85.9	85.3	81.5	80.3	77.9	70.6	70.5	60.4
acc+ori(PU)	91.8	90.3	87.7	86.2	86.1	83.3	82.0	80.6	77.3	72.2	69.1	67.1
mag+ori(PU)	92.8	91.1	87.7	86.7	84.7	86.5	81.3	74.0	69.1	65.9	63.2	58.3
all(PU)	93.9	92.8	90.1	89.1	87.2	85.2	84.3	82.7	78.7	72.4	70.8	67.2
acc(GCU)	91.0	88.4	87.8	87.9	87.5	82.4	83.1	77.8	78.3	80.2	75.3	73.0
mag(GCU)	92.3	91.2	91.0	85.7	85.2	83.4	79.5	76.7	75.3	72.2	69.8	69.5
ori(GCU)	64.2	63.9	63.8	60.8	60.7	60.6	60.0	60.0	59.1	58.0	57.5	57.3
acc+mag(GCU)	95.5	95.8	94.7	93.7	92.7	91.8	89.2	86.7	84.0	83.1	81.4	79.6
acc+ori(GCU)	96.4	96.6	95.5	94.3	93.1	92.0	90.0	87.1	84.7	83.5	82.7	79.4
mag+ori(GCU)	91.8	90.3	87.7	86.2	84.3	82.2	80.8	79.1	76.2	73.2	71.1	70.1
all(GCU)	97.4	97.1	96.7	95.7	95.3	93.1	90.0	89.1	87.5	85.9	83.1	80.2

Table 5. Time for training a user's profile by using the SVM algorithm for three sensors, for (a) the PU data set and (b) the GCU data set, respectively. We can see that the smaller sample interval (higher sampling rate) needs more time to train a user's profile. Therefore, we need to find a trade-off sampling rate to balance performance and complexity.

Sampling interval	1	2	5	10	20	40	60
training time (PU data set)	33502s	1855s	170.72s	39.85s	6.07s	1.19s	0.51s
training time (GCU Data Set)	23101s	485s	62.41s	9.43s	1.02s	0.21s	0.17s

4.5   Accuracy and Time vs. Data size

Figure 8 shows another trade-off between security and convenience. We choose a sampling interval of 10 min and a training data size ranging from 1 day to 5 days in the PU data set (and 1 day to 15 days in the GCU data set). The blue dashed line with triangles shows that the accuracy increases with the increase of training data size. The black solid line with circles shows that the training time increases with the increase of training data size.

4.6   Comparison with KRR

In order to compare our SVM performance with other machine learning methods, we apply another popular machine learning method, kernel ridge regression (KRR) to train the user's model. Figure 8 compares the performance of SVM

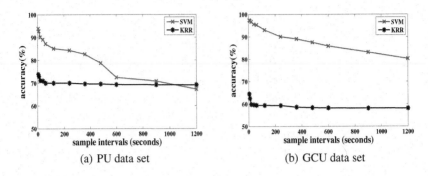

(a) PU data set

(b) GCU data set

Fig. 7. Comparison of authentication accuracy between SVM and KRR for a combination of three sensors, for (a) the PU data set, and (b) the GCU data set. Using SVM has much better performance than KRR.

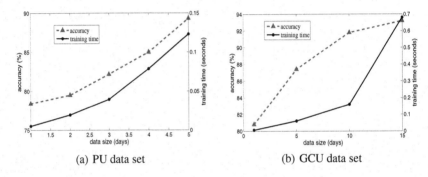

(a) PU data set

(b) GCU data set

Fig. 8. (a),(b) represent the authentication accuracy and the training time with different training data size for three sensors in the PU data set and the GCU data set. Blue dashed lines show that the larger data size has better accuracy because we use more information about the user. Black solid lines show that larger data size usually needs longer training time (Color figure online).

and KRR by using all three sensors. Figure 8 shows that using SVM gives much better authentication performance than using KRR.

5   Conclusions

In this paper, we utilize three sensors: the accelerometer, the orientation sensor and the magnetometer, which are all commonly built into smartphones today. We apply the SVM technique as the classification algorithm in the system, to distinguish the smartphone's owner versus other users, who may potentially be attackers or thieves. In our experiments, we compare the authentication results for different sampling rates and different data sizes, which shows a trade-off between accuracy performance and the computational complexity. Furthermore, we experiment with data from a single sensor and from a combination of two sensors, to compare their results with data from all three sensors. We find that the authentication accuracy for the orientation sensor degrades more than that of the other two sensors. Therefore, the data collected from the orientation sensor is not as important as that from the accelerometer and magnetometer, which tend to measure more stable, longer-term characteristics of the user's coarse-grained movements and his general physical location, respectively (Fig. 7).

We also compared using KRR versus using our SVM method, and found that SVM gave much better authentication accuracy.

Utilizing sensors to do implicit user authentication is very interesting and promising. Our work also suggests some other interesting research directions. First, we can use more detailed sensors' information to further improve the authentication accuracy. Second, we can try to combine the time information with frequency information to potentially achieve a better user profile. Many other issues relating to the user's privacy remain. It is also interesting to launch an attack through the sensors' information. Since our research shows that indeed, sensors can represent a user's characteristic behavior and physical environment, sensors can be used for both new security defenses, e.g., implicit authentication, and for new attacks. By understanding these potential attacks, we may be able to design more secure sensor systems to further improve smartphone security.

Acknowledgements. This work was supported in part by the National Science Foundation under grant NSF CNS-1218817. Any opinions, findings, and conclusions or recommendations expressed in this work are those of the authors and do not necessarily reflect the views of NSF.

References

1. ConsumerReports, Keep your phone safe: How to protect yourself from wireless threats, Consumer Reports, Technical (2013)
2. Kayacık, H.G., Just, M., Baillie, L., Aspinall, D., Micallef, N.: Data driven authentication: on the effectiveness of user behaviour modelling with mobile device sensors. In: Mobile Security Technologies (2014)
3. Zhu, J., Wu, P., Wang, X., Zhang, J.: Sensec: mobile security through passive sensing. In: International Conference on Computing, Networking and Communications (2013)
4. Buthpitiya, S., Zhang, Y., Dey, A.K., Griss, M.: n-gram geo-trace modeling. In: Pervasive Computing (2011)
5. Trojahn, M., Ortmeier, F.: Toward mobile authentication with keystroke dynamics on mobile hones and tablets. In: 2013 27th International Conference on Advanced Information Networking and Applications Workshops (WAINA) (2013)
6. Li, L., Zhao, X., Xue, G.: Unobservable re-authentication for smartphones. In: Network and Distributed System Security Symposium (2013)
7. Nickel, C., Wirtl, T., Busch, C.: Authentication of smartphone users based on the way they walk using k-nn algorithm. In: 2012 Eighth International Conference on Intelligent Information Hiding and Multimedia Signal Processing (IIH-MSP) (2012)
8. Wu, P., Zhu, J., Zhang, J.Y.: Mobisens: a versatile mobile sensing platform for real-world applications. Mob. Netw. Appl. **18**(1), 60–80 (2013)

9. Xu, Z., Bai, K., Zhu, S.: Taplogger: inferring user inputs on smartphone touch-screens using on-board motion sensors. In: Proceedings of the Fifth ACM Conference on Security and Privacy in Wireless and Mobile Networks (2012)
10. Marquardt, P., Verma, A., Carter, H., Traynor, P.: (sp) iphone: decoding vibrations from nearby keyboards using mobile phone accelerometers. In: ACM Conference on Computer and Communications Security (2011)
11. Michalevsky, Y., Boneth, D., Nakibly, G.: Gyrophone: recognizing speech from gyroscope signals. In: USENIX Security (2014)
12. Vapnik, V.N., Vapnik, V.: Statistical Learning Theory, vol. 2. Wiley, New York (1998)
13. Anguita, D., Ghio, A., Oneto, L., Parra, X., Reyes-Ortiz, J.L.: Human activity recognition on smartphones using a multiclass hardware-friendly support vector machine. In: Bravo, J., Hervás, R., Rodríguez, M. (eds.) IWAAL 2012. LNCS, vol. 7657, pp. 216–223. Springer, Heidelberg (2012)
14. Cristianini, N., Shawe-Taylor, J.: An Introduction to Support Vector Machines and Other Kernel-Based Learning Methods. Cambridge University Press, Cambridge (2000)
15. Gentile, C., Warmuth, M.K.: Linear hinge loss and average margin. In: Conference and Workshop on Neural Information Processing Systems, vol. 11, pp. 225–231 (1998)
16. Chang, C.-C., Lin, C.-J.: LIBSVM: a library for support vector machines. ACM Trans. Intell. Syst. Technol. **2**, 27:1–27:27 (2011)
17. Hastie, T., Tibshirani, R., Friedman, J., Hastie, T., Friedman, J., Tibshirani, R.: The elements of statistical learning, vol. 2(1). Springer, New York (2009)
18. Hoerl, A.E., Kennard, R.W.: Ridge regression: biased estimation for nonorthogonal problems. Technometrics **12**(1), 55–67 (1970)

Secure Communication in Civil Drones

Abdulhadi Shoufan[1]([✉]), Hassan AlNoon[2], and Joonsang Baek[1]

[1] Electrical and Computer Engineering Department, Khailfa University,
Abu Dhabi, United Arab Emirates
{abdulhadi.shoufan,joon.baek}@kustar.ac.ae
[2] Advanced Technology Consultancy L.L.C,
Emirates Advanced Investment Group L.L.C,
Abu Dhabi, United Arab Emirates
hassan.alnoon@eai.ae

Abstract. The drone technology is attracting an increasing attention in civil applications. Secure communication is a critical requirement in many scenarios to provide an acceptable level of data confidentiality, integrity, and availability. In this chapter we first present a security analysis of civil drones. Then, a light-weight hardware solution is proposed to assure the confidentiality and integrity of both command data sent by the ground station and payload data transmitted by the drone. Using the developed prototype, finally, we investigate the impact of hardware accelerators on the power consumption of these power-constrained devices. We show that the advantage of hardware as a power-efficient computation platform is not necessarily valid for drones due to the extra hardware weight.

Keywords: Civil drones · Security · Cryptoengine · Speedup · Power consumption

1 Introduction

Unmanned aerial vehicles have long been used for surveillance in homeland security. Due to their high costs, however, the effectiveness of UAVs in civil applications has always been under discussion. This circumstance contributed to the development of lower-cost platforms in the form of quadrotors or multirotors, which we refer to as civil drones (CD). The absence of mechanical linkages to vary the rotor blade pitch angle, the usage of multiple rotors and the improvements in the algorithms that controls its advanced electronic systems and sensors has allowed CDs to be of small-size and easy to fly, control, and maintain. Due to their ability to interact with the environment in close proximity safely, CDs are gaining an increasing attention in different civil application areas [1]. In environment monitoring CDs use sensors and cameras to collect information that is difficult to be obtained by helicopters because of space or cost reasons. An example for this application area is monitoring the woods, desert, animals, and agriculture. Disaster management is another application area where CDs can

© Springer International Publishing Switzerland 2015
O. Camp et al. (Eds.): ICISSP 2015, CCIS 576, pp. 177–195, 2015.
DOI: 10.1007/978-3-319-27668-7_11

give a quick overview of the size and the grade of a disaster caused by flooding, earthquake, or fire. Based on this information an efficient plan for rescue
activities can be defined and implemented. Especially in the surveillance and
law enforcement areas CDs are receiving an increasing acceptance to observe
restricted areas, state borderline, pipelines, private properties, or public events
for detecting suspicious actions and preventing terrorism.

Commercial CDs are penetrating and the importance of these devices was
recognized by the governments of many countries. Several research projects
were supported by governmental and non-governmental funding sources: USICO
(Unmanned Aerial Vehicle Safety Issues For Civil Operations) is a European
project that dealt with the operation and the safety of UAVs, e.g., for collision avoidance. CAPECON (Civil UAV Application & Economic Effectivity of
Potential Configuration Solution) is another European project, which aimed at
the specification of civilian applications for the UAVs. A major aspect of this
project is the integration of large-scale UAVs into the air traffic control system.
The design of a distributed control system for cooperative detection and monitoring using heterogeneous UAVs [2] was the subject of the project COMETS
funded by the European Union, too. μDrones is another European project which
focuses on microdrones for autonomous navigation for environment sensing. The
purpose is the development of hardware and software modules to ensure flight
stability, navigation, localization, and robustness to unexpected events. Several
topics related to networked UAVs were investigated at the Aerospace Controls
Laboratory at MIT [3]. These include sensor network design, adaptive control,
and model predictive control. Starmac is a project at Stanford University [4],
which works on autonomous collision and obstacle avoidance and task assignment
formation flight using both centralized and decentralized techniques. Additionally to these projects, an enormous amount of individual research chapters can
be found in the literature that address different topics such as specific control
systems [5–7] and obstacle avoidance approaches [8–10].

With all this attention to the functional aspects of this new technology, the
consideration of security aspects is still very limited. When it comes to security, the CD should be considered from two points of view: as a threat and as
a target. CDs are considered as security threat because they can be used for
mischievous or criminal activities. With the versatile technical possibilities, the
drones can be abused to spy on unaware individuals. Privacy and civil liberty
advocates have raised many doubts about the legitimacy of facial recognition
cameras, thermal imaging cameras, open Wi-Fi sniffers, license plate scanners
and other sensors. For example, the researchers at the London-based Sensepoint
security firm showed how to equip a drone with a software program called Snoopy
that allows the vehicle to steal data from surrounding mobile devices searching
for a Wi-Fi network. The researchers successfully demonstrated the ability of
the Snoopy application to steal Amazon, PayPal, and Yahoo credentials from
random citizens while the drone was flying over their heads in the streets of
London. Not only individual's privacy and security seem to be threatened by
the CD technology but also commercial, industrial, and governmental sectors.

Recently, a drone was used to leak behind the scenes footage of the filming of the new Star Wars movie series without the authority to be able to do anything about it. The penetration of new commercial products such as DroneShield, that help detect spying drones based on acoustic noise or radio signals is a clear evidence for the seriousness of these concerns.

CDs, however, can themselves be an attack target. The principal risks are represented by the possibility that criminals and cyber terrorists can attack unmanned aerial vehicles for several purposes such as hacking or hijacking. The chapter deals with the CD security from this latter point of view and provides an in-depth analysis of the CD communication security. Based on this analysis a hardware-based solution is proposed to obtain the required performance for cryptographic functions. The solution is investigated with respect to power consumption and compared with a software solution. This investigation shows that the cryptoprocessors advantage of low power consumption is suppressed in this application because of the additional power that is needed to carry and fly the additional hardware.

The chapter is structured as follows. Section 2 discusses the security vulnerabilities and threats of civil drones and presents a use-case based classification of the drone security requirements in terms of confidentiality, integrity, and availability. Section 3 describes the security controls built in our prototype. Section 4 describes the proposed hardware solution and Sect. 5 gives some implementation details. In Sect. 6 we analyze the performance and the power consumption of the developed prototype. Section 7 concludes the chapter.

2 Security Aspects in Civil Drone Communication

This section first describes the vulnerabilities of CDs and the threats they are exposed to, in general. Obviously, the level of threat highly depends the particular application of the drone and the security requirements on drone communication should be defined in the context of the particular use case. Therefore, this section also provides a use-case based analysis of the security level in terms of confidentiality, integrity, and confidentiality.

2.1 Civil Drone Vulnerabilities and Threats

As a flying platform, a drone is exposed to various passive and active attacks with specific impacts as summarized in the following:

Control Data Manipulation. Control data manipulation is perhaps the most critical active attack on a CMD. Sending fake control commands by an attacker may be motivated by one of the following:

1. Dislocating the CD: When CDs are used for surveillance and law enforcement purposes, then people under surveillance, who may be criminals, may work against that by trying to fly the CD away from the monitored area. Recently

GPS spoofing has been a focus of both media and academia. In the spoofing GPS attack, the counterfeit GPS signals, which resemble the real GPS signals, are broadcast to deceive a drone with a GPS receiver. These spoofed signals can cause the receiver to estimate its position to be somewhere other than the real position [11,12].

2. Physical theft (Hijacking): Some commercial microdrones are highly expensive and can fly to far distances. Having it under control, an attacker may fly a CD to a desired place where she or he can steal it physically. The physical theft may also be motivated by the intention to tamper with the device to disclose cryptographic keys or secret data.

3. Damage to persons and property: Due its light weight, a CD can fly with high speeds. A malicious attacker may use this feature to steer a CD and cause it to collide with high momentum with an arbitrary or certain target. In addition to the risk of person's injury and damage to property, such attacks may cause major legal liability problems to the CD owner or to his or her insurance provider.

Replay Attacks on Control Data. Adversaries may record control data and resend it later to misuse the CD. This kind of attack works even if control data are protected against manipulation.

Denial-of-Service Attacks (DoS). CDs are power-critical microcontroller-based systems. Any computation overhead causes additional power consumption and shortens the endurance of the CD. An attacker may use this vulnerability to flood the CD with faked or replayed commands and, thus, impair the availability of the CD. Even if the CD is able to identify these commands as fake or replay, e.g., using a verification process, this approach demands considerable computation power and time. In extreme cases, such a DoS attack may cause the CD to be completely engaged in the authentication process until the CMD battery is fully discharged. Note that flooding the CD with faked or replayed commands, as treated in this chapter, can be regarded as a DoS attack on the application layer. DoS attacks in wireless networks on lower layers such as the physical layer (jamming) and the MAC layer are well-studied in the literature [13,14] and out of the scope of this chapter.

Information Theft. The bird's-eye view provided by the CD is attracting professional photographers to take high-quality pictures or record videos from the sky. As a rule, these pictures or videos are sent to the ground station not only to save the memory usage on the CD but also for the photographer to control the picture taking or the video recording. Obviously, such data may be of high value and under copy right. Sending the data in plaintext opens the way for adversaries to record and distribute the data at low cost and to cause considerable financial loss to the professional photographer. Understandably, information theft may be exercised in many other CDs' application areas with different motives.

Information Manipulation. Information data sent by the CD may be used for critical purposes. For instance, pictures taken in surveillance and law enforcement applications may be used as means of evidence. Also, the success of a rescue plan for disaster management may rely on the picture taken by the CD. Obviously, any manipulation of these data including replay attacks may cause severe problems.

2.2   Use-Case Based Classification of CIA Security Requirement

The level of security requirements on drone communication depends on the particular application of the drone. We first developed a use-case independent classification scheme for these requirements as given in Table 1. The requirement level of confidentiality, integrity, and availability is classified into *High, Medium,* or *Low.* For that we differentiated between *control data* sent from the ground station to the drone and *information data* sent in the other direction.

Then, we conducted a research to create a comprehensive list of possible use cases as reported in media or research chapters. For each use case we tried to qualitatively assess the security risk arising through the communication channel between the drone and the ground station in both directions. Accordingly, we assigned a level for each security requirement as summarized in Table 2.

Table 1. CIA level classification scheme.

		High	Medium	Low
Control data	Confidentiality	Flight path and/or flight destination are secret or highly secret	Flight destination is roughly defined and flight path is semi-random	Flight path and flight destination are known or easily predictable
	Integrity	Manipulating commands causes high severity level such as injuries or loss of life	Manipulating commands causes medium severity level such as moderate asset damage or loss	Manipulating commands causes low or no violation
	Availability	Real-time human-controlled flight mode	Human-controlled flight mode but no hard real-time control is required	Autonomous flight mode
Information data	Confidentiality	Data is highly sensitive or has high commercial value	Data is not sensitive and has medium commercial value	Data is not sensitive and has no commercial value
	Integrity	Highly critical data with real-time requirements. Data manipulation causes high severity levels	Critical data, however, without real-time demands	Less critical data
	Availability	High data rates and real-time response to data content is required	Either high data rates or real-time response to data content are required	Low data rates and time-tolerant response (or no response) to data content is required

In the following we describe the thoughts behind the classification scheme given in Table 1 referring to some examples in the Table 2. Please note that the proposed classification of some use cases into some CIA levels may seem to be arguable. This is essentially because of the different angles from which the use case can be looked at and the different possible threats and attack scenarios. To reduce the uncertainty of our classification we followed the following approach. After agreeing on the classification scheme, each of the three authors has separately classified the uses cases. Then, we aggregated the three classifications in the following way:

1. If the three authors agreed on the same security level, we adopted it.
2. If two authors assigned the same level and the third one selected a different level, we adopted the level that was selected by two authors.
3. If the three authors selected three different levels, we assigned the level medium to the corresponding security requirement.

Apart from this, we believe that this investigation clearly reflects the sophistication of defining security requirements for drones. Identifying the appropriate security level is the first step towards selecting appropriate security controls.

CIA Levels for Control Data. The basic information embedded in control commands relates to three critical flight dynamic parameters referred to as the roll, pitch, and yaw angles; as well as to the throttle. Based on this information and on the embedded dynamic model and control mechanism, the drone moves from its current position to a new position following a certain trajectory. Thus, the control data sent by the ground station relates in the end to the new position of the drone and to the trajectory it follows to reach there. Obviously, the confidentiality level of this data is commensurate with the confidentiality level of the drone new position and trajectory. Depending on the use case this information can be critical if the attacker can model the drone and calculate the trajectory starting from sniffed commands. For instance, in the case of package delivery, this may give an attacker information about the delivery address. It is not unthinkable that drone-based delivery services will attract malicious groups to develop professional techniques for package theft. In such a case, the control data should be classified as highly confidential and appropriate security controls must be implemented. On the other hand, in many applications such as in the dam inspection scenario, the drone flight space is limited and its position in the air is almost always predictable. In such cases the control data confidentiality can be considered as low. In other cases, the drone can fly within a limited area but its trajectory should be kept secret, e.g., to reduce shooting risk. In such cases, the confidentiality level of the control data can be classified as medium. An example for these applications is the drone-based crowd surveillance and control.

Drones should follow the trajectory determined by the pilot. Manipulating the control data or sending false control data by an attacker may cause the drone to follow an undesired trajectory that may intentionally or unintentionally lead

Table 2. Classifying the CIA levels of reported use cases.

Use Case	Control Data			Information Data		
	Conf.	Int.	Ava.	Conf.	Int.	Ava.
Climate Monitoring	L	M	M	M	M	L
Glacier Dynamics Monitoring and Analysis	L	L	M	M	M	M
Volcano Monitoring and Analysis	L	L	M	M	M	M
Atmospheric Sampling	L	L	L	M	M	L
Journalism and News Gathering	M	H	M	M	M	M
Environmental Control and Monitoring	L	M	M	L	M	L
Mineral Exploration and Exploitation	M	M	M	H	M	M
Farm Monitoring / Agriculture	M	M	M	M	M	M
Remote Sensing	M	M	L	M	M	L
Pest Eradication	L	M	M	L	M	M
Predator deterrence	L	H	M	L	M	H
Scientific Research	M	M	M	M	M	M
Factory Production line malfunctions	L	H	M	L	M	M
Film Industry	M	H	H	H	M	H
Real Estate Photography	M	H	M	M	M	M
Invasive Species Identification	L	M	M	L	L	H
Archaeological / Historic Site Mapping and Inspection	L	M	M	L	M	M
Wind Turbine Inspection	L	M	M	M	M	H
Wildlife monitoring	L	M	M	L	M	M
Ship Inspection and Monitoring	M	M	M	M	L	M
library Bookshelf Monitoring	L	H	M	L	L	M
Package Delivery	H	H	M	M	H	L
Deep-Sea Fossil Fuels Scanning	H	M	M	M	M	M
Insurance Claim	L	M	M	M	H	M
Air Photography	M	M	M	M	M	M
Power lines inspection	M	M	L	H	M	H
Inspect Nuclear Installations	M	H	H	H	H	H
Nuclear Waste Transport	H	H	H	H	H	H
Dam Inspection	L	M	M	H	L	H
Railway Track Inspection	L	M	M	H	M	H
Road Inspection	L	M	M	M	L	M
Oil & Gas Pipeline Inspection	M	M	M	H	H	H
Bridge Inspection	L	M	M	H	M	M
Fire Scene Inspection	L	H	H	M	M	H
Search and Rescue	L	H	H	L	H	H
Emergency Response	M	H	H	M	H	H
Traffic Control	L	H	H	L	M	M
Poaching Activity	M	M	H	L	L	M
Disaster Site Monitoring	L	M	H	M	H	H
Forest monitoring	M	M	M	L	L	M
Perimeter Surveillance	H	M	M	M	M	M
Traffic Accident Analysis	L	M	M	M	H	M
Crowd Surveillance and Control	M	H	H	M	M	M
Borderline monitoring	H	H	L	H	H	M
Pollution Monitoring	L	H	L	L	M	L

to a damage or loss of properties (including the drone itself) or cause injuries or even loss of life. The level of control data integrity should be linked to the level of severity caused by sending false or manipulated commands. This severity level depends on the value of the drone itself, the mission costs, the value of objects that may be damaged, the density of humans or other animate being that may be injured. In many cases, the level of potential severity is obvious. This, for instance, applies to the use case Crowd Surveillance and Control, where many people can be gathered in relatively small areas. The risk of injuries by potential attacks is extremely high in this case. In contrast, a drone flying for Volcano Monitoring and Analysis is supposed to be less critical. In many applications, however, the severity level should be considered in the context of the particular use case. In the Farm/Agriculture Monitoring application, for instance, the severity level may depend on the kind of the agriculture or on the presence of farmers on field. This kind of use cases were assigned a medium integrity level in Table 2.

Drones must response to the ground station control commands whenever required immediately. The amount and the rate of control data sent to the drone depend on the use case and whether the drone flies in an autonomous mode or in a pilot-controlled mode. In the autonomous mode, the pilot usually loads mission data to the drone before starting. With the help of a GPS receiver, the drone then follows the defined path, altitude, and orientation to arrive at the final landing destination. Thus, use cases that assume autonomous flight mode do not require high-level availability for control data, as a rule. Examples for such use cases include Borderline Monitoring and Power Line Monitoring. Many use cases presume a real-time control of the drone by a human pilot for appropriate performance such as in Nuclear Waste Transport, Search and Rescue applications, or Film Industry. In such cases the availability of the control data must be provided on a high level. Some applications require human control. However, the real-time requirement on control data is not especially high because the drone mission is mainly performed in a hovering state or under very low speed. In the Air Photography, for instance, the pilot needs to find an appropriate perspective for her or his pictures. However, some amount of delay can be tolerated. So the availability level of control data can be regarded as medium.

CIA Levels for Information Data. Some commercial drones are supplied with actuators to perform some physical function on the fly such as Pesticide Spraying Drones. However, the majority of drones still serve sensory applications where data in different forms is collected on the fly and submitted to the ground station or stored on board for later processing and analysis. The confidentiality level of this data tightly relates to the use case. Images submitted by drones on missions for critical infrastructure inspection such as Oil and Gas Pipelines are classified as highly confidential, in general. Also, data collected in some commercial applications such as Mineral Exploration and Exploitation can be of high confidentiality level. In some commercial use cases such as in the Film Industry, the producer may prefer to keep the data secret within limited time frames and the confidentiality level can be classified as medium. In many other applications, the data provided by the drone is public or of less commercial and private value so that its confidentiality can be classified as low. Examples for such applications include Library Bookshelf Monitoring and Wildlife Monitoring.

Integrity is a fundamental requirement on any data. Nevertheless, the level of integrity is an important concept to describe the impact of the loss of data integrity. The integrity level required for information data gathered by the drone depends on the type of this data and its criticality in the context of the use case. In many applications, the data sensed by the drone is processed in ground station computers to determine an appropriate response. For example, drones can be supplied with thermal imaging sensors for Rescue Operations in the night or in invisible areas. Manipulating the sensor data may cause the rescue team to lose sight of injured or trapped people. In such cases the data integrity must be regarded as a high-level requirement. In some use cases the data integrity is essential to obtain accurate simulation results or precise future predictions but there is no real-time requirements or a need for urgent responses. In such cases the integrity level can be classified as medium. Examples for these use cases include Climate Monitoring and Glacier Dynamics Monitoring and Analysis. In some applications, the drone sends visual image data that are only inspected by the pilot or other operators for uncritical routine surveillance or inspection purposes. In such cases, the required level of data integrity can be described as low. Examples for such use cases are Dam inspection and Road Inspection.

The required availability level of information data mainly depends on the timing criticality of this data and its rate. Drones that send high-rate data in real-time to enable prompt response should show a high level of availability. Examples for such applications include Emergency Response and Film Production. When the data rate is low or the response time is not especially critical we classify the requirement on the availability level as medium. This is the case in many applications such as Ship Inspection and Monitoring or Air Photography. In use cases, where neither high data rates are required nor a real-time response to the data is expected, the data availability level can be classified as low. Examples for these cases include Climate Monitoring and Remote Sensing.

3   Security Controls

In this section we describe the security controls that we applied in our prototype to meet the different security requirements.

3.1   Data Confidentiality

Depending on the application, remote control data (Upstream), information data (Downstream), or both should be encrypted. For CD communication the AES algorithm is selected with a key length of 128 bit [15]. AES in its native operation mode (Electronic Code Book (ECB)) results in the same ciphertext block if the same plaintext block is encrypted, which presents a security risk. To avoid this, the Cipher Block Chaining mode (CBC) can be used. CBC encryption provides confidentiality against Chosen Plaintext Attack (CPA), which is a strong but essential requirement for secure symmetric-key encryption [16].

3.2 Data Integrity and Authenticity

To enforce Data Integrity and Authenticity we used a message authentication code scheme (MAC) that uses a symmetric key. A MAC scheme can be either proprietary, hash-based, or block-cipher based. We chose to use CBC-MAC which is block-cipher based MAC scheme so that is can share the same AES core used for encryption due to hardware resource constraints.

The high similarity between the MAC scheme and the CBC-mode of encryption is essential for the design of a compact cryptographic engine as will be detailed in Sect. 4.1. Note that message authentication code uses AES in encryption mode only in both the sender and receiver sides of communication. MAC also implicitly provides data integrity, as any change in the message will result in a different MAC value.

3.3 Resistance Against Replay-Attacks

Even encrypted and authentic messages may be captured by an attacker and replayed at a later point of time. Replayed data passes the authentication process successfully on the receiver side. Therefore, to detect replay attacks additional information is added to the message, which enables the receiver to verify the freshness of the message. The additional information can be a nonce (number used only once), time stamp, or a sequential number. In CD communication, we propose using sequential numbers against replay attacks, as these numbers can be deployed for additional purposes, specifically to detect packet loss and to restore the packet order.

3.4 Resistance to DoS Attacks

DoS attacks are versatile and can be carried out on different network layers. Countermeasures are usually specific to one or small number of attacks and operate on specific layers embedded in firewalls, network routers, switches, etc. As noted previously, we focus on a DoS on the application layer by assuming that the attacker is able to flood the CD with fake or replayed commands to affect the availability of the vehicle. In CD communication, command authentication and the replay attack countermeasure play a detective and a preventive role in the defense against DoS attacks. First, the CD keeps track of received commands and periodically determines the ratio of non-authentic commands and replay commands to the total number of received commands. If this ratio becomes higher than a specific value a DoS attack is assumed. Second, command authentication and the replay attack countermeasure perform a primary filtering of DoS commands. This means that the system components that follow the authentication process are preserved from the DoS effects. Using authentication to mitigate (not eliminate) DoS attacks is deployed in the IPSec protocol suite, for instance.

3.5   Tamper-Resistant Key Management

Key management is a challenging task that addresses key generation, key exchange, key storage, key update, and key revocation, in general. The following paragraphs describe how the proposed key management scheme works for CD communication.

Key Generation. The encryption and authentication keys are generated by the ground station based on the key generator specified in ANSI X9.17 which is a key management standard for financial institutions published by the American National Standard Institute [17]. This key generator relies on the block cipher 3DES but can use any other block cipher. In our case we use AES, as it is already available for other security functions.

Key Exchange and Storage. Key exchange and key storage are usually treated separately. In our case they are related due to the used hardware platform. As will be seen later, we use an FPGA to run the security functions on the CD. The used FPGA is SRAM-based, which means that the configuration data must be loaded to the FPGA at each start. The configuration data is stored in a small external configuration memory mounted on the same board. Thus, a permanent key storage on the FPGA is impossible. Furthermore, storing the keys in the configuration memory as a part of the configuration data poses two risks. First, if the attacker gets physical access to the CD she or he can temper with the memory chip to extract the key. Furthermore, the attacker may analyze the configuration data while transferred from the memory to the FPGA to obtain the key.

To avoid these risks we propose the following simple scheme. Before each flight, keys are generated by the ground station and written to the FPGA by wire. Wireless submission is improper as radio data can be intercepted by adversaries. The keys are stored in dedicated registers inside the FPGA. These registers can only be read by the cryptographic engine and has no read interface to outside. Writing the keys to the FPGA by wire may appear to cause an operational overhead. However, flying a CD is always preceded by a setup phase. The proposed key exchange approach can be seen as a step in this setup phase.

Key Update and Revocation. Updating symmetric keys is recommended to enhance security. The idea is to reduce the amount of data encrypted with the same key to limit the damage, if the key is compromised. Usually, symmetric keys are updated for each new message or for each new communication session. For the CD we propose updating the encryption and the authentication keys for each

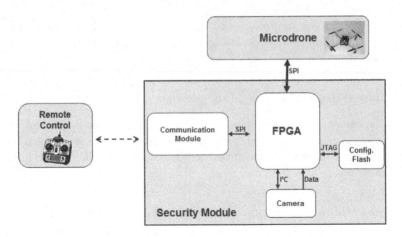

Fig. 1. General architecture of the secure CD system.

flight. The new keys are generated according to standardized key management algorithm (ANSI X9.17) and sent to the FPGA by wire as described in the previous paragraph.

The registers used to store the keys are provided by a reset input that can be activated by a special command from the ground station. The CD operator can submit this command in emergency cases when she or he loses control over the CD for any reason.

4   System Architecture

The system consists of three main components: The remote control, the drone, and an extension module connected to the drone that embeds the cryptographic engine, see Fig. 1. The hardware architecture of the extension module is depicted in Fig. 2. The architecture comprises a cryptographic engine; the on-chip JPEG encoder, which on its part embeds a camera controller; a video streamer and the control data receiver to manage the data communication; A Digital-2-PPM converter, which receives the digital control data extracted from the upstream packet and converts it back into a PPM signal (Pulse Position Modulation). In the following sections the different components of this architecture will be explained with more attention to the Cryptographic Engine as it provides the core of the security solution.

4.1   Cryptographic Engine

The Cryptographic Engine is the central part of the hardware architecture. The authentication key and the encryption key are written to the corresponding registers during the CD setup. The Cryptographic Engine serves the video streamer and the control data receiver. It expects from these modules an intermediate

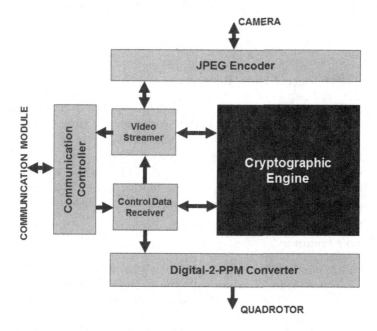

Fig. 2. General architecture of the FPGA hardware system.

MAC value, a plaintext block, and a cipher text block. The particular module indicates its need for data processing by sending a start signal, the cryptographic module also decides which module will be served next using a "fairness scheme" that was developed to prevent the data-intensive video streamer from occupying the cryptographic engine for a long time at the cost of the control data receiver. In the idle state the control data receiver is given priority over the video streamers. This is necessary because the control data includes some information for video control.

Processing Video Streamer Data. Video data are prepared and sent by the CD. Before sending the data, the Cryptographic Engine processes the video data in two stages for encryption and authentication. First, the Cryptographic Engine receives the video data block to be encrypted and either the cipher text block of the previous block or the encryption initialization vector (IV). Secondly the Cryptographic Engine is fed with the encrypted video data block and either with the intermediate MAC value or with the authentication initialization vector.

Processing Control Data. Control data are sent to the drone by remote control. The Cryptographic Engine processes the control data in two stages before sending it the to the drone. First, in the authentication stage the Cryptographic Engine receives the data block and either the intermediate MAC value or the authentication initialization vector. Secondly, in a decryption stage the

Cryptographic Engine processes either the encrypted control data block or the encryption initialization vector.

4.2   Remote Control Data Receiver

The Control Data Receiver receives control data from the communication controller in form of a 384-bit packet that is compound of three 128-bit blocks. The first block represents the encryption initialization vector IV_{enc} which is not encrypted but authenticated by the ground station. The second block is the control block that includes the actual control data in encrypted form. The third block is the MAC value of the first two blocks. These data are sent to the Cryptographic Engine for authentication and to decrypt the control data block.

4.3   Video Streamer

Control data are sent from the ground station at a low rate according to the PPM scheme. In contrast, video data are sent continuously at high rate. One image occupies many packets. The size of the packet relies on the used communication module.

Each video packet includes an 128-bit encryption initialization vector IV_{enc} (or the last cipher text block), a variable number of 128-bit video cipher text blocks, a 128-bit encrypted status block, and the 128-bit MAC value of the entire packet.

The Video Streamer receives the video data byte-wise from the JPEG Encoder through a first-in first-out memory (FIFO). Using a shift register, 16 bytes of these data are concatenated to construct a 128-bit data block. In addition to the video data, the Video Streamer constructs and appends a status block to each downstream packet. The VS controller also exchanges control signals with the Control Data Receiver, the Cryptographic Engine, the Communication Module, and the JPEG Encoder. Data is processed according to a developed abstract finite state machine which is responsible for creating the different block of encrypted data according to the stream.

4.4   Digital-2-PPM Converter

The used remote control generates a PPM frame with a length of 22 ms. For each control channel a rectangular pulse is produced, whereas the pulse width is proportional to the control value. The minimum and the maximum width is 0.7 ms or 1.5ms, respectively. The minimum distance between each two succeeding pulses is 0.4 ms. The remaining time of the 22 ms is used as a start signal.

The CD receives all the channel data at once embedded in the control block inside the control data packet. The PPM signal is generated using different counters. The first counter has a fixed preset value that depends on the clock frequency to produce the start pulse. The second counter produces the control pulse. It has a variable preset value to produce time values between the minimum and maximum width of a PPM pulse. The preset value of this counter is the 8-bit digital value of the corresponding control channel. The third counter produces the pause periods which vary between 1.8 and 0.4 ms.

4.5 Other Components

The FPGA hardware includes a communication module and a JPEG encoder that includes a controller for the camera. The JPEG encoder was adopted from [18] and adapted to suit our design.

5 Implementation

To evaluate our solution a complete system prototype was implemented. The system prototype consists of a radio transmitter, a personal computer, and a drone extended with the security module.

The drone was prototyped as a quadrotor based on the Next-Generation Universal Aerial Video Platform (NG-UAVP). The NG-UAVP is "a community-driven open source project to build a modern autonomously flying multicopter" [19]. The NG-UAVP has a special focus on expandability and configurability with a proprietary near real-time operating system and a hardware abstraction layer that enables the platform to support different hardware types and configurations. The NG-UAVP uses three microcontrollers for data acquisition and preparation on the sensor's board and for flight control.

The quadrotor is extended with the security module and a camera module. The camera used is the TCM8240MD from Toshiba with an image resolution of 640×480 pixel, a frame rate of 30 fps, and a color depth of 24 bit. One of the selection criteria of this camera was its small size of $6 \times 6 \times 4.5$ mm. The camera has an Inter-Integrated Circuit (I^2C) interface for configuration and delivers pixel data over an 8-bit parallel interface along with two lines for vertical and horizontal synchronization.

The security module is compatible with the other NG-UAVP boards. It contains mainly a communication module, an FPGA, and a flash memory for programming the FPGA. The used communication module (from the company Avisaro AG) is connected to the FPGA through a serial peripheral interface (SPI), which allows a maximum data rate of 2.8 MBit/s.

As an FPGA we use Spartan E from Xilinx. Image processing demands large memory size. The used open-source JPEG encoder works on 8×8-pixel blocks. However, data is read from the camera row by row. Thus, for the JPEG encoder to start, at least seven rows and the first 8 pixels of the 8-th row must be read first. With 640 pixel per row and 24-bit color depth a minimum memory space of $(7*640+8)*24 = 108$ kbit is required. To increase throughput, the JPEG encoder uses pipelined processing of 16 rows which demands a total memory usage of 163.840 kbit. Additional memory space is required for the encoder output buffer, for the AES Sboxes, and for the input and output FIFOs of the video streamers.

Instead of using external memory for data storage we decided to use the largest member of the Spartan E family. By this means, the design is kept simpler and data is transferred synchronously between the different FPGA components, which is essential for the performance. The FPGA works at 50 MHz clock frequency that is supplied by an external oscillator. The FPGA is configured using a SPI serial flash PROM (programmable read-only memory) from Atmel.

6   Results and Analysis

The hardware prototype was tested for the data given in Table 3. The raw frame size results from multiplying the image resolution by the color depth. Through encoding, the frame size is reduced 15 times. The encoded frame is divided by 128 to get the number of AES blocks that need to be processed for one frame.

Table 3. Image Parameters used in the Prototype Implementation.

Parameter	Value	Unit
Image resolution	640×480	pixel
Color depth	24	bit
Frame size before encoding	7372800	bit
Compression ratio	15	%
Frame size after encoding	491520	bit
No. AES blocks per frame	3840	Block

Table 4 shows a comparison between the hardware solution and a comparable software solution running on the drone microcontroller ARM7 LPC2148 clocked at 60 MHz. The comparison metrics are the timing, the power consumption, and flight time.

With respect to timing, the developed FPGA solution provides an approximately 20-time higher throughput than the software solution. The software solution only achieves a frame rate of 3.2 fps, which is clearly below acceptable rates for live feed, and therefore fails to deliver a moving picture.

With respect to power, the consumption of the hardware solution exceeds the consumption of the software solution by 3.356 watts. This amount comprises three components:

1. The power consumption of the FPGA chip as provided by the Xilinx Xpower Analyzer (0.22 watts).
2. The measured electrical power consumed by the FPGA board exclusive of the FPGA chip (0.64 watts)
3. The mechanical power needed to raise the additional weight caused by the FPGA card (2.5 watt). This value was determined using a commercial calculator as detailed below.

Table 4. A HW-SW Comparison of the Image Coding, Encryption, and Authentication.

Compared Value	Software	Hardware	Unit
Time needed to encode one JPEG frame	100	14.4	ms
Time needed to encrypt and authenticate one JPEG frame	209.6	1.54	ms
Time needed to encode, encrypt and authenticate one JPEG frame	309.6	15.9	ms
Throughput	3.2	62.8	fps
Measured drone power consumption while hovering	220	223.36	watt
Estimated flight time under maximum possible throughput	9.03	8.89	min

By comparing the pure computational power consumption, the FPGA with 0.22 watt is superior to the software solution that consumes 1.8 watt on ARM7 LPC2148. This is in line with the general understanding of FPGAs as power-efficient alternatives to software. This is valid even when we compare with the power consumed by the entire FPGA board $(0.64 + 0.22 = 0.88$ watt$)$.

In this application, however, we have to consider the power needed to carry the weight of the FPGA board. Apparently, this part is significant and it contributes to shortening the flight time by almost 1.5 %. The latter figure is based on the voltage and the capacity of the battery used in our model. These are 14 volts and 2300 mAh, respectively.

Note, however, that the actual impact on the flight time should be considered in the light of the required throughput. The advantage of the software solution is only valid when 3.2 fps or less are required. As stated before, this rate is not sufficient for moving pictures.

To determine the power needed to carry the FPGA we used eCalc which is a commercially available online tool that provides calculations for electrically driven remote controlled devices [20]. The vendor states that the calculation accuracy is 10 %. eCalc provides four different tools for RC model calculation: propeller airplanes, multicopters, ducted fan airplanes and helicopters. eCalc can be used for free however with limited capability in terms of supported models and components as well as provided output data. For our calculations we used the commercial edition of eCalc to be as specific as possible in the data entry.

It is important to note that the obtained throughput of the hardware implementation can be easily optimized by using different techniques such as parallelism and pipelining and/or by using more memory. However, for the sake of proof-of-concept implementation, the delivered throughput of 62.8 fps was satisfactory, as it is more than twice the rate needed for moving pictures.

7   Conclusions

The chapter presented a security analysis for civil drone communication. Considering security aspects of the drone technology is urgent at this stage because of the rapidly increasing interest in applying this technology in diverse private, commercial, and governmental areas. Unfortunately, civil drone vendors are still focusing on functional aspects of drones and we are not aware of any supplier that underlines the security requirements of civil drones.

The chapter highlighted that the security requirements on drones differ from one use case to another. That means that the concept of "one size fits all" should not be used when developing security controls for civil drones. This is because such a solution would be the one that provides the highest level of confidentiality, integrity, and availability regardless of the requirements of the use case. This would not only cause unnecessary costs but also affect the system performance and power consumption negatively. Furthermore, additional overhead would be caused to manage the security solution including key management.

Given the computational overhead of cryptographic operations and, at the same time, the required flexibility to add as much security controls as necessary, configurable hardware such as Field Programmable Gate Arrays offers a suitable alternative for fast and adaptable prototyping.

While developing hardware accelerators for light-weight drones, special attention should be paid to the contribution of the additional hardware weight to the total power consumption. While our case study showed this aspect as an example, more research is required to specify the relation between the speedup obtained by hardware and the additional power consumption and, thus, the flight endurance.

Although the GPS spoofing is one of the serious threats on UAV [21], it is not the focus of our chapter. This chapter is concerned more about providing information flow between CDs and ground station with confidentiality and authentication services. In order to achieve this, we used symmetric key cryptography. As mentioned previously, symmetric keys are generated by the ground station and are installed on the FPGA directly. This way, the shared keys can be protected as they will never be "online". Nevertheless, we are aware that there is a scalability issue here: If there are many CDs to deploy, sharing different keys with each drone will overload the ground station. To alleviate this, we may use public key cryptography. But this should cope with another operational issue of handling digital certificates. For this reason, we envision that identity-based cryptography [22] might be helpful. We leave this as our future work.

References

1. Quaritsch, M., Stojanovski, E., Bettstetter, C., Friedrich, G., Hellwagner, H., Rinner, B., Hofbaur, M., Shah, M.: Collaborative microdrones: applications and research challenges. In: Proceedings of the 2nd International Conference on Autonomic Computing and Communication Systems, p. 38. ICST (Institute for Computer Sciences, Social-Informatics and Telecommunications Engineering) (2008)
2. Gancet, J., Hattenberger, G., Alami, R., Lacroix, S.: Task planning and control for a multi-UAV system: architecture and algorithms. In: 2005 IEEE/RSJ International Conference on Intelligent Robots and Systems, IROS 2005, pp. 1017–1022. IEEE (2005)

3. How, J., Bethke, B., Frank, A., Dale, D., Vian, J.: Real-time indoor autonomous vehicle test environment. IEEE Control Syst. Mag. **28**, 51–64 (2008)
4. Hoffmann, G., Rajnarayan, D., Waslander, S., Dostal, D., Jang, J., Tomlin, C.: The stanford testbed of autonomous rotorcraft for multi agent control (STARMAC). In: The 23rd Digital Avionics Systems Conference, DASC 2004, vol. 2, p. 12-E. IEEE (2004)
5. Chiu, C., Lo, C.: Vision-only automatic flight control for small UAVs. IEEE Trans. Veh. Technol. **60**, 2425–2437 (2011)
6. Dierks, T., Jagannathan, S.: Output feedback control of a quadrotor UAV using neural networks. IEEE Trans. Neural Netw. **21**, 50–66 (2010)
7. Voos, H.: Nonlinear state-dependent riccati equation control of a quadrotor UAV. In: 2006 IEEE International Conference on Control Applications Computer Aided Control System Design, 2006 IEEE International Symposium on Intelligent Control, pp. 2547–2552. IEEE (2006)
8. Minguez, J., Montano, L.: Nearness diagram (ND) navigation: collision avoidance in troublesome scenarios. IEEE Trans. Robot. Autom. **20**, 45–59 (2004)
9. Yuan, C., Recktenwald, F., Mallot, H.: Visual steering of UAV in unknown environments. In: IEEE/RSJ International Conference on Intelligent Robots and Systems, IROS 2009, pp. 3906–3911. IEEE (2009)
10. Zsedrovits, T., Zarandy, A., Vanek, B., Peni, T., Bokor, J., Roska, T.: Collision avoidance for UAV using visual detection. In: 2011 IEEE International Symposium on Circuits and Systems (ISCAS), pp. 2173–2176. IEEE (2011)
11. Kim, A., Wampler, B., Goppert, J., Hwang, I., Aldridge, H.: Cyber attack vulnerabilities analysis for unmanned aerial vehicles. Infotech@ Aerospace (2012)
12. Shepard, D.P., Bhatti, J.A., Humphreys, T.E., Fansler, A.A.: Evaluation of smart grid and civilian UAV vulnerability to GPS spoofing attacks. In: Proceedings of the ION GNSS Meeting, vol. 3 (2012)
13. Pelechrinis, K., Iliofotou, M., Krishnamurthy, V.: Denial of service attacks in wireless networks: the case of jammers. Commun. Surv. Tutorials **13**, 245–257 (2011). IEEE
14. Bicakci, K., Tavli, B.: Denial-of-service attacks and countermeasures in IEEE 802.11 wireless networks. Comput. Stand. Interfaces **31**, 931–941 (2009)
15. Daemen, J., Rijmen, V.: The Design of Rijndael: AES-The Advanced Encryption Standard. Springer, Heidelberg (2002)
16. Katz, J., Lindell, Y.: Introduction to Modern Cryptography. Chapman & Hall, Boca Raton (2008)
17. NIST: American national standard for financial institution key management (wholesale) (1985). http://csrc.nist.gov/publications/fips/
18. Krepa, M.: Jpeg encoder, project, mkjpeg. http://opencores.org/
19. ANG-UAVP: Next generation universal aerial videoplatform. http://ng.uavp.ch/moin/FrontPage
20. Mueller, M.: ecalc, on-line calculator for electric driven RC models. http://www.ecalc.ch/
21. Mansfield, K., Eveleigh, T., Holzer, T.H., Sarkani, S.: Unmanned aerial vehicle smart device ground control station cyber security threat model. In: 2013 IEEE International Conference on Technologies for Homeland Security (HST), pp. 722–728. IEEE (2013)
22. Joye, M., Neven, G.: Identity-Based Cryptography, vol. 2. IOS Press, Amsterdam (2009)

Biometric Authentication

The Palm Vein Graph for Biometric Authentication

Arathi Arakala[✉], Hao Hao, Stephen Davis, and K.J. Horadam

School of Mathematical and Geospatial Sciences,
RMIT University, Melbourne, Australia
{arathi.arakala,hao.hao,stephen.davis,kathy.horadam}@rmit.edu.au
http://www.rmit.edu.au/mathsgeo

Abstract. We introduce the Palm Vein Graph, a spatial graph representation of the palm vasculature, for use as biometric identifiers. The palm vein image captured from an infra red camera undergoes several image processing steps to be represented as a graph. After image enhancement and binarisation, the palm vein features are extracted from the skeleton using a novel two stage spur removal technique. The location of the features and the connections between them are used to define a Palm Vein Graph. Palm vein graphs are compared using the Biometric Graph Matching (BGM) Algorithm. We propose a graph registration algorithm that incorporates the length of the edges between graph vertices to improve the registration process. We introduce a technique called Graph Trimming that shrinks the compared graphs to achieve faster graph matching and improved performance. We introduce 10 graph topology-based measures for comparing palm vein graphs. Experiments are conducted on a public palm vein database for full and trimmed graphs. For the full graphs, one of the introduced measures, an edge-based similarity, gives a definite improvement in matching accuracies over other published results on the same database. Trimming graphs improves matching performance markedly, especially when the compared graphs had only a small common overlap area due to displacement. For the full graphs, when the edge-based measure was combined with one of three other topological features, we demonstrate an improvement in matching accuracy.

Keywords: Biometric graph · Graph matching · Authentication · Palm vein

1 Introduction

Palm vein biometrics refers to the use of the unique vascular pattern in the human palm for authentication. Palm veins have the following advantages shared with most vascular biometrics:

1. Internal location, which makes it hard to to spoof or covertly acquire from an individual.

© Springer International Publishing Switzerland 2015
O. Camp et al. (Eds.): ICISSP 2015, CCIS 576, pp. 199–218, 2015.
DOI: 10.1007/978-3-319-27668-7_12

2. In-built liveness detection in the capture process. Palm-vein images are captured using infra-red (IR) cameras. The palm vein images are created by the property that infra red light is absorbed by the deoxygenated haemoglobin creating dark regions corresponding to the veins. The rest of the human tissues and skin reflect the IR creating bright regions in the image. This property ensures that a live subject is available for biometric capture.

3. The capture is harmless and often contactless.

4. The capture process is non-intrusive with respect to an individual's personal space and is therefore more socially acceptable.

5. A very low failure to enrol (FTE) rate.

Palm vein has been identified as the easiest [14] vascular biometric to work with as the palm area is free of hair and skin color variations thereby reducing capture noise. Also the palm vein pattern is very detailed and intricate and covers a larger area than other vascular biometrics like the dorsal vein, finger vein and wrist vein.

In this paper, which is an extension of Arakala et al. [17], we investigate the palm vein patterns captured in the PUT database [6]. The palm vein patterns are represented as biometric graphs. Biometric graphs have been used to represent fingerprints [4], retina patterns [8] and dorsal hand vein patterns [9]. The palm vein graphs are compared using Biometric Graph Matching [8]. The main contributions of this work are:

1. A novel image feature extraction process that creates a Palm Vein Graph representing the vascular structure.

2. An improved registration algorithm that enhances the speed and registration accuracy compared to the algorithm in [9].

3. Graph-based distance measures that effectively separate genuine and imposter comparisons of palm vein patterns.

4. A new approach called Graph Trimming, that speeds up graph matching and improves accuracy.

2   Image Preprocessing and Graph Extraction

2.1   The Database

This research uses palm vein images captured by researchers at the Poznan University of Technology (PUT) [6]. The database has vein pattern images from the left and right palms of 50 individuals. Each individual gave 12 samples of each palm, totalling 24 samples. Each set of 12 samples was acquired over 3 sessions with 4 images each, at least one week apart. The database was chosen for two main reasons - a large number of samples per individual palm (12 images) and 3 separate sessions, one week apart. Several other databases exist in the literature [7,12,13], but they all take samples within one session. The across session comparison is valuable to understand the natural variation that will occur in a practical scenario where individuals leave after enrolment and return after a period to be verified without remembering the exact location of their hand at enrolment.

2.2   Feature Extraction

The Infra Red (IR) capture process often generates noisy images with low contrast between the vein pattern and background. The challenges of feature extraction in the PUT database include noise of wrinkles and other skin features on the hand, non-uniform background brightness and palm displacement within and across the sessions. In order to extract features from the palm vein image, specific image processing steps are required to enhance the vein pattern. Initially, we used Discrete Fourier Transform based method, gradient-based method and thresholding method [3,5,15] to extract the vein pattern and found that they failed to provide the continuous rich structure of palm vein in the PUT database. This paper has modified and combined several noise reduction and vein enhancement methods for the better performance of palm vein graph extraction.

The automatic processing of graph feature extraction from palm vein images can be summarized in the following steps - Image pre-processing and vein enhancement; image binarisation; and skeleton and graph feature extraction. It is important to identify the Region of Interest (ROI): the spatial region where the vein patterns are most visible and useful. A well defined ROI will enable a good registration between compared palm vein graphs and will hence improve overall processing time. However, the PUT database has shown large displacements in captured images, especially between the sessions. In fact, the region in one image may only be partially present in another. In addition, if the ROI is too small, it limits the number of features that can be extracted from the image. This paper selects the entire captured image area as the ROI. Then, 40 pixels inwards from the border was masked to eliminate possible misidentification of the vein.

The palm vein image was first converted to greyscale. To avoid amplifying the noise in the image, especially in homogeneous areas, contrast-limited adaptive histogram equalization [16] was applied on a small window (8×8 pixels) to make image contrast uniform at different regions. The noise in the image was reduced using a linear anisotropic diffusion filter [10]. An example of the original image and vein-enhanced image is shown in Fig. 1(a)and (b).

Skeleton extraction requires image binarisation to distinguish vessel and background. We used the binarisation algorithm in [8] and a binarized image is shown in Fig. 1(c). The skeleton was extracted from the binary image by morphologically removing pixels on the boundaries and keeping pixels connected, shown in Fig. 1(d). Graph features of vertices and edges were then detected from the skeleton.

The Biometric Graph. The Biometric Graph is a spatial graph with features in a biometric represented as vertices and the connections between those features represented as edges. Often the spatial coordinates of the features become the spatial attributes of the corresponding vertices. In a vascular biometric, the vein bifurcations and crossovers represent the vertices and their locations in the image represent their attributes. A pair of vertices are connected by an edge if their features were linked by a vein in the original vein pattern. The biometric graph

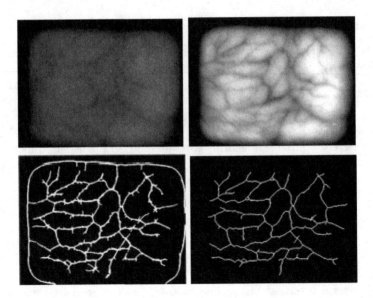

Fig. 1. This figure shows the stages that a palm vein image goes through before feature extraction. (a) (top-left) Original image; (b) (top-right) Palm vein enhanced image; (c) (bottom-left) Image after binarisation; (d) (bottom right) Skeleton extracted from binarised image.

representation for retina [8] and hand vein [9] have been shown to be extremely effective when compared to other existing templates. The main advantages of using a graphical representation is that it is concise and modular. There are no limits to the vertex, edge or graph attributes that can be added to the graph. Thus additional features deemed important for representing the biometric in the future can easily be added on the existing graph representation as new attributes.

To obtain the palm vein graph after skeletonisation, a 3 by 3 window was applied on each pixel of the skeleton to test if it was an end or a junction (crossing point or branching point). All junction and end points were marked as vertices of the graph. An edge is the link between two vertices. Edges were detected by neighborhood tracking along the skeleton. All possible branches were tracked from the junction vertex.

Palm vein graph features represent the vascular pattern with limited vertices and edges. The undesirable spurs caused by noise and tiny veins have an impact on the registration and matching process. There were two stages to remove undesirable spurs. Firstly, morphological operations were applied to remove undesirable short spurs on the skeleton. However, removing spurs also reduces the vertices on the major skeleton that may alter the shape of the skeleton. Therefore, the threshold for morphological operations involved in defining short spurs was set to 10 pixels to ensure correct representation of the vein shape. Secondly, there were a number of short to medium spurs in the skeleton due to palm principle lines and wrinkles. These lines and wrinkles vary in the captured

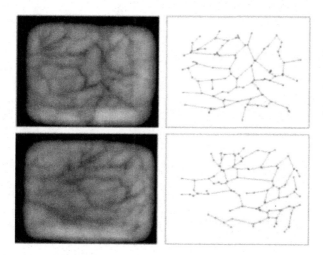

Fig. 2. This figure shows the extracted graph and the corresponding original image. Left figures are original images and right figures are extracted graphs with features of vertices (filled dots) and edges (line segments connecting a pair of vertices). (a) the top panel and (b) the bottom panel, show two palm vein images and corresponding graphs captured at different sessions from the same person. A large displacement is noticeable between the two images.

images at different sessions. Palm principal lines and wrinkles can be considered as part of the biometric and are difficult to completely remove; our experiments have shown that removing the short-medium spurs improves the process of registration and matching. The short-medium spurs were removed after the detection of vertices and edges. We used the following algorithm: (1) calculate the lengths of all branches. (2) identify the short-medium branches that are not linked to the end vertices (these branches should not be removed) 3) the short-medium branches, that are linked to end vertices and whose lengths are less than 40 pixels are removed. The connecting vertex was kept to form the correct vein shape while the edge and the vertex at the end of the edge was removed.

Examples of palm vein graphs from an individual captured at two different sessions are shown in the right panels of Fig. 2(a) and (b).

Fig. 3 shows the topological properties of the palm vein graphs. The Palm vein graphs from the PUT database have an average of 101 vertices and 112 edges. In reality, palm veins can never be discontinuous, noise in the image will impact the accurate capture of some sections of the image. Consequently, the graphs obtained may have some parts disconnected from the main component. The largest component size relative to the graph size indicates the level of noise present in the image. The average edge to vertex ratio is 1.11 and the average number of vertices of the largest component is 91. The average size of the largest component is almost equal to the average size of the palm vein graph. This indicates that the image processing can retrieve most of the features and connecting veins in a given image. Smaller disconnected components exist in a

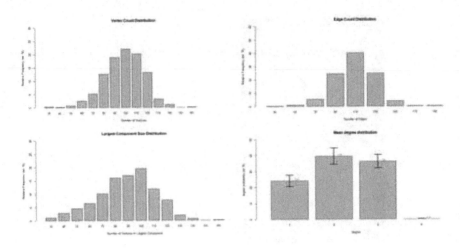

Fig. 3. This figure shows the distribution of the topological features of Palm Vein Graphs in our database. (a) Top Left. The distribution of the size of the palm vein graphs. Around 80 % of the graphs have between 90 and 130 vertices. (b) Top Right. The distribution of the number of edges in the palm vein graphs. Around 80 % of the graphs have between 100 to 140 edges connecting the nodes. (c) Bottom Left. The distribution of the size of the largest components. (d) Bottom Right. The average degree distribution of the palm vein graphs. There is more than 70 % probability that a vertex in a palm vein graph in this database has either have a degree 2 or degree 3.

palm vein graph because the quality of the image in certain parts is not good enough to retrieve the connecting veins. Figure 3(d) shows the average degree distribution of the Palm Vein Graphs. This describes the kind of connections the edges create between the nodes. The high proportion of degree 2 and 3 vertices is quite characteristic of palm vein graphs, indicating a high density of veins in the captured area. Figure 4 shows the average distribution of the lengths of the edges in the palm vein graphs. The median length of the edges in this database is 45 pixels. The majority of edges in a graph are short and medium length edges. This is because the vertex connections follow edges and have a greater probability to attach to a closer vertex than a faraway one. Therefore palm vein graphs show properties similar to proximity graphs. As seen in the figure, over 30 % of the edges have a length larger than 70 pixels. This shows there are a significant number of long connecting edges in these graphs which will give unique patterns to the palm vein graphs. This topological information will be used extensively in registering and matching graphs.

3   Biometric Graph Matching

Biometric Graph Matching (BGM) is a two-stage algorithm for the error-tolerant comparison of biometric graphs and is described in Lajevardi et al. [8]. The first stage is registration and the second is error tolerant graph matching.

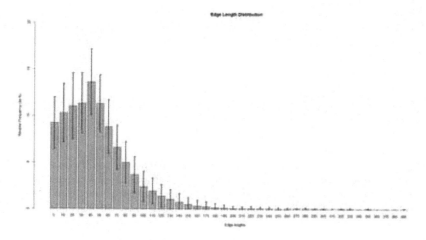

Fig. 4. Average distribution of the lengths of the edges in the palm vein graphs.

3.1   Registration

Registration is the process of bringing a pair of compared graphs into the same reference frame. The Iterative Closest Point (ICP) algorithm [1] and the Modified Hausdorff Distance (MHD) [2] are algorithms commonly used to register point clouds. It has been demonstrated by Lajevardi et al. [9] that the registration process in BGM is either as good as or does better than these standard algorithms, especially when the graphs are small. This paper uses a registration algorithm that is a slight modification of the one in Lajevardi et al. [8]. The registration process in [8] translates and rotates a pair of graphs based on a corresponding pair of edges that define the coordinate system. Every pair of edges with one edge from each compared graph, is given a score based on a function of their edge attributes of length and slope. The edge pairs are ranked on this score. This algorithm had one drawback that caused several genuine palm vein samples to be misaligned. Most edge pairs in the palm vein graph were short (See Fig. 4) and short pairs often scored a high rank compared to longer pairs. This caused longer pairs that could give a better registration to not appear on the top L shortlist. To overcome this, we modified the algorithm to split the set of edge pairs into long and short edge pairs. The mean of the medians of the edge lengths in the two graphs was selected as the threshold. If both edges of an edge pair had length greater than this threshold, the edge pair was categorised as long. All other edge pairs were labeled as short. The new shortlist comprised the top $\frac{L}{2}$ of long edge pairs and the top $\frac{L}{2}$ of short edge pairs. This modification ensured that long edge pairs that potentially gave better alignment could be included in the shortlist to get a better registration of the graphs. The algorithm is described in Algorithm 1. Figure 5 shows examples of registration between a pair of palm vein graphs using Algorithm 1.

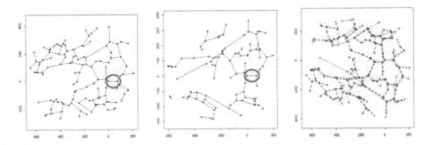

Fig. 5. This figure shows examples of registration of palm vein graph pairs. The third column of figures shows the two graphs superimposed and aligned on the best edge pair. The first graph is shown in blue and the second graph is shown in red. The best aligned edge pair is indicated by a black circle around it (Color figure online).

3.2   Graph Matching

Once a pair of graphs is registered, the graph matching process gives a numerical measure of the distance between the pair of graphs. Matching is done using an error tolerant graph matching algorithm adapted from one proposed by Riesen and Bunke [11]. The detailed process is described in [8].

Once the Hungarian algorithm computes the cheapest edit path to convert the source graph to the destination graph, this edit path is used to build the *maximum common subgraph* (*mcs*). The mcs is a vertex induced subgraph of the destination graph. The vertices of the destination graph could be associated with two operations from the edit path - substitutions of vertices from the source graph and insertions. In particular, the mcs will comprise only those vertices of the destination graph that were associated with substitutions in the edit path. An edge will exist in the mcs if the edge existed in corresponding vertex pairs of both the source and destination graphs. Figure 6 shows the mcses from a genuine graph comparison and an imposter graph comparison. Note the difference in topology of the two types of mcses. Mcses from a genuine comparison are observed to have more vertices and more edges with larger connected components than the mcses from an imposter comparison. It is this difference in topology that will be used to define similarity scores to distinguish genuine and imposter comparisons.

3.3   Graph Trimming

Graph matching is based on a sub optimal optimisation algorithm whose time increases with graph size. A technique to optimise the graph matching time is to trim the registered graphs to a radius r around the start vertex of the aligned edge pair, by deleting all vertices outside this radius. An advantage of graph trimming is that it improves the matching score from graph pairs where there is only partial overlap. This is because only the region of the graphs within the radius r will be considered in computing the similarity. The additional area of a graph that does not match any part of the partial graph will not penalise the

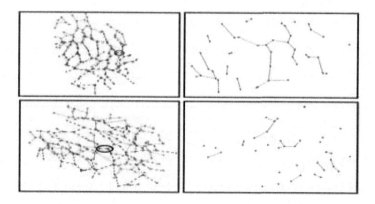

Fig. 6. Examples of registrations of a pair of graphs taken from the (a) (top - left) the same palm at different sessions and (c) (bottom-left) from different palms. The corresponding maximum common subgraphs are in (b) (top-right) and (d) (bottom-right).

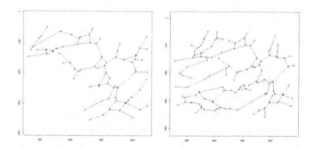

Fig. 7. A pair of genuine samples where the graphs have only partial overlap.

match score. Figure 7 shows an example of a graph pair where the two samples are from the same palm, taken at different sessions.

Figure 8 shows trimming applied to this graph pair. The radius r around the aligned edge is increased in stages. Figure 8 shows how increasing r increases the matching time almost linearly. In this case of partial overlap, a smaller r will allow the graphs to achieve a good match score (low d value) when compared to when more of the graphs are allowed to match. In contrast, we find that imposter comparisons have a large distance d even at smaller radii like $r = 200$ or $r = 300$. At $r = 200$ we found that some imposter comparisons had very small trimmed graphs, that could cause imposters to score high similarity on just an aligned edge. This could impact the matching accuracy. However, $r = 300$ or $r = 400$ would give enough graph structure in imposter comparisons to prevent this happening. Therefore, Graph Trimming could potentially improve the performance of genuine comparisons with partial matches without benefiting the imposter comparisons. In addition, we reduce the time required to match a pair of graphs.

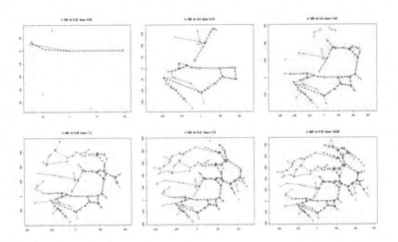

Fig. 8. Example of the effect of graph trimming on the match score and match time of a genuine comparison with partial overlap. Row 1 shows the compared graphs. Rows 2 and 3 show the registered graphs with r varying from 100 to 500 pixels. The graph matching score d and the time for graph matching t in seconds is also shown at the top of the images.

4   Graph Features

The topological features of the mcs are used to differentiate the comparisons of samples from the same palm and samples from different palms. Let $g_1 = (\mathbf{V_1}, \mathbf{E_1}, \mu, \nu)$ and $g_2 = (\mathbf{V_2}, \mathbf{E_2}, \mu, \nu)$ be the two graphs compared using the BGM algorithm and $g = (\mathbf{V}, \mathbf{E}, \mu, \nu)$ be the mcs of the graphs. Let $C1$ and $C2$ be the vertex counts of the largest and second largest components, c_1 and c_2 in g. We define a set of similarity scores that quantify the closeness of g_1 and g_2. As all these measures are normalised, they can be equivalently defined as distances by using $1 - S_*$.

Similarity scores based on the graph features are defined as follows:

1. Normalised vertex count, $S_n = \dfrac{|\mathbf{V}|}{\sqrt{|\mathbf{V_1}| \times |\mathbf{V_2}|}}$

2. Normalised edge count, $S_e = \dfrac{|\mathbf{E}|}{\sqrt{|\mathbf{E_1}| \times |\mathbf{E_2}|}}$

3. Edge to vertex ratio, $S_\rho = \dfrac{|\mathbf{E}|}{|\mathbf{V}|}$

4. Size of the largest component, $S_{c1} = \dfrac{C1}{\sqrt{|\mathbf{V_1}| \times |\mathbf{V_2}|}}$

5. Size of the second largest component, $S_{c2} = \dfrac{C2}{\sqrt{|\mathbf{V_1}| \times |\mathbf{V_2}|}}$

6. Ratio of the number of isolated vertices in the mcs to the number of connected vertices, S_i.

7. Total length of the edges in the largest component in the mcs. Let $L()$ be a function that takes a graph as input and returns the sum of the lengths of the edges in the graph. Then $S_l = \dfrac{L(c_1)}{\sqrt{L(g_1) \times L(g_2)}}$

8. sum of the sizes of two largest components in the mcs, $S_{c1c2} = \frac{C1+C2}{\sqrt{|V_1| \times |V_2|}}$
9. Edge to vertex ratio of the largest component, $S_{\rho c1}$
10. Ratio of the number of vertices with degree greater than 3 in the mcs, to the total number of vertices in the mcs, S_d.

We investigate if one or more of these features can be combined to achieve maximum separation between genuine and imposter scores of comparisons from the palm vein database.

5 Experiments

The PUT database has for left and right hands respectively, 600 palm vein images from 50 individuals, giving 6,600 genuine comparisons across all sessions, 1,800 genuine comparisons within same sessions and 352,800 imposter comparisons. To tune the parameters in the experiment, we chose a random sample of 150 genuine comparisons and 150 imposter comparisons from all possible genuine and imposter comparisons. This set of 300 comparisons is called the *training set* and will be consistently used throughout all the experiments described in this paper. The BGM algorithm has a few parameters to be tuned- the tolerance ϵ and shortlist length L in the registration algorithm; the insertion and deletion cost α in the graph matching algorithm and the radius r in the trimming process. The training set will be used to set up all these parameters.

The first experiment was to quantify the advantage of using both long and short edgepairs to register. To do this, we registered the graphs in the training set with both registration algorithms - [8] and Algorithm 1 and compared their accuracy and average registration time. The accuracy was measured using Receiver Operating Characteristic curves (ROC curves) of the minimum distance output from the Registration Algorithm (see line 32) between the graphs in the training set from genuine and imposter comparisons. For this experiment we fixed $\epsilon = 8$ and $L = 200$ for both algorithms. The results on the training set showed that both algorithms had similar accuracy, with Algorithm 1 getting a slightly better Equal Error Rate (EER) of 5.33 % over [8]'s 6 %. The process of sorting the edges into long and short does take additional time and therefore [8] does better on average registration time(11.52 sec, compared to 15.69 sec of Algorithm 1). Figure 12(a) and (b) illustrate a specific examples where Algorithm 1 gives a better registration than [8] by forcing the use of longer edge pairs.

The next experiment was to determine the best ϵ and L values for the registration algorithm. The genuine and imposter comparisons in the training set were registered using Algorithm 1 with a range of ϵ and L values. ϵ values are varied from $\epsilon = 4$ to $\epsilon = 14$ in steps of 2 units while the L values are varied from 50 to 300 in steps of 50. The distance measure d_{min} (See 32 in Algorithm 1) from the genuine and imposter comparisons is used to generate ROCs for all 36 the combinations of parameters and the Equal Error Rate for each are noted. The best parameters for the database was $\epsilon = 10$ and $L = 200$. The Equal Error Rate

(EER) on the training set for these parameters was 4.67 %. We next determine the parameter for graph edit distance matching α. Using the training set, with $\epsilon = 10$ and $L = 200$, α was varied between 5 and 15 in steps of 2 units. The similarity measure S_n from the mcs of the compared graphs was used in this experiment. This measure was chosen as it is a common measure of closeness to count the number of corresponding features between two biometrics and is comparable to non-graph based measures. The S_n values from the genuine and imposter comparisons for each of the six α values are used to evaluate the matching performance on the training set. From our experiment, the best parameter was $\alpha = 5$.

The next parameter to determine was the radius r when graph trimming is done. In order to determine the best r value for graph trimming, we used the training set at parameters $\epsilon = 10$, $L = 200$ and $\alpha = 5$ for registration and graph matching. We varied r from $r = 100$ to $r = 600$ in steps of 100 and determined the accuracy and average graph matching time for each value of r. We compared the performance to using the full graphs for graph matching. Again, we used the similarity measure S_n to quantify the closeness of the graph matching. Figure 9 shows that by trimming the graphs to $r = 200$ we can achieve the same performance as that when the full graph is used. There is a tremendous saving in graph matching time. At $r = 200$ and $r = 400$, the average graph matching time is .052 s and 6.5 s while it takes an average of 16 s to match the full graphs.

We tested the accuracy of our algorithm by applying these parameters on the rest of our database, which formed the test set. The BGM algorithm, on

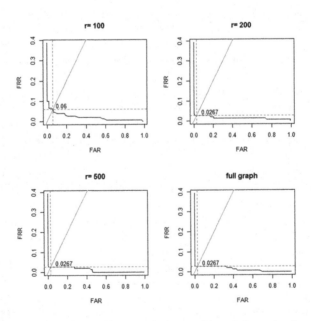

Fig. 9. The Receiver Operating Characteristics on the training set using the similarity measure S_n for a range of r values.

the full graphs (no trimming) was run on left and right palms separately. There were two distinct types of experiments based on the type of genuine comparisons made. First, *Across Session Genuines* using all the genuine comparisons including those across sessions and the second *Within Session Genuines*, with genuine comparisons taken only from within the same session. In both types of experiments, distances between a pair of graphs was measured using each of the 10 topological measures listed in Sect. 4. Table 1 shows the EER based on the the 10 topological features for across session and within session experiments for left and right hands. The Table 1 shows that S_e does the best job of separating the genuine comparisons from the imposters.

The next step was to determine if any combination of similarity scores could improve the performance compared to using a single similarity measure. To do this, first the pairwise Spearman's correlation coefficient between the 10 features was calculated. We found that most of the topological features were strongly correlated, with correlation coefficients between 0.8 to 0.95. In fact only $S_{\rho_{c1}}$ showed moderate correlations ranging between 0.58 and 0.78 with the other features. Nevertheless, in the absence of perfect correlation between features, there is a potential that pairwise combination of S_e with one of the other features could produce better matching results. To test this hypothesis, S_e was combined with every other feature to give 9 different pairings of topological features. For every pair of features, the following experiment was done. A Support Vector Machine (SVM) was used to build a classifier with a radial basis function (RBF) kernel that was tuned on the score pairs from the *training set* to determine the best parameters for the RBF kernel. The remaining comparisons on the database were divided into 10 parts and a 10 fold test was conducted where the SVM classifier was trained on 9 parts of the data and tested on the one other part. The false match rate (FMR), false non match rate (FNMR) and total misclassification error (TE) were computed in every fold. The average over 10 folds was taken as the matching performance using the chosen pair of features. The results for the 9 pairings are shown in the Table 2.

We next applied BGM on the testing set by allowing graph trimming at $r = 400$. Figure 10 shows the ROC curves for left palms for the measures S_n, S_e, S_ρ, S_{c1}, S_l and S_{c1c2}. These measures gave the lowest classification errors. Table 3 shows the corresponding EERs.

6   Results and Discussion

On comparing the registration algorithms for palm vein graphs, we find that Algorithm 1 improves the registration process over [8], evidenced by the better EER for Algorithm 1. This demonstrates that for palm vein graphs, a better registration could be achieved by considering longer edge pairs which represent longer vein segments that were often reliably captured across samples. The algorithm takes longer on average due to the additional step of separation of long and short edges.

When BGM is run on full graphs, Table 1 shows that for S_e, average EER for left and right palms is 2.63 % for across session comparisons and this markedly

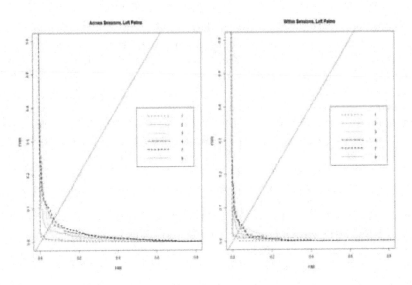

Fig. 10. The figure shows the across session and within session ROCs for graphs from the left palm when trimmed at $r = 400$. The indices in the legend correspond to the similarity measures described in Sect. 4. Results for measures S_n, S_e, S_ρ, S_{c1}, S_l and S_{c1c2} are shown here as they were the best performing ones for the trimmed graphs.

Table 1. Equal Error Rate as %, when comparing genuine and imposter palm vein graphs using each of the 10 graph measures.

Topological Measure	EER as %			
	Across session Genuines, Left	Within session Genuines, Left	Across session Genuines, Right	Within session Genuines, Right
S_n	4.18	2.02	4.17	2.13
S_e	**2.71**	**1.11**	**2.55**	**1.23**
S_ρ	5.32	2.9	5.27	3.42
S_{c1}	6.06	3.91	6.63	4.39
S_{c2}	7.33	5.49	7.76	5.58
S_i	8.43	5.66	8.25	5.93
S_l	5.64	3.5	6.59	4.19
S_{c1c2}	4.45	2.51	4.79	2.91
$S_{\rho c1}$	19.22	19.96	13.04	12.67
S_d	13.33	9.9	11.5	8.57

improves on the published benchmark of 3.86 % [6] on the same database. BGM performs on par with the published result 1.11 % for within session comparisons using S_e. Note the large difference between EERs of across session and within session data. Genuine samples of palm veins captured from different sessions tend to have large displacement in captured area. This reduces the common overlap area between genuine samples and hence causes a lower score. Comparing our

Table 2. Matching performance when combining S_e with each of the other 9 measures. The table represents the mean over 10 folds with the standard errors in brackets. All results are expressed as percentages. The rows corresponding to the combinations with lowest Total Error (TE) are highlighted.

Features	Left Palm			Right Palm		
	FMR	FNMR	TE	FMR	FNMR	TE
S_e, S_n	0.37($\pm$.07)	4.72($\pm$0.38)	2.34($\pm$0.17)	0.38($\pm$0.06)	4.29($\pm$0.25)	1.93($\pm$0.08)
S_e, S_ρ	0.52($\pm$0.09)	4.02($\pm$0.35)	2.1($\pm$0.13)	0.36($\pm$0.08)	4.23($\pm$0.24)	1.9($\pm$0.07)
S_e, S_{c1}	0.38($\pm$0.09)	3.90($\pm$0.32)	1.97($\pm$0.11)	0.29($\pm$0.04)	3.93($\pm$0.22)	1.74($\pm$0.07)
S_e, S_{c2}	0.41($\pm$0.06)	4.23($\pm$0.3)	2.12($\pm$0.12)	0.44($\pm$0.07)	4.26($\pm$0.21)	1.96($\pm$0.08)
S_e, S_i	0.31($\pm$0.08)	4.37($\pm$0.35)	2.15($\pm$0.12)	0.40($\pm$0.08)	4.20($\pm$0.25)	1.92($\pm$0.08)
S_e, S_l	0.38($\pm$0.1)	3.83($\pm$0.29)	1.94($\pm$0.09)	0.27($\pm$0.03)	3.79($\pm$0.22)	1.67($\pm$0.08)
S_e, S_{c1c2}	0.45($\pm$0.08)	3.82($\pm$0.3)	1.97($\pm$0.12)	0.36($\pm$0.03)	3.79($\pm$0.23)	1.72($\pm$0.09)
$S_e, S_{\rho c1}$	0.51($\pm$0.11)	4.02($\pm$0.33)	2.1($\pm$0.12)	0.46($\pm$0.09)	4.15($\pm$0.23)	1.93($\pm$0.06)
S_e, S_d	0.48($\pm$0.1)	3.87($\pm$0.35)	2.02($\pm$0.13)	0.44($\pm$0.07)	4.03($\pm$0.22)	1.87($\pm$0.08)

Table 3. Equal Error Rate as %, when comparing genuine and imposter palm vein graphs when graphs are trimmed at $r = 400$. The rows having the lowest error rates are in boldface.

	EER as %			
Topological	Across session	Within session	Across session	Within session
Measure	Genuines, Left	Genuines, Left	Genuines, Right	Genuines, Right
S_n	**1.15**	**1.38**	**0.99**	**0.43**
S_e	**1.80**	**1.38**	**1.85**	**0.53**
S_ρ	4.48	4.48	5.38	4.61
S_{c1}	6.24	4.01	6.47	3.54
S_l	6.97	4.71	5.71	4.29
S_{c1c2}	3.92	2.87	4.63	2.25

results to the published benchmark illustrates that BGM performs better than the benchmark when palm vein samples have only a partial overlap area. Five out of the 10 features give competitive EERs of under 5 % for within session comparisons while three of these features (S_n, S_e, S_{c1c2}) also give competitive EERs for across session comparisons.

Table 2 shows that there are three topological features, that when combined with S_e give a competitive matching performance with total misclassification rate under 1.9 %. To understand how much better feature combination does over using the single measure S_e, we adopt the following procedure. From the ROC curve when using single feature S_e (see Fig. 11) we locate the FNMR when using S_e, at a FMR value, close to that obtained using two features. If the FNMR value using two features is actually lower than the corresponding one feature value, that particular pair of features gives a better result than using a single feature for comparison. The performance comparison between two features and one feature S_e is shown in Table 4.

Table 4. Comparison of matching performance when using a pair of features and a single feature S_e. The rows where the FNMRs are in boldface show the feature pairs whose performance is better than using S_e alone.

Feature Pairs		FMR	FNMR	FMR (S_e)	FNMR (S_e)
S_e, S_n	Left	0.37	4.72	0.37	4.28
	Right	0.38	4.29	0.38	4.06
S_e, S_ρ	Left	0.52	4.02	0.51	3.98
	Right	0.36	4.23	0.36	4.21
S_e, S_{c1}	Left	0.38	**3.90**	0.38	**4.22**
	Right	0.29	**3.93**	0.23	**4.46**
S_e, S_{c2}	Left	0.41	4.23	0.41	4.16
	Right	0.44	4.26	0.44	4.03
S_e, S_i	Left	0.31	4.37	0.31	4.39
	Right	0.40	4.20	0.4	4.03
S_e, S_l	Left	0.38	**3.83**	0.38	**4.22**
	Right	0.26	**3.79**	0.26	**4.63**
S_e, S_{c1c2}	Left	0.45	**3.82**	0.45	**4.13**
	Right	0.36	**3.79**	0.36	**4.21**
$S_e, S_{\rho c1}$	Left	0.51	4.02	0.51	3.98
	Right	0.46	4.15	0.46	3.96
S_e, S_d	Left	0.48	3.86	0.48	4.04
	Right	0.44	4.03	0.44	4.03

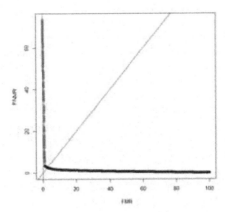

Fig. 11. The Receiver Operating Characteristic (ROC) curve, showing the plot of False Match Rates (FMRs) versus False Non Match Rates (FNMRs) over a range of operating thresholds. The matching algorithm uses a single feature S_e.

Table 4 shows that the topological feature pairs (S_e, S_{c1}), (S_e, S_l) and (S_e, S_{c1c2}) do better than using S_e alone, with (S_e, S_l) showing the maximum gain in performance.

Table 5. Multiple similarity measures for trimmed graphs.

Feature Pairs		FMR	FNMR	FMR (S_e)	FNMR (S_e)
S_e, S_n	Left	1.2	1.06	0.99	0
	Right	1.12	2.48	0.99	0
S_e, S_{c1}	Left	1.72	1.96	0.99	0
	Right	1.77	1.98	0.997	0
S_e, S_l	Left	1.69	1.88	0.99	0
	Right	1.14	2.23	0.99	0
S_e, S_{c1c2}	Left	1.74	1.96	0.99	0
	Right	1.44	1.72	0.997	0

Table 3 shows that the measures S_n and S_e give a significantly better performance when the graphs are trimmed at $r = 400$ compared to the full graphs. In fact S_n and S_e also have a similar matching performance, as seen in the Fig. 10. We also explored if combining S_e with the other similarity measures would give a further improvement in matching performance. Table 5 shows the results of combining S_e with S_n, S_{c1}, S_l and S_{c1c2}. In contrast to the full graphs, the trimmed graphs had no added advantage when features were combined. In fact the matching performance was worse than when using a single feature S_e. This shows that the topological properties of biometric graphs can be fully utilised when the graphs are large and have rich connections. Graph Trimming markedly improves the graph matching speed and accuracy when a single similarity measure is used.

7 Conclusion

This paper proposes a graph-based approach to represent a palm vein template and proposes the Biometric Graph Matching algorithm (BGM) to match the templates. We introduce a technique called Graph Trimming where the registered graphs are shrunk to a region around the registered edge pair. The BGM algorithm with and without trimming is tested on the PUT public palm vein database where each palm vein has 12 samples captures across 3 sessions. This gave us a good number of genuine comparisons that were within the same session and across different sessions, to estimate the difference in performance when biometrics are captured in different sessions. Note that multi session comparison is typical in a real-world scenario. The proposed method beats the existing state of art results on the PUT public palm vein database [6] for genuine samples captured across sessions when graphs are used in full and trimmed. In fact, trimming graphs shows better performance than when full graphs are used. This establishes BGM with trimming as an effective algorithm, especially when genuine palm vein samples have partial overlap.

We remark that as the graph edit algorithm we used gave significant results we did not need to try other cost functions. However, for future work these could be applied to help evaluate the efficiency tradeoff of graph matching.

The paper shows that using the graph representation and BGM matching approach for palm vein graphs is practical and efficient. The graph-based measure based on edge count outperforms the measure based on vertex count for full graphs. This reinforces the advantage of using the edge information in representing the palm vein graph. For trimmed graphs the node-based measure does as well as the edge-based measure. We further demonstrate that for full graphs by combining graph features, the matching performance can be improved over using just a single feature. Trimmed graphs do not show this property. The ability to explore and combine different graph features based on the spatial characteristics of the palm vein graph is one of the biggest advantages of using the graph-based approach.

Acknowledgements. We thank the anonymous referees for comments which improved the clarity of the paper. This research was funded by ARC grant DP120101188.

A   Appendix: BGM Registration Algorithm

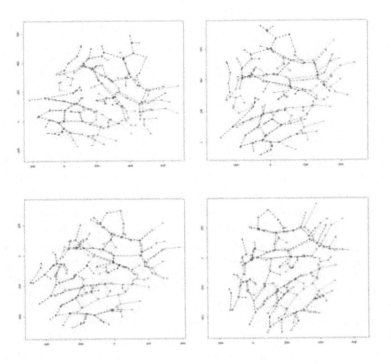

Fig. 12. The (a) top and (b) bottom rows show examples of a pair of graphs from the same palm where Algorithm 1 (left column) gives a better registration than [8] (right column). Observe that in both cases the better registration occurs with a long edgepair in Algorithm 1.

Algorithm 1. Graph registration module.

Require: Graphs g and g' with vertex sets $\mathbf{V} = \{v_1, v_2, \cdots, v_m\}$ and $\mathbf{V}' = \{v'_1, v'_2, \cdots, v'_{m'}\}$ and edge sets $\mathbf{E} = \{e_1, e_2, \cdots, e_n\}$ and $\mathbf{E}' = \{e'_1, e'_2, \cdots, e'_{n'}\}$ respectively. Let p be the percentage of top scoring edges to shortlist and let ϵ be the tolerance to match vertex pairs.

Ensure: Aligned graphs g_a and g'_a having same edge links as g and g' but with new spatial coordinates.

1: $g_a \leftarrow \varnothing$ and $g'_a \leftarrow \varnothing$. $\triangleright$ Initialise the registered graphs that will be returned at the end of the algorithm
2: $\mathbf{L} = \{l_1, l_2, \cdots, l_n\}$ is the list of lengths corresponding to edges in g.
3: $\mathbf{L}' = \{l'_1, l'_2, \cdots, l'_{n'}\}$ is the list of lengths corresponding to edges in g'.
4: $\Theta = \{\theta_1, \theta_2, \cdots, \theta_n\}$ is the list of orientations of the edges in g.
5: $\Theta' = \{\theta'_1, \theta'_2, \cdots, \theta'_{n'}\}$ is the list of orientations of the edges in g'.
6: $M_{dist} \leftarrow 0$ $\hspace{3cm}$ $\triangleright$ Initialise a matrix of size $n \times n'$ with zeros.
7: **for** $a = 1$ to n **do**
8: $\quad$ **for** $b = 1$ to n' **do**
9: $\quad\quad d_{ab} = \frac{1}{0.5(l_a + l'_b)} \sqrt{(l_a - l'_b)^2 + (\theta_a - \theta'_b)^2}$ $\hspace{1cm}$ $\triangleright$ s_{ab} is the distance score between edges e_a and e'_b
$\quad\quad$ with l_a and l'_b in pixels and θ_a and θ'_b in degrees.
10: $\quad\quad M_{dist}[a, b] \leftarrow d_{ab}$
11: $\quad$ **end for**
12: **end for**
13: Sort the contents of M_{dist} in increasing order.
14: $M_{shortlist}$ is a matrix with 3 columns. $\hspace{1cm}$ Every row m_i stores the 3-tuple (d_{ab_i}, a_i, b_i).
$\quad d_{ab_i}$ is taken from the sorted M_{dist} with the first row of $M_{shortlist}$, m_i having d_{ab_1}, the smallest distance.
$\quad a_i$ and b_i indicate the corresponding row and column of s_{ab_i} in M_{dist}.
15: l_{th} will be the mean of the median edge lengths in g and g'.
16: $M_{shortlist}$ is split into two sub matrices, M_{long} and M_{short}.
17: A row m_i belongs to M_{long} if $l_{a_i} > l_{th}$ and $l_{b_i} > l_{th}$. Otherwise m_i is assigned to M_{short}.
18: $d_{long} \leftarrow (0, 0, \cdots, 0)_{1 \times L/2}$
19: **for** $i = 1$ to $L/2$ **do**
20: $\quad a = a_i, b = b_i$ where $m_i \in M_{long}$
21: $\quad g_o = \text{TRANSROT}(g, e_a)$.
22: $\quad g'_o = \text{TRANSROT}(g', e'_b)$.
23: $\quad d_{long}[i] = \text{QUICKSCORE}(g_o, g'_o, \epsilon)$
24: **end for**
25: $d_{short} \leftarrow (0, 0, \cdots, 0)_{1 \times L/2}$
26: **for** $i = 1$ to $L/2$ **do**
27: $\quad a = a_i, b = b_i$ where $m_i \in M_{short}$
28: $\quad g_o = \text{TRANSROT}(g, e_a)$.
29: $\quad g'_o = \text{TRANSROT}(g', e'_b)$.
30: $\quad d_{short}[i] = \text{QUICKSCORE}(g_o, g'_o, \epsilon)$
31: **end for**
32: $d_{min} = \text{MIN} (\text{MIN}(d_{long}), \text{MIN}(d_{short}))$.
33: a_{min} and b_{min} are the row and column in $M_{shortlist}$ corresponding to d_{min}.
34: $g_a = \text{TRANSROT}(g, e_{a_{min}})$.
35: $g'_o = \text{TRANSROT}(g', e'_{b_{min}})$. **return** g_a, g'_a and d_{min}.
36: **function** TRANSROT(g, e)
37: $\quad g_o \leftarrow g$
38: $\quad$ The start vertex of e will be the origin of the coordinate system.
39: $\quad$ The edge e will be define the positive direction of the x-axis.
40: $\quad$ Recalculate all the vertex attributes of g_o in the new coordinate system. **return** g_o.
41: **end function**
42: **function** QUICKSCORE(g, g', ϵ)
43: $\quad$ Label all vertices of g and g' as unmatched.
44: $\quad C = 0$ $\hspace{2cm}$ $\triangleright$ Counter for number of vertex pair matches between g and g'
45: $\quad$ **for** $i = 1$ to m **do**
46: $\quad\quad$ **for** $j = 1$ to m' **do**
47: $\quad\quad\quad$ **if** v_i is labeled unmatched and v'_j is labeled unmatched and EUCDIST(q_i, q'_j) $\leq \epsilon$ **then**
48: $\quad\quad\quad\quad C = C + 1$. $\hspace{3cm}$ $\triangleright$ v_i matches with v'_j.
49: $\quad\quad\quad\quad$ Label v_i and v'_j as matched. $\hspace{0.5cm}$ $\triangleright$ $q_i = (q_{1i}, q_{2i})$ is the vertex attribute of v_i and q'_i is the vertex attribute of v'_i.
50: $\quad\quad\quad$ **end if**
51: $\quad\quad$ **end for**
52: $\quad$ **end for**
53: $\quad d = 1 - \frac{C}{\sqrt{m \times m'}}$. **return** d.
54: **end function**

References

1. Chen, H., Lu, G., Wang, R.: A new palm vein matching method based on ICP algorithm. In Proceedings of the 2nd International Conference on Interaction Sciences: Information Technology, Culture and Human, pp. 1207–1211. ACM, New York (2009). http://doi.acm.org/10.1145/1655925.1656145

2. Dubuisson, M.P., Jain, A.: A modified hausdorff distance for object matching. In: Proceedings of the 12th IAPR International Conference on Pattern Recognition, p. 566. IEEE (1994)

3. Gaikwad, D.P., Narote, S.P.: Multi-modal biometric system using palmprint and palm vein features. In: Annual IEEE India Conference (INDICON), p. 15 (2013)

4. Horadam, K.J., Davis, S.A., Arakala, A., Jeffers, J.: Fingerprints as spatial graphs: nodes and edges. In Proceedings of International Conference on Digital Image Computing Techniques and Applications (DICTA), Noosa, Australia, pp. 400–405 (2011)

5. Kabaciński, R., Kowalski, M.: Human vein pattern segmentation from low quality images – a comparison of methods. In: Choraś, R.S. (ed.) Image Processing and Communications Challenges 2. AISC, vol. 84, pp. 105–112. Springer, Heidelberg (2010)

6. Kabacinski, R., Kowalski, M.: Vein pattern database and benchmark results. Electron. Lett. **47**(20), 1127–1128 (2011)

7. Kumar, A., Prathyusha, K.V.: Personal authentication using hand vein triangulation and knuckle shape. IEEE Trans. Image Process. **9**, 2127–2136 (2009)

8. Lajevardi, S., Arakala, A., Davis, S.: Horadam, K: Retina verification system based on biometric graph matching. IEEE Trans. Image Process. **22**(9), 3625–3635 (2013)

9. Lajevardi, S., Arakala, A., Davis, S., Horadam, K.: Hand vein authentication using biometric graph matching. IET Biometrics **3**, 302–313 (2014). doi:10.1049/ietbmt.2013.0086

10. Perona, P., Malik, J.: Scale-space and edge detection using anisotropic diffusion. IEEE Trans. Pattern Anal. Mach. Intell. **12**, 629–639 (1990)

11. Riesen, K., Bunke, H.: Approximate graph edit distance computation by means of bipartite graph matching. Image Vis. Comput. **27**(7), 950–959 (2009)

12. Shahin, M., Badawi, A., Kamel, M.: Biometric authentication using fast correlation of near infrared in hand vein patterns. Int. J. Biomed. Sci. **2**, 141–148 (2007)

13. Wang, L., Leedham, G., Cho, S.Y.: Infrared imaging of hand vein patterns for biometric purposes. IET Comput. Vis. **1**(3–4), 113–122 (2007)

14. Watanabe, M., Endoh, T., Shiohara, M., Sasaki, S.: Palm vein authentication technology and its applications. In: Proceedings of Biometrics Consortium Conference, Arlington, VA, p. 12 (2005)

15. Wenxiong, K., Qiuxia, W.: Contactless palm vein recognition using a mutual foreground-based local binary pattern. IEEE Trans. Inf. Forensics Secur. **9**, 1974–1985 (2014)

16. Zuiderveld, K.: Contrast Limited Adaptive Histogram Equalization. Academic Press Professional Inc., San Diego (1994)

17. Arakala, A., Hao, H., Davis, S., Horadam, K.: The palm vein graph - feature extraction and matching. In: Proceedings of The First International Conference on Information Systems Security and Privacy(ICISSP), Loire Valley, France, 19–21 February 2015 (2015)

Impact of External Parameters on the Gait Recognition Using a Smartphone

Josselyn Le Moing[(⊠)] and Ingo Stengel

School of Computing and Mathematics, Plymouth University, Plymouth, UK
josselyn.lemoing@postgrad.plymouth.ac.uk,
ingo.stengel@plymouth.ac.uk

Abstract. This paper identifies possible impacts of a couple of external parameters on gait recognition when a build-in smartphone accelerometer is used. Some parameters like the types of shoes impact gait recognition significantly while others like the type of surfaces has only a minor impact. A correlation between accelerometer's data and the phone position was identified. For this, data originating from the Z-axis as well as from the X-Y-Z – axes was used together with Dynamic Time Warping (DTW) for template generation and matching tests.

Keywords: Gait recognition · Biometric authentication · Accelerometer

1 Introduction

Security often refers to the process of asset protection. In this context, verification of identities, known as authentication, is used as a mean to ensure the right person is able to access information. Authentication mechanisms are used on almost any device. Especially on mobile devices, authentication is "not user friendly enough to be widely adopted" [1]. As a consequence non-invasive, continuous methods of authentication like gait recognition are currently being explored.

Gait recognition is an emerging biometric technology that does not explicitly involve users' actions. It evaluates the manner of walking over a certain distance [2] and can be used to identify persons [3]. First approaches used a visual evaluation of the recorded movements [4], while later approaches used sensors like accelerometers in mobile devices to record specific data [5]. Factors originating from users (e.g. illnesses as Parkinson disease, etc.) as well as from the environment (e.g. ground the user is walking on, etc.) can impact the process of gait based authentication [7].

The aim of this research project is to find out how strong the impact of parameters like, e.g. types of shoes, types of floors and phone position, is on the process of gait recognition. The problem is worth giving attention since these environment-related parameters have an impact on the quality of the authentication process and as such on the level of Security provided.

Even if it is shown that the analysis in frequency domain gives a better match result than the analysis in the time domain [7], the latter has been chosen in our experiment because it gives a better representation of the user's physical gait (acceleration as function of time) and it is assumed that the impact of external parameters would be

© Springer International Publishing Switzerland 2015
O. Camp et al. (Eds.): ICISSP 2015, CCIS 576, pp. 219–233, 2015.
DOI: 10.1007/978-3-319-27668-7_13

more visible using this method. However, the use of frequency based methods is planned for the future in order to refine these results.

2 Previous Works

Significant research in gait recognition was done by several researchers. Indeed, according to a research carried out in Germany [8], the gait contains a periodical pattern which is almost identical for every step of a same person at a constant speed. Furthermore, in addition to these similarities for a same person, the research shows also that for two different subjects, patterns are significantly different [9].

Another research made in USA [10] shows that when two normal speeds, for a same person, are compared, the results are excellent with 99.4 % match against 96.8 % with two fast gaits. However, results are not the same when fast gaits are compared with normal gaits and the difference is very significant with a match of only 61.1 %. This research shows a first weakness when the speed is different for a same person but confirms results of the first one [8] for a constant speed. A research made in USA by Boyle and his colleagues [11] confirms previous analyses for a constant speed and also confirms the first weakness (with different speeds) but shows the impact of another parameter on gait recognition. Indeed, when the user is subjected to a modification of the way (flat hallway, circle, hill...) the gait is significantly different and the match rate is low. However, very few research projects took into consideration the impact of external parameters like type of floor/surface, different footwear and the position of the phone.

Details show that results with regard to the impact of surfaces on gait recognition are not as clear as they seem to be at the first sight [6] identified that the modification of the surface does not have a significant effect on gait recognition but they showed that gait recognition is more efficient on gravel and grass than on indoor surfaces. Later, Muaaz and Nickel [12] showed that walking on grass and on inclined surfaces impacts significantly gait recognition. Walking on gravels - although impacted - produced comparable results to normal gait.

In two studies, the impact of different footwear was examined using video analysis. The first report shows that all shoes excluding strapless open-toed sandals do not impact gait recognition [4].

However, flip-flops have a significant impact. The second research highlights the significant impact of the type of shoes in the recognition process using the video analysis method [13].

None of the previous studies analysed the impact of shoes and the position of the smartphone on gait recognition using the accelerometer in a smartphone.

3 Research Methodology

In order to use the smartphone as a gait recognition device, an Android application was developed. Its main objective is to collect data from different sensors in the phone that was worn by the participant during the experiment, see Fig. 3. After that, data will be processed and interpreted using MatLab scripts. The impact of the different parameters used was analysed using data from two experiments.

3.1   Number of Participants

The identified impact of the parameters should be independent of the person who wears the phone. Therefore 19 volunteers within an age from 18 to 25 years participated in this experiment. Should the results be promising, a further evaluation with significant numbers (100 volunteers) will be implemented. The experiment is anonymous and each volunteer is represented by a number in the experiment. An additional letter identifies the type of experiment done.

3.2   Research Procedure

The research procedure is similar to the one used in [7], where first a reference gait (called normal gait) is identified before additional measurements can be done, e.g. measuring the gait with different types of shoe.

In order to determine a reference gait for each participant the first step for each user consists in several measurements during walks on the pavement with the phone tied to the leg using a leg band (Fig. 1).

Fig. 1. "Leg band" (Side view).

The next measurements helped to identify the impact of the selected parameters like floors on gait recognition, e.g. by walking on grass with the smartphone tied to the leg with the leg band.

To measure the impact of shoes two extremes will be used: normal, closed shoes and flip-flops. Featured templates will be extracted from these recordings.

Finally, the impact of the smartphone positioning in the trousers' front pocket will be tested. In this third part, participants with adequate trousers (tight to the body) will walk with the smartphone in their trousers' front pocket. This will help to identify potential differences in measurements based on the position on the phone.

The second aim will be to understand how reliable the accelerometer's data is when the smartphone rotates around its Z-axis (Fig. 2). This device will allow a rotation

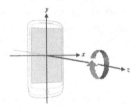

Fig. 2. Smartphone axis [14].

Fig. 3. Data collection around the Z axis (Side view).

around the Z-axis of the phone (one degree of freedom) and be attached to the leg using a strap.

The last step of this methodology is the interpretation of data. Several choices will have to be made in order to select a suitable method. First of all, MatLab will be used for the interpretation of results. It was chosen because it simplifies handling of large amounts of data.

3.3   Selecting the Analysis Method

In this research area two analysis methods are traditionally used: the Dynamic Time Warping (DTW) method in the time domain and the Fast Fourier Transform (FFT) method in the frequency domain.

Even though it was shown that the analysis in frequency domain (FFT) gives better matching results than DTW [7], the latter was chosen for our experiment. It gives a better representation of the user's physical gait (acceleration as function of time) and is more suitable for the comparison of curves [7].

Additionally, DTW is a non-linear time alignment technique that allows matching of similar shapes out of phase in the same time axis [15] and thus avoids gait cycle length normalisation. This approach allows the measurement of similarities between two series of data that do not have the same length and as such fits our requirements.

4   Results and Discussion

Before discussing results, it is necessary to explain how a confusion matrix works and to address decisions linked to measurements and evaluation that were made.

4.1   Confusion Matrix

A confusion matrix contains two inputs in which each letter (A – Z) is a label of a participant. The horizontal input represents each participant's featured template which is obtained after a training phase or by extracting the most representative vector of a record. This featured template is the curve which the vertical entry will be compared with. Indeed, the vertical input contains all curves representing each step for a specific record.

Each vertical input contains all the curves of the record for one person (one curve represents one step) and each curve is compared with all the featured templates of all participants. The comparison is done by calculating the distance between these curves using the DTW method, additionally the table's cell corresponding to the featured template is incremented by one.

The last column of this matrix contains the percentage of matches for each vertical entry. It shows the number of curves that match with the good featured template (corresponding to the same person) compared to the number of curves tested. Figure 4 illustrates in detail the operation on this type of matrix.

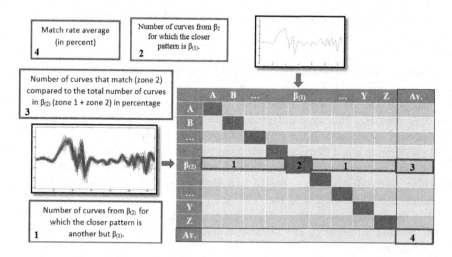

Fig. 4. Explanation of the confusion matrix operation.

In this step three records belonging to normal gait records are used for comparison. The featured template is extracted from the first record and compared to the curves representing the second and the third record. The average matching rate is 73.41 % against 73.85 % when the featured template is extracted from the second records.

4.2   Choice of the Time Interpolation Frequency

The gait recognition algorithm developed collects data from the accelerometer sensor of the smartphone at the speed set by the phone.

A quick analysis of the first data extracted using the accelerometer showed that the smartphone does approximately a hundred measurements per second. In the first approach the closest time interpolation frequency (128 Hz) to one hundred (in power of 2) was selected.

This choice had to be confirmed by comparing matching results with other time interpolation frequencies. The algorithm was tested with the first two lower frequencies which are 64 Hz and 32 Hz. A higher frequency has not been tested for two reasons.

Firstly, with this amount of points (256 points per second), the algorithm's execution time would have been too long and data interpretation would not have been possible with the laptop used. Secondly, such a frequency would have created too many missing points in the original recording and it might have influenced negatively the collected data (Table 1).

Table 1. Average match rate evolution depending on the time interpolation frequency.

Average values	1	2	Trim. mean 1	Trim. mean 2
128 Hz	73.41	73.85	80.30	80.61
64 Hz	63.52	56.38	68.95	62.03
32 Hz	45.65	40.09	50.26	44.22

Comparisons of these three frequencies (128 Hz, 64 Hz and 32 Hz) are done using a confusion matrix. For the same recording, the average matching rate is 80.61 % with a frequency of 128 Hz against a rate of 44.22 % with a frequency of 32 Hz and with 62.03 % at 64 Hz. This large difference shows clearly that the average matching rate considerably increases with the number of points per second.

In addition to this difference, the variation between two recordings is also impacted by the time interpolation frequency. Indeed, with a frequency of 128 Hz, the average matching rate difference between the two samples is 0.31 % while for 64 Hz the difference is 6.92 % and for 32 Hz, 6.04 %.

The time interpolation frequency initially chosen is finally the best of the three tested because it produces the highest matching rate and will provide significant recognition results.

4.3   Detecting the Starting Point

In order to determine this starting point of gait, data collected following the Y axis of the accelerometer was analysed. This data is used to detect vertical acceleration.

Moreover, in previous work [5] indicates that, from a standing position, starting to walk involves an acceleration of around 1.3 g. It was suggested to identify the starting point when the measurement on the Y axis exceeds 12.74 m/s^2 (1.3 g × 9.8 m/s^2) (Fig. 5).

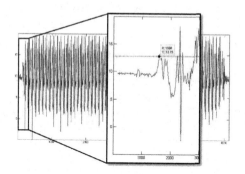

Fig. 5. Starting point detection using Y-axis data.

4.4   Cycle Detection and Step Extraction

For cycle detection, data from mainly one axis (Y-axis) was used. Indeed, data originating from several dimensions makes the detection of cycles hard. However, filtering one dimensional data will result in a sinusoidal curve that will allow the identification of cycles [7]. The measurement of each pattern length in this sinusoid will identify the cycle time of each step.

As such the first step of cycles' detection is to filter the Y component of accelerometer using a moving-average filter with a 50 points window to clearly identify peaks. Each of these peaks represents the starting point of one step. The time interval between two peaks is the time of one step (Fig. 6).

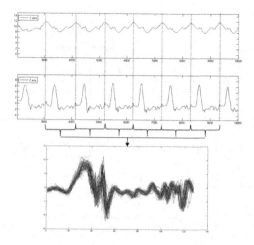

Fig. 6. Steps extraction.

All these landmarks are then applied to the Z-axis. Steps and data between two consecutive landmarks are extracted. To avoid any error in this important extraction phase, the length of each step is compared to the cycle time of a normal person which is a value between 0.87–1.32 s [16]. The multiplication of this time value with the time interpolation frequency indicates the range of acceptable values for a step.

4.5   Determination of the Featured Template

Once each step is extracted, the distance between them is calculated using the Dynamic Time Warping method [17] which is a method to calculate the distance between two curves. Unlike Euclidean or Manhattan methods which align the x-th point of one curve with the x-th point of the other, the DTW method uses a non-linear time alignment (Fig. 7).

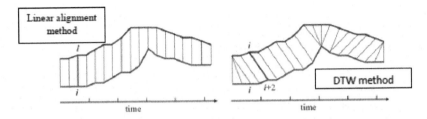

Fig. 7. Differences between linear alignment methods and the DTW method [15].

The distances between each curve are placed in a matrix and the average distance of each curve is calculated. The curve which has the lowest average distance is considered to be the featured template of the record (Fig. 8).

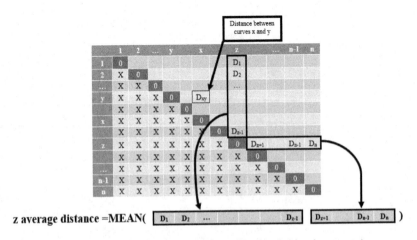

Fig. 8. Calculation of a curve average distance (with other curves).

4.6   Impact of the Smartphone's Position on Gait Recognition

The technical challenge when the phone is placed in a random position is to recognize this position and to adapt the algorithm to proceed with gait recognition. Each position has its own pair of X and Y central values, which makes the identification of the smartphone's position easily possible. Furthermore, the step detection is based on Y axis data when the phone is in its normal position (top of the phone oriented upwards) and each cycle time is delimited by two peaks of this axis. This axis has been chosen because its direction is parallel to the user and detects up and down variations. However, when the inclination of the phone is modified, this axis does not detect these variations anymore. As a result, a phase difference seems to exist between curves along the same axes in different position. This difference could be due to a different sampling of the original data. In order to avoid this problem, the selection of the axis which will determine the cycle time has to be linked to the phone position detection: Y-axis when the phone is oriented upwards, absolute value of the X axis when it is oriented forwards, absolute value of the Y axis when it is downwards and X-axis when the phone is oriented backwards (Fig. 9).

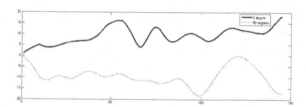

Fig. 9. Y axis in position 0° and X axis in position 90°.

4.7   Impact of the Curve Filter

The degree of filtering impacts the analyses of curves and as such the achieved results. Filtering is intended to reduce the existing error rate.

The application of filtering techniques gives several results depending on the filters applied. These results show a progressive increase of the average matching rate when the value of the filter is incremented. Furthermore, it proves that filtering has a positive impact on gait recognition.

This positive impact can also be identified by the increase of perfect matches. Indeed, when gait is analysed without filters, a perfect match occurs for one participant out of thirteen only, while with a filter of 90 %, a perfect match occurs for ten volunteers. Furthermore, the use of an important filter removes intermediate values. Indeed, the average matching rates using an important filter are close to 100 % or 0 % which gives a binary answer to the gait recognition question (Fig. 10).

Even if the highest filter seems to be the best solution, it is preferable to select an intermediate one in order to diversify the answer. Indeed, the binary answer provided by the highest filter avoids any interpretation of the result while it can be interesting, in a future application, to make a difference between a perfect match and an intermediate one.

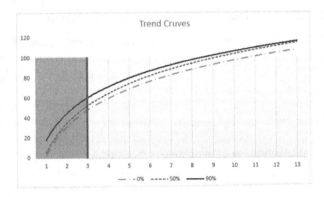

Fig. 10. Trend curves of three filters (0 %, 50 % and 90 %).

4.8 Elimination of Abnormal Steps

Abnormal steps are steps for which representing curves have the highest average distance with the other curves using the DTW method. As they are not representative to the average gait, the curves with the highest variance from the average were removed. Indeed, these curves represent abnormal actions done by the user during the walking process (obstacle, loss of balance…).

During evaluation the presence of a few extreme values were noted. Whereas most of the values are included between 60 % and 100 %, some average matching rates are close to 0 %.

The presence of these values is due to mis-measurement during the experiment and mainly with the use of the "leg band". Indeed, this "leg band" slid down along few participants' leg and they had to hold it to avoid this problem. The cause of this mismeasurement was confirmed by the experiment.

In order to avoid a misinterpretation of these errors, 10 % of the extreme values are filtered when the sample of participant permits it.

4.9 Evaluating the SVM, DTW and Average Value Algorithms in Our Context

The definition of the sample's featured template is crucial in for the implementation of the algorithm. Indeed, if the featured template is not representative for the participant's gait, all the comparisons and all the further analysis become insignificant as they would be based on a wrong template.

For this experiment, three methods have been tested and compared: the Support Vector Machine (SVM) method, the Dynamic Time Warping (DTW) method and the simple calculation of the average which calculate the average of all the gait in the same recording. The results of this comparison is clear because using the SVM method, the average match rate is 56.27 % and the trimmed mean is 61.54 % whereas the average match rate using the average method is 50.39 % and its trimmed mean is 56 %. The DTW method is by far the most conclusive with an average match rate of 73.41 % and a trimmed mean of 80.30 % for the same dataset.

4.10   Results

Impact of Shoes. When gait using shoes is compared to the normal gait, the average matching sample obtained for each recording is relatively low (49.21 % and 49.8 %) as shown in Table 2.

Table 2. Average values of shoe measurement series.

Average values	1	2
Normal gait vs. 2 samples of normal gait	70.56	69.54
Normal gait vs. 2 samples of gait with flip-flops	49.21	49.8
Gait with flip-flops vs. 2 samples of gait with flip-flops	84.13	80.24

However, when gait data series are compared to each other, the result is significantly higher.

The significant decrease of the average match using flip-flops means that the use of this type of shoes significantly impacts gait. Furthermore, the good match of two gaits using flip-flops confirms that the shape of the gait is linked to the type of shoes used and the strongest result identified with flip-flops shows that gait is more specific for each person using flip-flops making the recognition easier by not limiting movement as strongly as regular shoes do.

Flip-flops give a lot of freedom of movement, which leads to a stronger characteristic of movements. On the other hand, more sturdy, more closed shoes limit the movement. This can lead to higher false positives or negatives as the measured values might not differ strongly.

Impact of Different Floors. The comparison of the normal gait with gait on the grass gives a relatively high average match as shown in Table 3.

Table 3. Average values of different floors measurement series.

Average values	1	2	Trim. mean 1	Trim. mean 2
Normal gait vs. 2 samples of normal gait	74.2	74.92	83.34	83.92
Normal gait vs. 2 samples of gait on grass	72.73	62.62	79.43	71.96
Gait on the grass vs. 2 samples of gait on grass	72.13	71.92	77.19	77.67

Whereas the variation of normal gait between two recordings is almost non-existent, a significant variation is identifiable when gait on the grass is compared to gait on normal surface.

Contrary to the conclusion made in previous research [6], when participants walk on the grass, the recognition probability is more variable and less predictable because of floor irregularities. Furthermore, the comparison of the two records on the grass to each other (Table 3) shows that, for a same itinerary on this surface, the average matching rates are similar to normal gait recognition and the level of variation observed previously disappeared. For the same person, the gait is characteristic to the type of floor. The comparison of two gaits recorded on two different floors implies a decrease of the recognition probability.

Impact of Positioning the Phone in the Pocket. The comparison of normal gait with gait with the phone in the pocket (Table 3) gives a weak result with an average matching rate of 26.28 % for the first recording and 22.96 % for the second one. These weak matches are in contrast to the result of the comparison between the two recordings of the gaits with the phone in the trousers' pocket (Table 4): 82.29 % and 76.77 %.

The comparison of normal gait with gait with the phone in the pocket may seem disappointing at first sight since there are low average matching rates (Table 4). But these results have to be interpreted in context. Indeed, the modification of the position when the smartphone is placed in the pocket produces a modification of the phone's coordinate system and this difference changes the conditions of comparison (Fig. 11). The matching rates are calculated with regard to variations along the Z axis which is oriented to the user's right side, whereas with the phone in the pocket the orientation of the Z axis is slightly different. Indeed, in Fig. 4, $\Delta 1$ and $\Delta 2$ represent the same data variation but with a rotation of the reference system. The impact of this rotation implies a significant difference on the Δ variation.

Table 4. Normal Gait vs. 2 samples of Normal Gait.

Average values	1	2
Normal gait vs. 2 samples of normal gait	70.37	69.64
Normal gait vs. 2 samples of gait with the phone in the pocket	26.28	22.96
Gait with phone in the pocket vs. 2 samples of gait with the phone in the pocket	82.29	76.77

However, when the two recordings of gait data with the phone in the pocket are compared to each other, the results are very successful. These matching rates are even

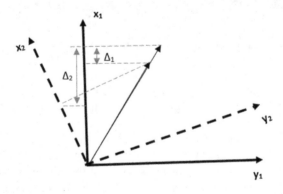

Fig. 11. Impact of the modification of the phone position on the reference system.

higher than normal gaits. This improved result is probably due to a better stability in the pocket than with the leg band avoiding up and down movements of the phone. This hypothesis tends to be confirmed by the absence of extreme values when the phone is placed in the pocket. Indeed, the shape of the pocket ensures a better stability by holding the phone on each side.

4.11   Gait Recognition – Three-Dimensional Data vs. the Initial Approach

The gait recognition algorithm developed to analyse data from the smartphone uses the Y axis to determine the starting point of the recording as well as the cycle time of each step. These cycle times are then applied to the data recording from the Z axis in which each step is extracted in order to be compared.

Another approach that was tested uses more than one axis to achieve the comparison. This is why, after the analysis of the Y axis in order to know the cycle time of each step, the three axes X, Y, Z are sampled step by step.

The results with the algorithm using three-dimensional data are more conclusive than the previous one. Indeed, for the normal gait, the comparison of data from three axes gives an average matching rate of 86.7 % (against 73.41 % with the previous method) and a trimming mean of 94.64 % (against 80.30 %). Regarding the gait on the grass, results are similare with 85.9 % against 72.73 % for the average matching rate and 92.89 % against 82.57 % for the timing mean. However, the most surprising result concerns gait using a different pair of shoes. While the first comparison method gave a match of 49.21 %, the use of the three dimensional data gives a better result of 84.76 %.

While the recognition following the Z axis is widely affected by the use of a different pair of shoes, the X and Y axes seem to be almost unchanged to ensure a similar recognition to normal gait. This seems logical since Z characterises a sidewise movement. Sturdy shoes reduce this movement significantly, while flip-flops offer freedom of movement on this axis.

Naturally, processing of three-dimensional data requires more computing power than data from fewer dimensions. While the initial approach needed only a couple of seconds for the analysis, the approach using three-dimensional data needed more than one minute to process data. As such the initial approach constitutes a tradeoff time vs. security. With current hardware none of these approaches can be used in real-time.

5   Conclusion

This pilot project addresses a couple of factors, e.g. types of shoes, types of floors and phone position that might have an impact on gait recognition and as such on the security provided through authentication mechanisms using gait recognition.

While most of the factors do not have a significant impact on gait, a few factors like shoes can have a big impact. Gait is significantly modified if the user does not use close pairs of shoes. Open shoes produce impressive results.

A varying surface has only a limited impact on gait recognition. However, three-dimensional data can help to mitigate variations generated by the factors mentioned. In some cases they tend to disappear leading to a very good recognition rate.

Finally, when the phone is positioned in the trousers' pocket rather than tied to leg with a leg band, huge differences appear in the recognition process because of the modified position. Up and down movements along the leg introduce extreme values which impact the results.

Not all results identified were those expected. This means the problem is worth giving attention in the future, especially by observing new parameters together with new recognition algorithms.

References

1. Schloeglhofer, R., Sametinger, J.: Secure and usable authentication on mobile devices. In: MoMM 2012, 3–5 December 2012. ACM (2012)
2. Nambiar, A. M, Correira, P., Soares, L.D.: Frontal gait recognition combining 2D and 3D data, In: MM&Sec 2012, 6–7 September 2012, Coventry, UK (2012)
3. Lu, H., Huang, J., Saha, T., Nachman, L.: Unobtrusive gait verification for mobile phones. In: ISWC 2014, 13–17 September 2014, Seattle, USA (2014)
4. Bouchrika, I., Nixon, M.S.: Exploratory factor analysis of gait recognition. In: 8th IEEE International Conference on Automatic Face & Gesture Recognition, pp. 1–6 (2008)
5. Gafurov, D., Snekkenes, E., Bours, P.: Gait authentication and identification using wearable accelerometer sensor. In: IEEE Workshop on Automatic Identification Advanced Technologies, pp. 220–225 (2007)
6. Holien, K., Hammersland, R., Risa, T.: How Different Surfaces Affect Gait Based Authentication (2007). http://rune.hammersland.net/tekst/gait_surfaces.pdf
7. Thang, H., M., Viet, V., Q., Thusc, N., D., Choi, D.: Gait identification using accelerometer on mobile phone. In: International Conference on Control, Automation and Information Sciences (ICCAIS), pp. 344–348 (2012)
8. Nickel, C.: Accelerometer-based biometric gait recognition for authentication on smartphones. Ph.D. thesis (2012)
9. Buch, C.: Gait Recognition. Presentation for the BCC Conference, Tampa (2013). http://www.biometrics.org/bc2013/presentations/int_busch_wednesday_1100.pdf
10. Juefei-Xu, F., Bhagavatula, C., Jaech, A., Prasad, U., Savvides, M.: Gait-ID on the move: pace independent human identification using cell phone accelerometer dynamics. In: 5th IEEE International conference on Biometrics: Theory, Applications and Systems (BTAS), pp 8–15 (2012)
11. Boyle, M., Klausner, A., Starobinski, D., Trachtenberg, A., Wu, H.: Gait-based user classification using phone sensor. In: MOBISYS 2011, pp. 395–396 (2011)
12. Muaaz, M., Nickel, C.: Influence of Different Walking Speed and Surfaces on Accelerometer-Based Biometric Gait Recognition (2012). http://www.usmile.at/sites/default/files/publications/06256346.pdf. Accessed 26 Aug 2014
13. Matovski, D.S., Nixon, M.S., Mahmoodi, S., Member, IEEE, Carter, J.N.: The effect of time on gait recognition performance. In: IEEE transactions on information forensics and security, pp. 543–552 (2012)
14. Developer Android: Sensors Overview (2014). http://developer.android.com/guide/topics/sensors/sensors_overview.html

15. Danias, V.: Dynamic Time Warping (DTW) (2014). http://homepages.inf.ed.ac.uk/group/sli_archive/slip0809_c/s0562005/theory.html
16. Levine, D., Richard, J., Whittle, M.: Gait Analysis, 5th edn. Elsevier, Oxford (2012)
17. Lemire, D.: Faster retrieval with a two-pass dynamic-time-warping lower bound. Pattern Recogn. **42**(9), 2169–2180 (2009)

EvaBio a New Modular Platform to Evaluate Biometric System

Benoit Vibert[1,3]([✉]), Zhigang Yao[1,3], Sylvain Vernois[1,3], Jean-Marie Le Bars[2,3], Christophe Charrier[2,3], and Christophe Rosenberger[1,3]

[1] ENSICAEN, Caen, France
{benoit.vibert,zhigang.yao,sylvain.vernois,
christophe.rosenberger}@ensicaen.fr
[2] UNICAEN, Caen, France
{jean-marie.lebars,Christophe.Charrier}@unicaen.fr
[3] UMR 6072 GREYC, 14032 Caen, France

Abstract. when someone wants to make a payment with a smartcard, the user has to enter a pin code to be identified. Only biometrics is able to authenticate a user; yet biometric information is sensitive. To ensure the security and privacy of biometric data, OCC (On-Card-Comparison) has been proposed. This approach consists in storing biometric data in a secure zone on a smartcard and computing the verification decision in a Secure Element (SE). The purpose of this paper is to propose an evaluation platform for testing biometric systems such as the analysis of performance and security on biometric OCC. Based on four examples, we illustrate its different uses in an operationnal context. The first example focus on the "Quality module" which allows to choose the enrollment by considering the fingerprint quality with one proposed metric. The second one addresses the minutiae reduction of the fingerprint template when the number of minutiae is higher than expected by the OCC. The third is based on sensors acquisition module to create databases and made attacks on sensors. The last one is the evaluation module, it permit to visualize results after an evaluation.

Keywords: Evaluation of biometric systems · Evaluation platform · Minutiae template selection · Fingerprint quality metric

1 Introduction

Nowaday, biometrics is often used in our daily life, (passport, border control, smartphone...). This kind of applications requires in general the use of large online biometric databases which may cause many security and privacy problems. In order to avoid these problems, the secure storage of biometric data and OCC verification are increasingly deployed on a SE (Secure Element) such as the French passport chip. The main benefit of this solution is to avoid the transmission of the biometric reference template of the user. The user has also the

O. Camp et al. (Eds.): ICISSP 2015, CCIS 576, pp. 234–250, 2015.
DOI: 10.1007/978-3-319-27668-7_14

control of its own biometric data stored in the SE. A secure element guarantees many security issues of the biometric reference (confidentiality, integrity).

The SE is frequently used for several applications such as border control or face to face bank payment. Thus, to avoid misused identity for example, it becomes very important to define a general methodology for evaluating these embedded systems. Some standards have been proposed as guidelines of biometric systems [1,2] but the definition of a certification process is not yet done. Industrial demand to have an efficient tool to evaluate and compare OCC and sensors to choose the best is increasing. We need a platform embedding performance and security tools to analyze existing biometric systems and to help research in this area. This platform should be modular, able to process embedded biometric systems and strongly connected with existing standards. This is why we proposed in this paper, this evaluation platform of biometric OCC for analyzing its performance and security.

The paper is organized as follows. Section 2 is devoted to the state-of-the-art of evaluation platform of biometric systems. Section 3 describes the proposed platform by emphasing on specific modules. In Sect. 4, we illustrate the benefit of the proposed platform through four examples of uses cases. We conclude and give some perspectives in Sect. 5.

2   State-of-the-Art

In the literature, only few platform exist for assessing the performance and security of biometric systems. We can cite the NIST platform [3], which is used in many research competitions. It allows researchers or manufacturers to test their OCC or minutiae extractors, in term of interoperability. NIST reports disseminate information on FMR (False Match Rate) and FNMR (False Non Match Rate) for each OCC and extractor. The purpose of this platform is to compare existing algorithms or systems by a trusted third party.

We can also mention the online FVC-Ongoing platform [4] dedicated to algorithms for fingerprint verification (evolution of the FCV competitions). The platform offers multiple databases grouped into two parts. The first one (Fingerprint Verification) quantifies both enrollment and verification modules, while the second one (ISO Fingerprint Matching) quantifies only the verification module on ISO Templates [5] based on minutiae. Performance metrics are: the failure to acquire rate (FTA) and the failure to enroll rate (FTE), the false non match rate (FNMR) for a defined false match rate (FMR) and vice versa, the average enrollment and verification times, the maximum size required to store the biometric template on the SE, the distribution of legitimate and impostors users scores and the ROC curve with the associated equal error rate (EER). The main drawback of this platform is that it is necessary to submit the executable or source code of the OCC algorithm to the online platform which can cause confidentiality issues.

Another platform is currently in development within the BEAT (Biometric Evaluation And Testing) European project [6]. At the end of the project,

	No Source Code needed	Use Real SE	Modular Platform	Reproductibility of research results
NIST	✓	✗	✗	✓
OnGoing	✗	✗	✗	✓
BEAT	✓	✗	✓	✓

Fig. 1. Summarize state-of-the-art platform capabilities.

a framework to evaluate the performance of biometric technologies using several metrics and criteria (performance, vulnerabilities, privacy) will be proposed. The goal of this project is to provide a common platform for industrial and researchers to evaluate their products and to have an independent and certified result with common criteria. This platform is not yet released and does not focus embedded biometric systems.

To compare the three platforms, we have used four criteria: (1)no source code needed, (2) Use real SE, (3) Modular platform, (4) Reproductibility of research results. These four criteria are important on an evaluating platform because researchers and industrials do not want to send the source code for example. They are more able to send to us a smartcard with the OCC inside or a dll to evaluate their OCC. The NIST and OnGoing platform could reproduce research results but it is not easy to use in opposite BEAT platform is principally design around this idea. We have seen the main platforms in the state-of-the-art and we have presented their possibilities and drawbacks summarize in Fig. 1. However, no platform answer to our criteriae (usability, modularity,...). This is why we have decided to develop our platform we present here.

3   EvaBio Platform

EvaBio platform permits to make the link between industrial companies and researcher. This strong link with industrial permits to improve the platform to respond to their needs and also permit to share results with academics. Figure 2 illustrates this idea.

3.1   General Scheme

The general architecture of the proposed platform is given in Fig. 3. This is the evolution of the first platform previously developed by [7] providing more functional modules such as Sensor, Computing, Quality metrics, Security for OCC and Audit. Those new modules offer to developers or researchers different methods to evaluate any OCC or to choose a sensor.

3.2   Modules

As previously mentioned, the platform is composed of different modules with specific treatments. All those available modules are independent. In addition,

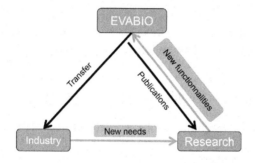

Fig. 2. EvaBio platform interactions with industrial and research.

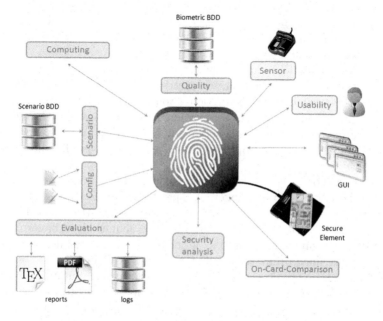

Fig. 3. General architecture of the EvaBio platform.

this modularity allows us to modify and/or add any module without changing the overall architecture of the platform. For example we can quantify the benefit of quality checking of the fingerprint during the enrollment process. The platform uses active mechanisms of communication by event allowing multiple modules simultaneously access data exchanged between the client application and the OCC, thus offering "on the fly" analysis of results. All the main modules such as Core, GUI interface, Sensor, Computing, Evaluation, Quality, Security Analysis modules are described thereafter.

The Core module is the main module in green with a fingerprint on Fig. 3 that is connected with all modules. It manages the interaction with the different modules. It only knows the type of data as input of a module and the type of data returned by it. As for example, to communicate with the Secure Element, the `Core` transparently manages the connection and communication with the OCC, that is realized by Personal Computer/Smart Card (PCSC) communication or Java Card OpenPlatform (JCOP) simulator with the software library developed through WSCT in [8].

The `Scenario` module permits to create or use an evaluation scenario. It defines the biometric database to query, the number of biometric data to be used for enrollment or the number of users to consider. This allows us to make reproducible testing only by setting these elements.

The `Security analysis` module contains various methods of attacks on the OCC. It is possible to use fuzzing approaches [9] consisting in injecting fault data to the biometric OCC. It can be a biometric template respecting the ISO format but containing random biometric data (brute force attack). It is also possible to test the interoperability of the OCC by providing biometric templates ISO in which faults have been injected.

The proposed platform has a main `Graphical Interface` that allows to choose the test scenario and evaluation metrics. From the main interface, many plugins can be used to get information about one or more data (e.g., minimum, average and maximum time for enrollment and verification). As mentioned above, the proposed platform uses active communication by event mechanisms. That way, plugin can be developped by users to get any specific information of interest for him.

The `Sensor` module is a little platform which permits to acquire real and fake fingerprint databases with real finger and specific protocols. This module is used to evaluate the performance of a sensor and to provide attacks on it. We also went on mortuary to test if the sensor is able to acquire dead fingerprint [10]. This sensor platform could be used as input for the `Core` module, to acquire in live one or more fingerprints to be compare on an OCC algorithm.

The `Computing` module yields to have a distributed computation to improve the efficiency of the evaluation of OCC. For example, from three OCC on three smartcards, we are able to run three different tests in parallel. In such a case, we divide by three the evaluation time within a campaign.

The `Quality` module is devoted to the quality metric of fingerprint images or minutiae templates. Fingerprint quality metric is an auxiliary solution to guarantee the matching performance by dropping the bad quality samples [11] in both the enrollment and matching sessions. This purpose can be simply achieved since good fingerprint quality could provide more precise and reliable features. Obviously, this is also beneficial for OCC operations, especially when it is necessary to consider minutiae selection. There is a much higher probability that a minutiae extractor can correctly localize minutiae points within good quality images than within bad quality prints [12]. Therefore, a reduced minutiae template can preserve correctly detected minutiae as much as possible rather than the spurious points, and the performance could be ensured as well. The quality metric module in the platform is combined with a validation component which allows the user to measure the performance of variant metrics, which enables making a further decision to choose an appropriate metric. The module has an interface witch permit to manages all biometric databases. The `Core` requests to the interface the next biometric data with quality filter for processing and delegates to the interface the connection and management of all biometric databases. This allows to abstract the storage format of biometric data for example.

Two image quality assessment algorithms are available in the `Quality` module: (1) NFIQ [13] and (2) GREYC Q metric [14]. The NFIQ generates five quality levels from 1 to 5, where the best quality is indicated by the lowest value and the maximum level denotes the samples of very poor quality. GREYC Q metric, estimates the quality of fingerprint with five score groups, poor (0–20), bad (20–40), medium (40–60), good (60–80) and very good (80–100). Such a continuous quality score could generate a better distribution of sample qualities than those using only few quality levels. This module is also a modular unit so that if other quality metrics will be released, it could be employable in the experiments.

The `Evaluation` module proposed different metrics commonly used in both the literature and ISO [1] with more specific ones:

- False Match Rate (FMR): it measures how many times the biometric data of a user provides positive verifications with biometric data of another user.
- False Non Match Rate (FNMR): it measures how many times the biometric data of a user gives a negative verification of biometric data with the same user,
- Success rate of attack: it measures the ratio of successful attacks (number of positive result over a number of transactions).
- Measuring interoperability: it quantifies the ratio of successful tests when providing an ISO template to the OCC.
- ROC curve: It describes the behavior of the biometric OCC for each value of the decision threshold (from which a test is positive). This implies that it is possible to obtain the comparison score from the OCC or to set decision threshold. For industrial OCCs, this is rarely the case but for research ones, this information is always available.
- Verification Time: we measure the time required to achieve a OCC enrollment or to obtain a verification result (after sending the ADPU (Application Data Protocol Unit defined in [15]) to the SE. It is also possible to generate several statistics on computation times such as histogram verification time, average, minimum or maximum time.

The Fig. 4 shows the main results come from a previous performing evaluation on keystroke dynamics. On input of this module, we have to select the formatting log file to compute and show the results of the evaluation. Most of time to compare two evaluation results we used the ROC curve, FNMR FMR vs Threshold and Score distribution. This is why these metrics are computed and displayed in a window. A calculating part which permits to obtain the value of FMR for a specific FNMR value and the opposite is also proposed.

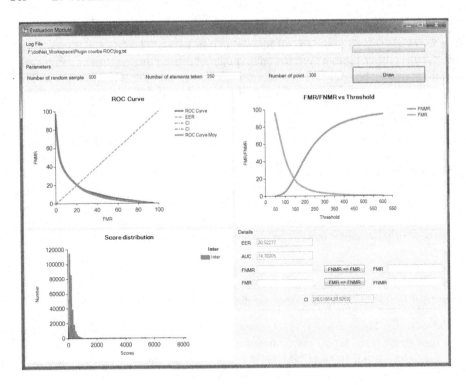

Fig. 4. Snapshot of the evaluation module display window.

4   Example of Uses Cases

In this section, we present four uses cases, (1) Quality checking during enrollment, (2) Minutiae selection, (3) Sensor acquisition module, (4) Evaluation of
OCC. This is four representative uses of the platform.

4.1   Quality Check During Enrollment

For this purpose, we address the problem of the selection of the best template
in terms of quality and number of relevant minutiae for OCC enrollment. This
selection process is performed using both NFIQ and Greyc Q metrics, and we
obtain a better result only with the selection of enrollment template. Figure 5,
shows the used process to choose a template without quality selection Fig. 5(a)
and when using a quality assessment process Fig. 5(b).

Concerning the protocol, the used biometric data have been collected in
earlier experiments with 39 individuals. We have made three capture sessions
with two fingers: left and right index finger, with five captures per session per
individual. In total, we captured 1170 fingerprint images and ISO Compact Card
templates. On each image, we compute the NFIQ and Q quality metrics an
processed by the evaluation module of the EVABIO platform. To choose the

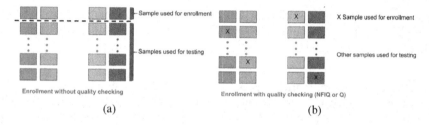

Fig. 5. Selection protocol on the reference template enrollment with and without quality checking where one column corresponds to samples from an individual.

reference templates, we have selected, for each person, the template with the best quality value considering the two metrics and the most number of minutiae under the maximum size allowed by the OCC.

The performance without template selection is also computed [7]. Table 1 presents the results of the evaluation on a commercial OCC with and without quality selection.

Table 1. Performance values for each quality metric selection method.

	FMR	FNMR
Without selection	0.41 %	17.36 %
NFIQ selection	0.05 %	14.36 %
Q selection	0.003 %	4.75 %

As a conclusion of the performance, there is a fairly good robustness to imposture for all methods and the FNMR is relatively good with Greyc Q selection but not with others. We observed quite satisfactory results without quality selection, in terms of false match rate compared to those found in [3] and a very good performance with quality selection. The false non match rate appears too high, however by improving the selection of the enrollment template, we are able to reduce the FNMR around 10 % with NFIQ selection and an other 10 % with Q selection in comparison with NFIQ. This experiment shows that the selection of enrollment template is very important to achieve good performance.

In the EVABIO platform, a quality metric is used as filter to choose the reference template for each user in the database. We can quantify the gain of operational quality checking during the enrollment process. It also helps us to improve quality metrics by considering on different databases similar experiments detailed in Table 1.

4.2   Minutiae Selection

A module to reduce the ISO Compact Card template when we have too many minutiae. The truncation method defined in the state-of-the-art [16] has been initially embedded in the module. To determine if the truncation is the best method in computation time and performance, we have compared with a clustering method called barycenter.

Selection by Truncation. This method is based on a simple truncation *i.e.*, we only keep minutiae from the initial template the first N_{max} minutiae. The efficiency of this simple approach depends on the method used to generate the fingerprint template. For many commercial biometrics systems, a fingerprint template is generated with a specific method. It can be generated considering minutiae with the ascending locations Y as for example. In the case where multiple captures have been made, high quality minutiae (always present in the different captures as for example) can be placed at the beginning of the template. Selecting the N_{max} first minutiae could be in this case a very efficient and simple.

Barycentre Selection. This method based on a pruning mechanism is simple and fast (few milliseconds). It has been proposed by the NIST for minutiae selection in [16]. It has been shown that minutiae located near the core of a fingerprint minutiae are the most useful ones for the matching process [17]. Given a fingerprint template, the core location is usually unknown. However, the centroid of minutiae can be a good estimate (when no other information is available). This minutiae selection approach tends to only keep minutiae near the centroid for this reason. We have four steps for the computation process:

1. Compute the centroid of the minutiae from the fingerprint template (containing N_j minutiae);

$$Centroid = (X_c, Y_c) = \frac{1}{N_j}(\sum_{i=1}^{N_j} X_i, \sum_{i=1}^{N_j} Y_i) \tag{1}$$

2. Compute the distance of each minutiae to the centroid;

$$r_i = \sqrt{(X_i - X_c)^2 + (Y_i - Y_c)^2}, \ i = 1 : N_j \tag{2}$$

3. Sort in ascending order minutiae according to the distance r_i, $i = 1 : N_j$;
4. Select the first N_{max} minutiae.

Performance Evaluation. Concerning the protocol, the FVC2002DB2 [18] database has been used to illustrate results. This database is composed of 8 fingerprints per person and 100 individuals, with a total of 800 fingerprints. All minutiae templates used in the experiments have been extracted using the NBIS tool, MINDTCT [19] from the NIST. In order to realize the matching of fingerprint templates, we used a very well known minutiae matching algorithm proposed in 1997 by Jain et al. [20]. This method consists of an alignment stage (translation and rotation estimation between the two templates to compare) and a matching stage after transformation.

To evaluate the performance of minutiae selection algorithms, we use the AUC (Area Under the Curve) metric since it is often considered as global performance criterion. We use this value to quantify the efficiency of a minutiae selection method. We compute the AUC value for each selection method with N_{max} varying from 30 to 50 by step of 2. The Confidence Interval (CI) is also used to weight the results of AUC value.

We show in Fig. 6 the results of minutiae selection using the two tested methods. Selected minutiae are represented by a red star and others with a blue circle. We can see with the barycentre approach, select minutiae are near the estimated CORE. With the truncation method, we loose the right part of the template.

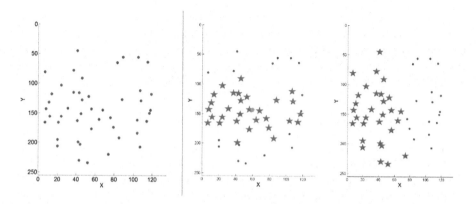

Fig. 6. Example of minutiae selection on a fingerprint sample: stars represent selected minutiae by the different methods. For the barycenter selection approach, the green point represents the estimated CORE point (barycenter of minutiae) (Color figure online).

Table 2 details the AUC value for each minutiae selection method for the FVC2002 DB2 database. On this database, the two selection methods permit to obtain a better performance (Cf. Fig. 7) compared to the initial template (no selection).

Table 2. AUC values for each minutiae selection method for different values of N_{max} on FVC2002DB2.

N_{max}	30	34	38	42	46	50
No selection (%)	11.2 ± 0.15	11.2 ± 0.15	11.2 ± 0.15	11.2 ± 0.15	11.2 ± 0.15	11.2± 0.15
Truncation (%)	10.2 ± 0.28	9.97 ± 0.2	9.29 ± 0.14	**8.93 ± 0.11**	9.41 ± 0.07	9.48 ± 0.05
Barycentre (%)	**8.73 ± 0.31**	**9.01 ± 0.2**	**9.00 ± 0.15**	9.26 ± 0.10	**9.17 ± 0.07**	**9.47 ± 0.04**

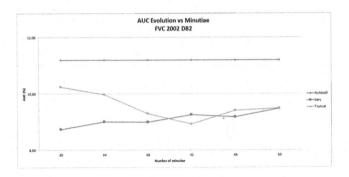

Fig. 7. Evolution of the AUC value face to minutiae selection on FVC2002DB2.

To conclude, we observe that the minutiae selection approach based on barycenter is better than the truncature method even if this later is preconised the standard method. The minutiae selection method can be seen as a pre-processing to the enrollment process in an operational application. Of course, EVABIO platform allows to test other selection methods.

4.3 Sensor Acquisition Module

Another module dedicated to the acquisition of biometric templates is offered with the EVABIO plateform. Furthermore, this module permits to collect raw data and store them in databases. During an acquisition campaign, we have used several sensors and the proposed module can detect which sensor the finger has been placed on. This module offers the possibility to acquire fingerprint on several sensors during a campaign. Each acquisition generates fingerprint images and minutiae ISO templates. These data are saved with an identification number, the hand, the finger and user's profile information. The sensor acquisition module is shown in Fig. 8. Many different sensors and the display screen indicating to the user the hand and finger to used for the capture are shown. We are able to run an acquisition directly on a real sensor.

With regard to security, a biometric sensor has vulnerabilities. Ratha and al. [21] have combined attacks of a generic biometric system in 8 classes: (1) falsified biometric data, (2) interception of biometric data during its transmission, (3) attack on the extraction module parameters, (4) altered extracted parameters, (5) matching module replaced by a malicious software, (6) alteration of the database, (7) man in the middle attack between the database and the matching module, (8) alteration of the verification decision. For each point, there are different types of attacks. Figure 9 illustrates the possible locations of the attacks in a generic biometric system. We have tested 2 attacks on sensor, one with fake fingerprint data taken on a genuine user and the other on a dead finger.

Fake Fingerprint: A fake fingerprint database from real fingers and fingerprints has been designed (see Fig. 10). To build this database, we have used wax

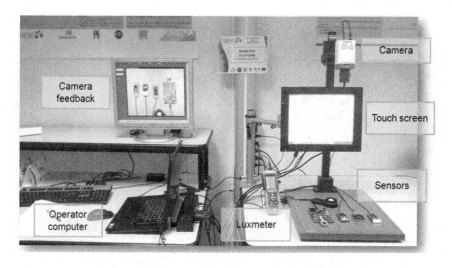

Fig. 8. Sensor acquisition platform in working.

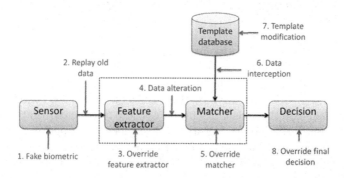

Fig. 9. Vulnerabilities locations of a biometric system (defined from [21]).

and gelatin because these materials are not thick. To verify the robustness of the trial sensors, we compute the FTAR and we determine if the trial sensors provide a negative verification or if they are able to detect fake fingerprints or a spoofing attack.

Dead Fingerprint: We created a fingerprint database only using dead fingers. We went to the mortuary of the Caen Hospital and we acquired fingerprints of 4 dead people. The acquisition protocol is the following:

- 3 sensors have been used
- 4 fingers (except the thumb) have been used
- the 2 hands (left and right) have been used
- 6 captures per individual per finger per sensor have been performed

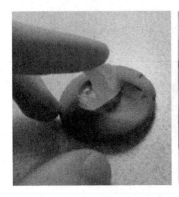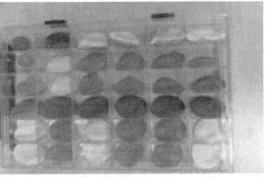

Fig. 10. Example of fake fingerprint.

Finally, we got 144 (6*2*4*3) data (fingerprint images and ISO template) per individual for all the sensors. For the 4 individuals, we have in total 576 (144*4) data. We have calculated the Failure To Acquire Rate (FTAR) and equals 36.11 %.

Illustrations: We have tried the fake and dead fingerprints on four sensors to check if this kind of attack works on them. The sensor 1 is a swipe model, and the others are optical. For fake fingerprints, we got a FTAR equal to 100 % for sensors 1, 3 and 4. Consequently, for these sensors, the tested spoofing attacks are not working. For the sensor 2, the FTAR is 0 % meaning that there is no problem to acquire the biometric data. 96 tests have been performed, 65 % led to a negative verification and 35 % to a positive one.

For the dead fingers, we have used the Q quality metric, because it has been shown in [14] that it provides a better quality assessment than NFIQ in Table 1.

Table 3. Average Greyc Q metric value for fingerprint coming from a senior database the deade fingers one.

	Metric Q results			
	Sensor 1	Sensor 2	Sensor 3	Sensor 4
Mortuary	38.3	81.9	72.3	68.3
Senior database	32.1	84	78.6	73.7

We note for sensors 2, 3 and 4 that the dead fingers have a lower fingerprint quality (Table 3) (the higher value is greyc Q, the better is the quality). For the sensor 1 (the only swipe sensor), it is not the case and the quality is largely worst than the three others. We think, this is due to its use, the operator for the dead fingers used correctly the sensor (see Fig. 11) contrary to real users.

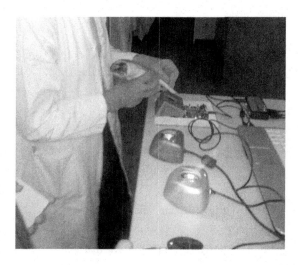

Fig. 11. Acquisition in Mortuary.

4.4   Evaluation

To illustrate how the EVABIO platform works, we have evaluated a commercial OCC on a fingerprint database acquired with the sensor module. We obtained the performance of the OCC, the operating point Fig. 12 with False Match Rate (FMR) and False Non Match Rate (FNMR), the distribution of FMR FNMR vs the Greyc Q metric on Fig. 14. We also have additional informations such as Q distribution on the database, time distribution Fig. 13.

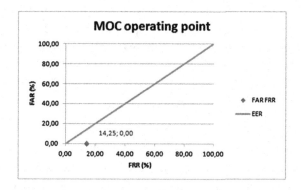

Fig. 12. Operating point for Greyc Q metric.

We are able to compare OCC because we use the same testing scenario for each OCC. When we have a high FNMR value, a good user is rejected frequently and it has a high impact on acceptability. If you have a high FMR, an impostor

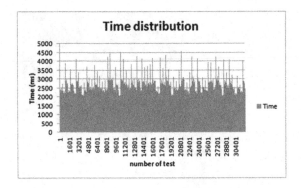

Fig. 13. Time distribution.

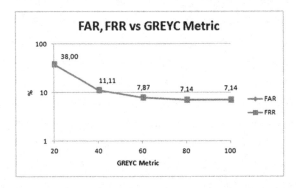

Fig. 14. FMR FNMR versus Greyc Q metric: the more high is the Greyc Q quality metric, the better are the samples, the lower are the FNMR values.

user is accepted by the system and it is a vulnerability. The time is another important information because it has an impact on user acceptance. Considering the evolution of the FNMR value face to the quality of samples is important to consider especially during the enrollment to guarantee a good operational performance.

5 Conclusions

In this paper, we have presented the benefits of the EVABIO biometric evaluation platform, and we have illustrated with four examples the capability of the platform. The first one quantifies how the use of biometric quality metrics on enrollment template selection is influenced performance. The second is a brief comparative study of fingerprint minutiae selection algorithms. The third is the sensor module witch permit to acquire and create fingerprint databases and test for example if sensor acquire dead fingerprint or not. And the last one is the evaluation of a biometric system. To conclude, we demonstrate the facility to obtain results with the proposed platform.

In perspective, we plan to develop new modules to evaluate the OCC and sensor on smartphone and to design new attacks on OCC and sensors. We will also improve the scenario module to propose new tests.

References

1. ISO/IEC 2382–37: Information Technology - vocabulary - part 37: Biometrics (2012)
2. ISO/IEC 19795–7: Information Technology - biometric performance testing and reporting - part 7: testing of on-card biometric comparison algorithms (2011)
3. Grother, P., Salamon, W., Watson, C., Indovina, M., Flanagan, P.: Minex ii performance of fingerprint match-on-card algorithms. phase iv: report NIST interagency report 7477 (revision ii) (2011)
4. Biolab: FVConGoing (2009). https://biolab.csr.unibo.it/FVCOnGoing
5. ISO/IEC 19795–2: Information Technology - biometric data interchange format - part 2: Finger minutiae data (2004)
6. Project, B.: Beat project (2013). https://www.beat-eu.org/
7. Vibert, B., Rosenberger, C., Ninassi, A.: Security and performance evaluation platform of biometric match on card. In: 2013 World Congress on Computer and Information Technology (WCCIT), pp. 1–6. IEEE (2013)
8. Vibert, B., Alimi, V., Vernois, S.: Analyse de la sécurité de transactions à puce avec le framework winscard tools. In: SAR-SSI 2012, p. 8 (2012)
9. Lancia, J.: Un framework de fuzzing pour cartes à puce: application aux protocoles EMV. In: Symposium sur la Sécurité des Technologies de lInformation et des Communications (SSTIC), p. 82 (2011)
10. Vibert, B., Lebouteiller, J., Keita, F., Rosenberger, C., et al.: Biometric sensor and match-on-card evaluation platform. In: International Biometric Performance Testing Conference (IBPC) (2014)
11. Grother, P., Tabassi, E.: Performance of biometric quality measures. IEEE Trans. Pattern Anal. Mach. Intell. **29**, 531–543 (2007)
12. Chen, Y., Dass, S.C., Jain, A.K.: Fingerprint quality indices for predicting authentication performance. In: Kanade, T., Jain, A., Ratha, N.K. (eds.) AVBPA 2005. LNCS, vol. 3546, pp. 160–170. Springer, Heidelberg (2005)
13. Tabassi, E., Wilson, C.L.: A novel approach to fingerprint image quality. In: IEEE International Conference on Image Processing, ICIP 2005, vol. 2, pp. II-37. IEEE (2005)
14. El-Abed, M., Hemery, B., Charrier, C., Rosenberger, C.: Evaluation de la qualité de données biométriques. Revue des Nouvelles Technologies de l'information (RNTI), pp. 1–22 (2011)
15. ISO/IEC: ISO/IEC 7816-1 to 15: Identification cards - Integrated circuit(s) cards with contacts(Parts 1 to 15). http://www.iso.org
16. Grother, P., Salamon, W.: Interoperability of the ISO/IEC 19794–2 compact card and 10 ISO/IEC 7816-11 match-on-card specifications 11 (2007)
17. Weiwe, Z., Wang, Y.: Core-based structure matching algorithm of fingerprint verification. In: International Conference on Pattern Recognition (2002)
18. Maio, D., Maltoni, D., Cappelli, R., Wayman, J.L., Jain, A.K.: FVC2002: second fingerprint verification competition. In: Proceedings 16th International Conference on Pattern Recognition, vol. 3, pp. 811–814. IEEE (2002)

19. Watson, C.I., Garris, M.D., Tabassi, E., Wilson, C.L., Mccabe, R.M., Janet, S., Ko, K.: Users guide to nist biometric image software (nbis). Technical report, NIST (2007)
20. Jain, A.K., Hong, L., Pankanti, S., Bolle, R.: An identity-authentication system using fingerprints. Proc. IEEE **9**, 1365–1388 (1997)
21. Ratha, N.K., Connell, J.H., Bolle, R.M.: Enhancing security and privacy in biometrics-based authentication systems. IBM Syst. J. **40**, 614–634 (2001)

Author Index

Printed in the United States
By Bookmasters